PHENOMENOLOGICAL BIOETHICS

Emerging medical technologies are changing our views on human nature and what it means to be alive, healthy, and leading a good life. Reproductive technologies, genetic diagnosis, organ transplantation, and psychopharmacological drugs all raise existential questions that need to be tackled by way of philosophical analysis. Yet questions regarding the meaning of life have been strangely absent from medical ethics so far. This book brings phenomenology, the main player in the continental tradition of philosophy, to bioethics, and it does so in a comprehensive and clear manner.

Starting out by analysing illness as an embodied, contextualized, and narrated experience, the book addresses the role of empathy, dialogue, and interpretation in the encounter between health-care professional and patient. Medical science and emerging technologies are then brought to scrutiny as endeavours that bring enormous possibilities in relieving human suffering but also great risks in transforming our fundamental life views. How are we to understand and deal with attempts to change the predicaments of coming to life and the possibilities of becoming better than well or even, eventually, surviving death?

This is the first book to bring the phenomenological tradition, including philosophers such as Martin Heidegger, Edith Stein, Maurice Merleau-Ponty, Jean-Paul Sartre, Hans-Georg Gadamer, Paul Ricoeur, Hans Jonas, and Charles Taylor, to answer such burning questions.

Fredrik Svenaeus is Professor of Philosophy at Södertörn University in Stockholm, Sweden.

'Drawing on the insights and methodologies of existentialism, phenomenology, and hermeneutics to deepen our understanding of health and illness, *Phenomenological Bioethics* is a timely and path-breaking work. With his signature clarity and accessibility, Fredrik Svenaeus illuminates the situated and experiential aspects of suffering, embodiment, empathy, and death that are all too often neglected in current bioethical debates.'

— *Kevin Aho, Professor of Philosophy, Florida Gulf Coast University*

'A ground-breaking development in medical bioethics, this book is the first to use phenomenology to analyse and understand contemporary bioethical issues, such as organ transplantation and assisted reproduction. This book announces the birth of a new field – phenomenological biomedical ethics – and is an important development for both philosophy of medicine and for phenomenology.'

— *Havi Carel, Professor of Philosophy, University of Bristol*

'Hitherto, few Anglo-American bioethicists have benefitted from the riches to be found in philosophical phenomenology. This can perhaps be traced to the phenomenologists' inhospitable language. Fortunately, in invitingly clear language, Svenaeus now offers a wonderfully thoughtful and accessible introduction to phenomenology – and shows how it can illuminate questions of bioethics.'

— *Erik Parens, Senior Research Scholar, The Hastings Center, Garrison, NY*

PHENOMENOLOGICAL BIOETHICS

Medical Technologies, Human Suffering, and the Meaning of Being Alive

Fredrik Svenaeus

Routledge
Taylor & Francis Group
LONDON AND NEW YORK

from Routledge

First published 2018
by Routledge
2 Park Square, Milton Park, Abingdon, Oxon, OX14 4RN

and by Routledge
711 Third Avenue, New York, NY 10017

Routledge is an imprint of the Taylor & Francis Group, an informa business

British Library Cataloguing-in-Publication Data
A catalogue record for this book is available from the British Library

Library of Congress Cataloging-in-Publication Data
Names: Svenaeus, Fredrik, author.
Title: Phenomenological bioethics : medical technologies, human suffering, and the meaning of being alive / Fredrik Svenaeus.
Description: Milton Park, Abingdon, Oxon ; New York, NY : Routledge, 2018. | Includes bibliographical references and index.
Identifiers: LCCN 2017010129| ISBN 9781138629950 (hbk) | ISBN 9781138629967 (pbk) | ISBN 9781315210131 (ebk)
Subjects: LCSH: Medicine--Philosophy. | Medical ethics. | Bioethics.
Classification: LCC R723 .S85 2018 | DDC 174.2--dc23
LC record available at https://lccn.loc.gov/2017010129

ISBN: 978-1-138-62995-0 (hbk)
ISBN: 978-1-138-62996-7 (pbk)
ISBN: 978-1-315-21013-1 (ebk)

Typeset in Bembo
by Saxon Graphics Ltd, Derby

CONTENTS

7 Surviving death 121

PREFACE

My aim in this book is to show how the tradition of phenomenology, including philosophers such as Martin Heidegger, Edith Stein, Maurice Merleau-Ponty, Jean-Paul Sartre, Hans-Georg Gadamer, Paul Ricoeur, Hans Jonas, and Charles Taylor, can be brought to the field of biomedical ethics. The continental tradition of philosophy, including the neighbouring fields of phenomenology, existentialism, hermeneutics, and post-structuralism, has been strangely absent in bioethics so far. There are probably several reasons for this, but two main ones are undoubtedly differences in philosophical style and disciplinary context; continental philosophy has migrated to several fields of the humanities and social sciences but has rarely teamed up with the natural sciences, which have been rather the companions of analytical philosophy.

This book is an attempt to close these gaps of style and disciplinary context in introducing phenomenology in the field of bioethics. It is not a book primarily aimed at philosophers who are already familiar with the phenomenological tradition – although I hope it will prove interesting to some of them, too – but written rather for scholars and laypersons professionally involved or interested in bioethical themes and without prior knowledge in the field of phenomenology. The explorations and analyses found in the book are inspired by some of the main philosophers in the phenomenological tradition, but they are systematic in manner and meant to be accessible in style, proceeding from main problems and themes of contemporary bioethics, including questions regarding human nature, suffering, empathy, and how we are to deal with medical technologies in our present situation and the future to come. The problems and themes addressed involve questions discussed in association with, for instance, new reproductive technologies, embryo ethics, genetic diagnosis, brain death, organ transplantation, and human enhancement, and also questions found in clinical ethics dealing with patient autonomy, euthanasia, abortion, medicalization, and the goals of medicine. In the book I want to show how phenomenology can enrich present bioethical debates and bring a new perspective to burning problems by focusing upon embodied, social, cultural, and existential aspects of human life and medical-technology development.

The book is, to my best knowledge, the first single-authored monograph to offer a sustained phenomenological approach to biomedical ethics. Phenomenology has previously been put to work in philosophy of medicine and medical humanities, in order to comprehend the nature of illness and the clinical encounter, but it has rarely been used in directly addressing questions of medical ethics. Emerging approaches in bioethics include traditions close to phenomenology, such as caring ethics, biopolitical studies, and narrative bioethics, but phenomenology offers a more fundamental viewpoint than any of these alternatives – an approach that is more comprehensive in dealing with bioethical dilemmas. The phenomenologist famously gives privilege to the *first-person* perspective in understanding embodied experiences, but the real beauty and strength of bringing phenomenology to bioethics consists in showing how this first-person perspective is systematically related to a second-person dialogical perspective of empathy and narrative, and a third-person scientific perspective investigating and manipulating biological processes of our living bodies. This is what I will try to do in this book.

I will start by introducing the phenomenological project and distinguishing three different ways to do phenomenological bioethics (chapter one). The version I will settle with proceeds by scrutinizing and thickening the – often implicit – *philosophical anthropology* at work in contemporary bioethics. This conceptual thickening indirectly includes two other versions of phenomenological bioethics: one that aims at providing rich descriptions of dilemmatic situations, the other at criticizing and moving beyond a simplified applicative paradigm in bioethics. In chapter two my phenomenological exploration of human nature will take on a concept absolutely central to bioethics – namely, suffering. This analysis will introduce interconnected types of human suffering that may occur in the life of a person due to illness or some other unwanted life event, *alienating* the person from her body, life world, or core life-narrative values. By way of this analysis the concept of autonomy, so central and dear to contemporary bioethics, will be embedded in a phenomenology of human flourishing.

In chapter three the *embodied* nature of human being will be scrutinized further by distinguishing different ways in which the body may turn up as alien in a human life. The lived body involves forces of nature that are experienced in an uncanny way when we fall ill, but the body may also be objectified and made other through the experienced *gaze* of other persons or by way of medical technologies. In chapter four the clinical encounter is brought into focus – a meeting in which a suffering patient presents his complaints to a health-care professional who is aiming to understand the reasons for ailments in *empathic* dialogue with the person and through medical investigations. The *hermeneutics* of medicine envelop scientific investigations of the potentially diseased, living body of the patient, but such medical investigations always relate back to the meeting with the suffering person who is being treated. The goal of medicine is to make the experienced body, world, and life story of the patient less alien, and this goes beyond the mission of treating diseases, in some situations even involving actions that will shorten rather than lengthen the life of a person in relieving suffering (palliative care).

Chapter five addresses a concept that is central to phenomenological bioethics and that has often been poorly understood in medicine: *instrumentalization*. Medical technologies are currently changing our everyday life predicaments and reshaping notions of human life and health in dramatic ways. In doing so, not only can the different diagnostic and therapeutic devices and drugs be immensely helpful in alleviating suffering, but they can also lead to a change in the *perception* of what we essentially are. The risk is not only that some human beings, or parts of human bodies, become instruments for the well-being of others. The risk is that we come to view human life as such as a medical resource or even a commodity on a market.

In chapters six and seven I explore the relationship that holds between a living human body and the experiencing, self-reflective, narrative person it will become in successive developmental stages of functional complexity. I also explore the way a human person goes out of existence when her living body becomes diseased and ceases to function, suddenly or gradually. This will bring us to the beginning as well as the end of human life, attempting to understand what kind of beings embryos, foetuses, newborn babies, and severely demented, comatose, and brain-dead patients really are. It will also bring us back to questions regarding the kind of relationship we have to our own bodies, and to the bodies of other persons, and under what conditions we are obliged to solidarily *share* parts of our bodies with others. The concept of *responsibility* is launched to better understand what empathy with suffering or vulnerable others may mean and consist in.

The chapters of the book can be read independently, but they are meant to develop a successive argument and image of phenomenological bioethics through the way they are located and connect to each other. Each chapter closes with a short summary, making it easier to move between the chapters and take shortcuts if the reader so wishes.

Finally, I want to point towards some limitations of phenomenological bioethics in the version found here. First, this is a book about biomedical ethics; I say close to nothing about issues belonging to animal ethics and environmental ethics. Second, the chosen topics aim to cover a vast area of biomedical ethics, but the reader will not find very much related specifically to research ethics or questions of distributive justice. These are large and important parts of bioethics, and I do reach some conclusions concerning ways in which medical research may be ethically problematic and what actions may be fair to suffering parties. However, I do not want to pretend that these thoughts offer more than beginnings in these two subfields.

Third, phenomenological analysis does not always make us able to formulate detailed ethical guidelines or law proposals in bioethics, since practical concerns and political issues also need to be taken into consideration in establishing ethical/legal rules. In this sense phenomenological bioethics may not be sufficiently applied in character to suit all tastes. But this, I think, is characteristic of many valuable philosophical contributions to bioethics, not only of the phenomenological attempt. What phenomenology is able to offer is a *perspective* that will make us see things differently and, I hope, more comprehensibly in bioethics, not a set of new rules to be applied in place of the standard principles of respecting autonomy, doing good, avoiding harm, and being just, or a new catalogue of virtues in place of the ones articulated by Aristotle and his successors. However, a fresh perspective is not necessarily a bad or even a small thing. If you are interested in medical technologies, human suffering, and the meaning of being alive, I think you should give phenomenology a chance.

ACKNOWLEDGEMENTS

This book has been on my mind for a long time. Although I did not sit down to actually start writing it until about a year ago, I have presented and discussed the thoughts and arguments found in the different chapters at seminars and conferences during the last seven years or so. I want to thank the participants in the annual conferences of The European Society for the Philosophy of Medicine and Health Care and The Nordic Network for Phenomenology who have visited the sessions in which I have presented my material for constructive criticism and enjoyable dialogue. I also want to thank the members of two research projects which I have been in charge of at Södertörn University for stimulating discussions and helpful suggestions: The Body as Gift, Resource, and Commodity (2008–2012) and The Phenomenology of Suffering in Medicine and Bioethics (2015–2018), both funded by The Baltic Sea Foundation.

Some of the crucial ideas behind this book were developed when I spent four months as a visiting fellow at the Bioethics Centre, University of Otago, New Zealand, in 2013–2014. Thanks to all the participants in the seminars and lectures in which I presented my tentative ideas, and thanks to the staff at the Centre for providing such a hospitable and stimulating academic environment. Likewise, I thank my colleagues at the Centre for Studies in Practical Knowledge and the Department of Philosophy, Södertörn University, with whom I have enjoyed many formal and informal discussions regarding phenomenological bioethics over the years. In particular I want to mention Rolf Ahlzén, Jonna Bornemark, Martin Gunnarson, Martin Gustafsson, Jonna Lappalainen, Eva Schwarz, and Patrick Seniuk, who provided feedback on different parts of the manuscript at a late stage. I also owe thanks to Anne Cleaves, who has proofread the whole manuscript, checking and improving my English. And, finally, thanks to Lina Svenaeus for love, support, inspiration, and the idea of the hospital waiting room for the book cover.

I thank the publishers of the following papers for allowing me to reuse parts of the material in reworked format:

Chapter one:
Phenomenology, in Henk A. M. J. ten Have and Bert Gordijn, eds., *Handbook of Global Bioethics* (New York: Springer, 2014), 2225–2233.

Chapter two:
The Phenomenology of Suffering in Medicine and Bioethics, *Theoretical Medicine and Bioethics*, 35/6 (2014), 407–420.

Chapter three:
Anorexia Nervosa and the Body Uncanny: A Phenomenological Approach, *Philosophy, Psychiatry, and Psychology*, 20/1 (2013), 81–91.

Chapter four:
Empathy as a Necessary Condition of *Phronesis*: A Line of Thought for Medical Ethics, *Medicine, Health Care and Philosophy*, 17/2 (2014), 293–299.
Hermeneutics, Health and Medicine, in Jeff Malpas and Hans-Helmuth Gander, eds., *The Routledge Companion to Philosophical Hermeneutics* (London: Routledge, 2015), 550–560.

Chapter five:
The Relevance of Heidegger's Philosophy of Technology for Biomedical Ethics, *Theoretical Medicine and Bioethics*, 34/1 (2013), 1–16.

Chapter seven:
The Body as Gift, Resource, or Commodity: Heidegger and the Ethics of Organ Transplantation, *Journal of Bioethical Inquiry*, 7/2 (2010), 163–172.
Organ Transplantation Ethics from the Perspective of Embodied Selfhood, in John Arras, Elizabeth Fenton, and Rebecca Kukla, eds., *The Routledge Companion to Bioethics* (London: Routledge, 2015), 570–580.

1

PHENOMENOLOGICAL BIOETHICS

Phenomenology of medicine and health care

In what ways is the philosophical tradition of phenomenology able to contribute to the field of bioethics? This is the question I aim to explore in the present book. In using the term 'bioethics', my intention is to address not only the classic medical ethical questions revolving around the clinical encounter, but also the type of ethical challenges that arise when medical technologies are used to support and control human life. Phenomenology has been rather absent in the bioethical field up to the present date, but some examples of phenomenology are found in the neighbouring fields of philosophy of medicine and medical humanities and in qualitative studies of medical phenomena carried out in disciplines such as nursing, medical psychology, medical sociology, medical anthropology, and science and technology studies. Phenomenology has also had an impact in certain subfields of bioethics, such as caring ethics, narrative ethics, and feminist ethics. These subfields have played important roles as alternatives to the principle-based bioethics that have developed into the mainstream tradition in the field (Jonsen 1998). This chapter will provide an overview of the different ways in which phenomenology could prove to be useful as a method and philosophical inspiration for bioethics. The possibilities, as will become obvious, are multiple, and to a large extent they still remain to be realized. After providing this overview, I will present my own strategy for bringing phenomenology to work in bioethics by navigating within this field of possibilities.

Phenomenology is a tradition more than one hundred years old of exploring and answering philosophical questions by proceeding from an analysis of what the phenomenologist calls 'lived experience'; important classics are written by philosophers such as Edmund Husserl, Martin Heidegger, Maurice Merleau-Ponty, and Jean-Paul Sartre (Moran 2000). The starting point for phenomenology is not the world of science, but the meaning structures of the everyday world – that which the phenomenologist calls a 'life world'. Contemporary phenomenology has branched out into many different disciplines from the tree that started growing in philosophy with Husserl and his successors. Scholars and researchers of art, literature, psychology, sociology, anthropology, pedagogy, history, and, recently, also nursing and medicine, have tried to make use of phenomenology in investigating phenomena of concern in their fields.

The main topic of phenomenology in medicine and health care so far has been *bodily* experiences – experiences of phenomena such as illness, pain, disability, giving birth, and dying (Meacham 2015; Toombs 2001; Zeiler and Käll 2014). Everybody has a body – a body that can be the source of great joy but also of great suffering to its bearer, as patients and health-care professionals know more than well. The basic issue that the phenomenologist would insist upon clarifying in this context is that not only does everybody *have* a body, everybody *is* a body. What is the difference?

That every experience is 'embodied' means that the body is a person's point of view and way of experiencing and understanding the everyday world. Not only can I experience my own body as an *object* of my experience – when I feel it or touch it or look at it in the mirror – but the body is also that which makes a person's experiences possible in the first place. The body is my place in the world – the place where I am which moves with me – which is also the zero-place that makes space and the place of things that I encounter in the world possible. The body, as a rule, does not show itself to us in our experiences; it *withdraws* and by way of this opens up a focus in which it is possible for things in the world to show up to us in different meaningful ways. When I am, for instance, cooking, reading, or talking to my friends, I am usually not attending to the way my body feels and moves; I am focused upon the thing I am momentarily *doing*; this is made possible, however, by the way my body silently performs in the background. The body already organizes my experiences on a subconscious level; it allows me to experience the things that are not me – the things of the world that show up to my moving, sensing body in different activities through which they attain their place and significance (Gallagher 2005).

Thus phenomenology can be understood as transgressing any dualistic picture of a soul living in and directing the ways of the body like some ghost in a machine. The body is me. But phenomenology, despite its anti-dualism, has also, from its beginnings, been an anti-naturalistic project; that is, the phenomenologist would contest any attempt to reduce experience to material processes *only*. Experience, to the phenomenologist, must be studied by acknowledging its form and content for the one who is having the experience. Experience carries meaning in the sense of presenting objects in the world *to* a subject (self, person). It is certainly possible to study experience from the third-person (or, rather, non-person) perspective of science also – we could study the ways light rays trigger nerve firings in my brain by way of the retina when I look at a person right now (if we hook me up to a technological device), but this picture of my brain in action would not be the experience of 'me seeing her right now'. The picture could catch neither the 'me-ness' nor the content of the experience that I am having – this is the first-person perspective of *intentionality*, which the phenomenologist takes as the starting point of the analysis.

Among the medical themes that can profit from a phenomenological analysis we find not only embodiment, but also related phenomena such as illness, suffering, dying, and giving birth (Aho and Aho 2008; Carel 2008; Leder 1990, 2016; Slatman 2014; Svenaeus 2000, 2011; Zeiler and Käll 2014). One finds elements of such analyses in the works of major classic phenomenologists, such as Husserl, Heidegger, Merleau-Ponty, and Sartre, and even more in some less well-known figures, such as F. J. J. Buytendijk, Hans Jonas, Herbert Plügge, and Erwin Straus, but the idea of a phenomenology of medicine as a distinct field of academic studies is younger than that, maybe thirty years old or so (Spiegelberg 1972; Toombs 2001). Long before that, however, phenomenology had a certain influence in one specific medical speciality, psychiatry, with scholars such as Karl Jaspers (Stanghellini and Fuchs 2013). Jaspers, in his *General Psychopathology*, published as far back as 1913, famously separated two different angles and frameworks that the psychiatrist needs to explore and combine in his practice: understanding and explanation (Jaspers 1997). This way of describing medical practice is very much similar to stressing the need for a focus upon the lived body and the everyday world of the patient in health care to complement the causal explanations explored by medical science in investigating the body as a diseased organism.

Phenomenology of illness

The contrast between understanding and explanation also mirrors the familiar distinction between illness and disease made in medical philosophy, psychology, and sociology. Illness is the name for the experience of the person being ill, and disease is the name for the pathological processes and states possibly inhabiting his body. Diseases are often taken to be the causes of illness, but the experience of illness can protrude in spite of the doctors' being unable to detect any diseases; and the illness experience, in turn, can have biological effects, just as the experience of negative stress in many cases leads to diseases and shortens life. Phenomenology of medicine explores the illness perspective – the first-person perspective – without denying the importance and reality of the biological functions of the body – the third-person perspective on diseases. In this way phenomenology is, indeed, anti-naturalist in vehemently denying that the meaning of lived experience could be reduced to patterns of material processes (causal explanation), but it remains material and anti-dualistic in the sense of proceeding from the *embodied* perspective of the ill person.

The first-person perspective of the ill person – what it is like to be ill in this particular way – is in fact exactly what the doctor explores when entering into empathic dialogue with the patient (see chapter four). When doing so, the doctor (or other health-care professional) adopts a *second*-person perspective on the experiences of the patient. The second-person perspective on the patient's experiences is an empathically imagined first-person perspective, in contrast to a third-person perspective on the patient, which is rather a *non*-person perspective – that is, a perspective that aims to steer free of all idiosyncrasies in a natural scientific way. As we will see, good medical practice consists of navigating in-between the second-person and the third-person perspectives on the patient, combining phenomenological understanding with scientific explanations.

Normally the lived body remains in the background of our experience, and our attention is instead focused on the things in the world that we are engaged with. In Merleau-Ponty, to mention the most well-known 'body phenomenologist', we find penetrating descriptions and conceptual analyses of such everyday experiences that are bodily in nature even though we are not focused upon the body: seeing, listening, walking, talking, reading, and the like (Merleau-Ponty 2012). In some situations, however, the body calls for our attention, forcing us to take notice of its existence in pleasant or unpleasant ways. This experienced body can be the source of joy, as when we enjoy a good meal, play sports, have sex, or just relax after a day of hard work. However, the body can also be the source of suffering to its bearer, as when a person falls ill or is injured and experiences pain, nausea, fever, or difficulties in perceiving or moving (Leder 1990; Zaner 1981). When I have a headache, an example most famously explored by Sartre in *Being and Nothingness*, the pain in question invades my entire world – my attempts to concentrate, perceive, communicate, move, and so on (Sartre 1992; Svenaeus 2015a). If the doctors examine my body with the help of medical technologies they may be able to detect processes going on in my brain and the rest of my body that are responsible for the pain in question, but they will never find my headache *experience*, the feeling and meaning the pain has for me in my 'being-in-the-world', to speak in a phenomenological idiom invented by Heidegger in his magnum opus, *Being and Time* (1996). The hyphens are put in place by Heidegger in order to stress that a person (other terms used here are 'self' or 'subject'), in experiencing and doing something, is always immersed in the things at hand. Consequently, things that we encounter in the world are first and foremost 'tools' (in German, 'Zeuge') that are 'ready to hand', according to Heidegger (1996: 66 ff.).

The concept of tool in *Being and Time* is introduced as Heidegger is analysing what he calls the 'being-there' – 'Da-sein' – of human beings as a 'being-in-the-world' (1996: 41 ff.). What is a world in the phenomenological sense? It is the pattern of meaning, the horizon in which we come to see things as such-and-such things. No phenomenon shows up alone; it is always embedded – temporally and spatially – in a background pattern that makes it possible for the object to stand out and show itself to us with a certain significance. The things of the world attract our attention from out of such meaning patterns: a chair can only show up within a room, on the floor, in front of a wall, beside the table at which we eat while sitting on it, and so on.

One of Heidegger's most important observations in *Being and Time* is that such 'showing itself to us' is as a rule not played out in the manner of our being conscious of objects in the world, in perceiving or thinking about them. The most basic access, rather, relies on our *handling* the stuff of the world in various ways to attain things. The chair is not first and foremost an object with such-and-such a shape and colour; it is something to sit on, and we approach it in such a way when we take a seat or offer it to somebody else in inviting her for a cup of coffee. The similarities and differences between the limbs and organs of the lived body and the 'outer' tools of the world will be an important subject in later chapters of this book, when I aim to explore the ethical conundrums that arise when we are able to transfer organs and tissues between bodies, or even to create fleshy 'body tools' in the laboratory (Diprose 2002; Malmqvist and Zeiler 2016; Sharp 2007; Slatman 2014; Waldby and Mitchell 2006).

The difference between the first-person and the third-person perspective is an important one. The first-person perspective makes it possible to understand not only how human experience is meaningful and material simultaneously, but also how the body belongs to a person in a stronger and more primordial sense than a pair of trousers, a car, or a house does. The body is not only ours, it is *us*; and this insight will, as mentioned, have important repercussions in facing ethical dilemmas associated with technologies that make it possible to keep a human body alive when the person, whose body it is, appears to be permanently gone (chapter seven). How should we treat and look upon such bodies? How should we consider the possibilities of using parts of such bodies to help other persons in need of new organs? A phenomenological take on embodiment is also helpful in understanding pregnancy and the way medical technologies are involved in assisted reproduction and maternal care (chapter six). How can phenomenology inform our views about embryo and stem-cell research and about abortion? How can it inform our views about the ethical dilemmas having to do with choosing what (type of) children should be born?

In this book we will return many times to how one could approach and better understand various forms of human suffering in health care by way of phenomenology and the importance such analyses carry for bioethics. Medical-ethical dilemmas revolving around issues of providing information and obtaining consent occur in situations involving people who are vulnerable, dependent, and out of control because they are suffering. To understand not only why but also how these people suffer is necessary to be able to help them. Empathy on the part of the health-care professional is a matter not only of informing patients about their medical condition and respecting their ability to make decisions about the medical care they are offered, but also of understanding and helping persons who suffer. As we will see in chapter two, suffering is an existential issue that occurs when we become alienated from the things that are most important and dear to us in life. Empathic understanding of human suffering in health care will in most situations need to proceed beyond medical body matters into everyday life matters and issues concerning persons' self-understanding. New medical technologies pushing or changing the forms and limits of human self-understanding as such raise further questions of responsibility when they are tested or implemented on a societal level.

Phenomenological bioethics

Phenomenological bioethics can be regarded as the part of the phenomenology of medicine and health care that focuses on ethical dilemmas arising in connection with understanding and helping suffering persons, and in connection with dealing with medical-technological dilemmas involving human bodies and their parts. Since phenomenological philosophers in the process of their explorations of lived experience and the life world of human beings have already developed various types of ethical arguments, phenomenological bioethics could, indeed, turn to these philosophers and make use of their moral reflections more or less directly in bioethics (Drummond and Embree 2002; Sanders and Wisnewski 2012). Since we find many different types of ethical analyses in the works of phenomenologists, the choices would then come down to whom, among the master phenomenologists, to follow. Such phenomenological heritages are already at work to some extent in fields such as caring ethics, feminist ethics, and narrative ethics.

As mentioned above, in addition to these heritages, phenomenology has entered bioethics via the philosophy of medicine and medical humanities in studies of such themes as illness, empathy, and medical technology. What follows will provide an overview of how the points of connection between phenomenology and bioethics should be considered. My main concern is the question of what it may mean to do bioethics in a phenomenological manner, and the aim is to offer a structure that can encompass many different understandings of phenomenological bioethics by offering a generous interpretation of both concepts. Phenomenology will be considered to be a tradition that is related to existentialism, hermeneutics, and post-structuralism, and such neighbouring schools will be included in my overview at certain points. The ways in which phenomenological bioethics is related to older traditions that have influenced phenomenology as well as bioethics will also be taken into account to some extent, mainly in the case of Kantian ethics and Aristotelian virtue ethics.

Different understandings of phenomenology in medicine and health care

Proceeding from the way the term phenomenology has been used in studies in and of medicine and health care, at least three different understandings of the concept might be discerned. These three, more or less established, understandings of phenomenology are helpful in drawing a map of phenomenological bioethics.

The first, and probably most dominant, understanding of phenomenology in medicine concerns giving *adequate and detailed descriptions* of experiences and situations of importance. A doctor may speak about 'the phenomenology of a case', for instance. This is certainly a correct and important understanding of phenomenology, but as has become obvious already from the brief overview above, it is insufficient for grasping the full meaning of the concept. The second understanding of phenomenology, less well known in medicine, is that phenomenology is a *research programme in philosophy* starting out with Husserl in the early twentieth century and including not only philosophers such as Heidegger, Merleau-Ponty, and Sartre, but also names such as Max Scheler, Edith Stein, Hans-Georg Gadamer, Karl Jaspers, Hans Jonas, Paul Ricoeur, Charles Taylor, Emmanuel Levinas, Hannah Arendt, Michel Foucault, Jacques Derrida, Jean-Luc Nancy, and many others. According to such an understanding, phenomenology is not only a descriptive but also a theoretical and conceptual endeavour. The third understanding of phenomenology common to studies in and of medicine and health care is phenomenology in the sense of a *qualitative research method* – a method inspired by the philosophical tradition of phenomenology in which the researcher aims to give voice in an unbiased way to the experiences of research subjects. The phenomenological method can be applied in gathering and analysing empirical materials consisting of interview transcripts, video recordings, field notes, diaries, and so on. This is a common understanding of phenomenology in nursing research and other fields of empirical health-care studies.

The three understandings of phenomenology obviously have much in common, and they support each other in offering a more complete account of what phenomenology is about in medicine and health care and, also, in bioethics. The conceptual endeavour is dependent upon having access to adequate and detailed descriptions of the type of lived experiences to be investigated, and the empirical research method proceeds from some of the conceptual points of departure stressed by Husserl and other phenomenological philosophers from the very start.

To see this more clearly, a practical example will be enlightening: consider a person seeking help and being hospitalized with the diagnosis of depression. What does it mean to develop a phenomenology of depression in contrast to other ways of understanding this psychiatric disorder? The phenomenologist will not primarily be interested in the ways in which the brain works when somebody is depressed. Nor will she take as her starting point the cataloguing of typical symptoms of depression, in contrast to the symptoms of other psychiatric disorders or somatic diseases, the way it is typically done in contemporary diagnostic psychiatry (DSM-5 2013). Instead, the phenomenologist will be interested in what Heidegger calls the 'being-in-the-world' of the depressed person (1996). What does it feel like to be depressed? How does the world appear to the depressed person, and what sorts of thoughts does he have? What does he want to do (or, rather, not want to do), and how does he communicate and feel related to other persons (or rather not communicate and feel related to other persons)? To investigate these issues thoroughly the phenomenological researcher needs to talk to depressed (or formerly depressed) people, at least if she is not (or has not been) depressed herself. Through the phenomenological analysis, in which the typical structure and meaning of the lived experience of depression should be revealed, the researcher will perhaps come to the conclusion that depression consists in a particular form (or maybe several forms) of suffering in which the autonomy (and possibly also the dignity and authenticity) of the depressed person has become threatened. To be depressed means to live in a world that appears senseless and fearsome and in which the depressed person is losing his bearings and sense of self-worth and self-respect (Ratcliffe 2015).

Phenomenology and the application of principles

Please note that already in this sketchily developed phenomenology of depression, two central concepts in bioethics are encountered: suffering and autonomy. In principle-based bioethics, the central notions are phrased in the manner of prima facie principles that are applied in situations in order to reach a moral decision (the principles most often stressed are the duties of doing good, avoiding harm, respecting autonomy, and being just) (Beauchamp and Childress 2013; Jonsen 1998).

Let us say that a depressed person finds his life so hopeless and horrible that he wants to die. Should his decision be regarded as autonomous, and is he right about his current situation and prospects in life? Leaving aside the question of whether health-care professionals should ever assist patients in ending their lives, it is obvious that the answers to these questions depend on the understanding we are able to develop of what the depressed person's life looks and feels like and what ways exist to improve his situation. In this exploration we would have to enter into a dialogue with the depressed person and also with other parties engaged in the current situation (e.g. family, friends, health-care workers who have been in contact with the depressed person in the past, etc.). To ask the questions of whether the depressed person is to be considered autonomous in his wanting to die, and whether the suffering that he experiences can be remedied in some manner by intervening, is most often phrased as an *application* of bioethical principles to the current situation (other important principles in bioethics besides respecting autonomy, doing good, avoiding harm, and being just are the creeds of empathy, responsibility, veracity, dignity, confidentiality, and fidelity) (Beauchamp and Childress 2013).

In this context of the practice of bioethics as the application of ethical principles to morally problematic situations in order to better understand the situations at hand and deciding what to do in them, one important role for phenomenology in bioethics can already be discerned. Phenomenological bioethics, according to such an understanding, consists in carrying out investigations of the lived experiences – being-in-the-world – of the persons involved in morally problematic situations in order to better see how the main principles of bioethics will apply. It means very little to say that autonomy should be respected if you have not developed an understanding of a particular person's situation and self-understanding. Likewise, it means very little to say that a patient should be helped and not harmed if you have not developed an understanding of the more precise ways this particular person is suffering. In this book I will make use of several penetrating descriptions of illness experiences taken from novels or self-biographic accounts (mainly, Drakulić 1993; Gustafsson 1990; Halse et al. 2008; Nancy 2008; Tolstoy 2015). Such phenomenological descriptions are crucial when the scope of phenomenology in bioethics is expanded to the other two possible versions I consider in the following pages.

Phenomenological bioethics in this form will be a close relative to what has been known since the 1990s as *narrative* bioethics (Charon 2006; Lindemann 1997). To provide the phenomenology of an ethically complex situation in health care means to give voice to the stories of the participants in the drama, throwing light on the different perspectives and experiences of the situation and problem at hand. The phenomenological analysis will supplement and strengthen the narrative approach, since phenomenology proceeds from an *embodied* life-world account, which makes up the basis of every narrated life plot (Rehmann-Sutter et al. 2008; Wiggins and Allen 2011) (see further chapters two and three). Phenomenology done by way of stories will develop into a hermeneutical undertaking, because the embedded character of every lived experience in culturally narrated patterns will lead to questions regarding the relationship between human understanding and scientific explanations (see chapter four).

Phenomenology as a critique of principle-based bioethics

In the first version of phenomenological bioethics delineated in the preceding section, phenomenology forms a part of applicative ethics by providing the careful and adequate descriptions of the terrain in which the principles are to be applied. Phenomenology takes care of one of the balancing scales of what is referred to as a 'reflective equilibrium' – namely, the side on which our moral intuitions are taken into account (Arras 2007). Phenomenological bioethics accordingly studies the lived experience of moral conundrums that are then to be determined via application of prima facie principles originating from ethical theories, such as utilitarianism, Kantian ethics, and liberal-based rights ethics. Other principles in bioethics in addition to the famous four of respecting autonomy, doing good, avoiding harm, and being just are tied to characteristics of the moral agent (virtue ethics) rather than to the action itself, but they can nevertheless be reframed as ethical principles: be empathic and friendly, tell the truth, show courage and integrity, respect the confidentiality and dignity of the patient, be trustworthy, and the like (Beauchamp and Childress 2013; Pellegrino and Thomasma 1993).

In the process of applying ethical principles there is a mutual process of explication and illumination going on. To apply the principle of respecting autonomy to the case of the depressed patient makes us see new aspects of the situation, but the phenomenological investigation of the lived experience of being depressed also informs the matter of what it means to be an autonomous person. The reason we try to stop the depressed person from committing suicide instead of respecting his choice or even providing euthanasia is that his wish is *not* considered autonomous. Depression apparently clouds autonomy since the suffering involved locks the patient into a desperately sad mood of hopelessness, which prevents him from seeing the true potentials of the future (see chapter two). In this process of balancing the understanding of the case and the principles to be applied to it, phenomenology can take on a more critical role than simply providing the details of the case. Phenomenology may be regarded as an attempt to set up bioethics by way of *alternative* principles (e.g. the case of the classic medical virtues reframed as principles above), or in a manner that is *not* understood as a procedure of application of principles in the first place (Welie 1999; Wiggins and Allen 2011).

Inspiration for such endeavours can be found by proceeding from the ethical theories found in classic phenomenologists such as Max Scheler, Edith Stein, Emmanuel Levinas, Jean-Paul Sartre, Hans Jonas, Hannah Arendt, and others (Drummond and Embree 2002; Sanders and Wisnewski 2012). These phenomenological moral theories have different emphases, but they are all united in questioning the firm distinction between what *ought* to be done (ethical principles) and what *is* the case (the situation we are applying the principles to in the moral analysis). The next section of this chapter will offer brief introductions to the most well-known moral philosophers from the phenomenological tradition. In this book, I will make use of concepts and ideas coming from some of these philosophers but will also turn to other major phenomenologists, who did not present their philosophies chiefly in terms of ethics but are nevertheless of great interest in terms of phenomenological bioethics – mainly, Martin Heidegger, Maurice Merleau-Ponty, Hans-Georg Gadamer, Paul Ricoeur, and Charles Taylor.

Some examples of major phenomenological moral philosophers

In the works of Max Scheler we find an attempt to extract norms from the phenomenological analysis itself – what philosophers refer to as 'objective value theory' (2009). This is done mainly via an understanding of the *feelings* we experience in situations in which we encounter other persons and important life goals. Empathy, sympathy, compassion, and love are examples of such feelings, which provide a path to the most important values to be realized in a human life. The concept of personhood is interpreted to include a hierarchically determined set of values involved in the endeavour of living in an ethically respectable or even excellent manner. The challenge to such a phenomenological framework, as we find it in Scheler, is to prove the ethical values to be objective in nature in contrast to just reflecting particular sets of culturally established norms. Scheler's moral philosophy is nevertheless of particular interest to bioethics because of its starting point in strong feelings connected to situations involving suffering, death, empathy, and compassion.

This emphasis on moral feelings is also true regarding Edith Stein, who provided a more comprehensive and detailed analysis of empathy than Scheler did, proceeding from the works of her teacher, Edmund Husserl, but also making a unique and highly relevant analysis of the phenomenon as related to the powers of the lived body and the structure of human personhood (1989). Empathy, according to Stein, is an emotional process in which a person feels and perceives the experiences of another person and attempts to follow these experiences of the other by understanding their content (e.g. why is the other sad, afraid, cheerful, etc.) (Svenaeus 2016a). Empathy, according to Stein, is related to having feelings *for* and *with* the other person (e.g. sympathy, compassion), but also differs from for- and with-feeling in providing a more basic experiential understanding *of* the predicament of the other person. Stein in her later philosophy proceeded to develop a phenomenological analysis of different forms of human sociality and also aimed to understand the relationship which, after converting to Roman Catholicism, she increasingly took to be the most ethically important one – namely, the relationship with the Christian God.

In Emmanuel Levinas we also find a phenomenological ethics that takes its starting point in the interpersonal meeting, spelling out the norms that are at stake there. However, this time the phenomenology of encountering the other person is interpreted as a radical asymmetry in which the 'face of the other' forbids me to do any violence to him (Levinas 1991). This violence potentially done to the other person in the meeting is understood not only as a physical violation, but also as an imposing on him of any norms that belong to my point of view rather than his. Levinasian ethics can be understood as an ethics of integrity, defending the rights of the weak and vulnerable, but in essence it rests on a more radical claim that makes me the hostage of every other person I encounter. The critical questions to ask the advocates of Levinasian ethics are as follows: whether such an ethics places demands that are too high upon the persons who are to exercise it; and whether it is possible that the other person may have some obligations to me in the meetings we enjoy. Nevertheless, the asymmetrical set-up of Levinasian ethics appears to fit the obligational structure of health-care meetings between professionals and patients in important ways and is therefore worth consideration in bioethics.

Levinas and Jean-Paul Sartre developed their moral philosophies at roughly the same time – the 1940s and 1950s, which were also the heyday of existentialism. In Sartre the primary ethical concepts are freedom and responsibility (1973, 1992). Not an infinite responsibility for the other person – the way things are framed in Levinasian ethics – but an infinite responsibility for my own life and what I choose to do with it (including my interactions with other persons, certainly). The existentialist ethics of freedom appears to resemble autonomy-based approaches to ethics, such as we find them in versions inspired by Kantian ethics or liberal, rights-based ethics. However, Sartre is critical of Kantian philosophy, since he does not believe that any universal moral norms can be philosophically defended – for example, categorical duties such as the prohibition of killing or the obligation to always tell the truth. For Sartre, what makes a decision ethical is that *I* aspire to the action in question no matter what public norms and duties may prevail. This looks suspiciously similar to a liberal, autonomy-based ethics – do with your life whatever you find fit as long as you do not interfere with the capability of others to do the same – but it really is not, since Sartre understands every choice to be considered not only as a contingent wish but as an expression of who I really am. Sartrean ethics is an ethics of *authenticity* rather than an ethics of autonomy.

The criticism of existentialist ethics could certainly be voiced in many ways. Are people with different histories and abilities free to realize their potentials to an equal extent? In what manner are the perspectives and situations of other persons taken into account in my endeavour to live authentically? It should be mentioned that in a later phase of his philosophical career, Sartre abandoned existentialist ethics in favour of a Marxist-inspired alternative, focusing on human need rather than freedom, but this alternative will not concern us here.

The second question in the previous paragraph is precisely the point of departure for Hans Jonas in *The Imperative of Responsibility*, a work written in the late 1970s in which he takes on the challenge of how to face the threats of modern technology (including biomedical technologies) that could make the planet uninhabitable (1984). Jonas, a former student of both Husserl and Heidegger, claims that we have an overarching ethical responsibility to save and protect the earth for future human generations. This responsibility becomes visible with a special acuteness in certain key situations – such as when we welcome and care for a newborn child. Jonas's work is of special concern for bioethics, since his endeavours to develop a phenomenology of life and death during the 1960s were of interest to the founding fathers of the field, and he was probably the first phenomenologist to later combine such studies of medical phenomena with the development of an ethics (1984). Medical technology is increasingly the topic of various forms of bioethical studies, and Jonas can be considered an inaugurator in this subfield of bioethics, as we will see in chapters six and seven.

The most widely read work by Hannah Arendt, friend and colleague of Jonas at the New School in New York for many years, is her philosophical analysis of the 'banality of evil' following the 1961 trial in Jerusalem of the Nazi war criminal Adolf Eichmann (2006). Arendt claims that the evil of Eichmann, who was in charge of transporting millions of Jews to the concentration camps, consists in his inability to reflect upon and take responsibility for his own actions. Eichmann pleaded not guilty in the trial (he was found guilty, however, and was executed in 1962) on the grounds of having only performed his duties as a citizen and soldier at the time, and exactly in this inability, or perhaps unwillingness, to understand what he was really doing we find his 'banal' evilness, according to Arendt. Such a moral perspective, distinguishing between a philosophically examined way of life and a life in which you merely think and do as everybody else thinks and does, is found in Sartre as well, and before him in the famous book that inspired both of them: Martin Heidegger's *Being and Time*, first published in 1927 (Heidegger 1996). To live authentically, to flourish, is to know and be true to yourself and to the core life values that you have more or less explicitly chosen to live by (see chapter two).

In works other than the Eichmann report, Arendt went on to develop her ideas about a philosophically examined, authentic life into a political philosophy (1998). This political philosophy of Arendt's is inspired not only by her readings of the phenomenologists, Kant, and Marx, but also notably by Aristotle and his idea of a 'practical wisdom' – '*phronesis*' – central to moral human interaction. In Arendt's phenomenological ethics we consequently find links not only to Kantian ethics but also to virtue ethics – a tradition that has been voiced as a complement to principle-based bioethics from the very start (Hursthouse 1999; Pellegrino and Thomasma 1993). We will return to practical wisdom and virtue ethics when we explore the role of empathy and interpretation in the clinical encounter (chapter four).

The most influential figure in bioethics descending from the tradition of phenomenology is without doubt Michel Foucault. Foucault did not name himself a phenomenologist, and in many ways he rebelled against the Husserlian tradition of phenomenology in France (e.g. Sartre, Merleau-Ponty), but he belongs nevertheless to the twentieth-century continental tradition of philosophy of which phenomenology forms the backbone.

The Foucauldian idea that has been most influential in bioethics – and also in what in Foucault's legacy is named 'biopolitics' – is that our thinking and our actions in the modern age are governed by repressive norms that make what is natural, good, and just appear to us in a certain, unquestioned manner (Meacham 2015). Such norms, which he named 'technologies of power', govern the way we handle questions of health, sexuality, productivity, and so on (Foucault 1990). In a Foucauldian analysis, the set of principles applied by bioethicists would form an important part of the contemporary prevailing power technologies that are used to keep the population under control. The principles thus need to be critically scrutinized from historical and cultural perspectives, rather than uncritically applied, if bioethics are to prove to be a liberating endeavour, according to Foucault.

Continuing in the critical, post-structuralist vein in bioethics, we should also mention the inaugurator of what is known as 'deconstruction', Jacques Derrida. Deconstruction is the term for critical readings of master texts aiming to uncover their implicit presuppositions, fundamental principles that remain unquestioned in launching claims about meaning, presence, and selfhood (Derrida 1978). During the 1980s and 1990s Derrida developed his theories to increasingly address fundamental ethical and political matters concerning human societies and their 'others'. Such questions of citizenship, human rights, and what he calls 'the bare life' are also addressed by Giorgio Agamben (1998), who can be viewed as the second major contributor to the field of biopolitics aside from Foucault (Meacham 2015). Agamben is an heir of both Foucault and Derrida, but he is particularly a critical disciple of the inaugurator of modern hermeneutics – Hans-Georg Gadamer (1994), a philosopher to whom we will return in the following chapters.

Finally, I would like to mention a prominent French scholar in the phenomenological tradition of Heidegger and Merleau-Ponty – namely Jean-Luc Nancy (Devisch 2013; Slatman 2014) Nancy has developed a theory of intersubjectivity that is potentially interesting for bioethics, not least because it stresses the embodied aspects of human life and togetherness. In the collection of essays titled *Corpus*, Nancy brings fresh meditations on human embodiment that proceeds, in the last chapter of the book, from the experience of undergoing a heart transplant (2008).

Phenomenological bioethics as philosophical anthropology

In the two main versions of phenomenological bioethics outlined so far, the field is understood either as an integrated part of, or as a critical outside perspective on, principle-based bioethics. Phenomenology can be used either to inform the application of principles or to criticize the contemporary set-up of bioethics and offer alternative approaches. The critical alternatives (namely, offering alternative principles or abandoning the systematic set-up of application altogether) may be more or less radical in nature concerning the way bioethics should be done. It is typical of the phenomenological moral philosophies presented above that they offer meta-ethical – or, perhaps, proto-ethical – approaches rather than a normative theory in the sense of utilitarianism or of liberal rights-based or Kantian ethics. Ethics is pursued not as a development of rules to guide actions, but as a spelling out of the meaning of the good and the just in the first place. Levinas's philosophy is prototypical in this regard: the face of the other is what informs and gives meaning to human existence, not something that appears subsequent to identifying the other human being (and myself) as persons. In the same way, the radical freedom approach of existentialist ethics is built up as a philosophy of personhood that needs to be developed in order to even formulate the question of what actions are good or just in an institutional framework à la contemporary bioethics. In these regards phenomenological bioethics will be similar to the forms of criticism and alternative ways of doing bioethics found in caring ethics and feminist bioethics (Zeiler and Käll 2014).

We will certainly return to questions of what self- and personhood mean from a phenomenological perspective in the ensuing chapters of this book, since such an exploration opens up a third avenue regarding how phenomenological bioethics could be pursued in comparison and combination with the two I have identified so far. Phenomenological bioethics may be viewed as the task to scrutinize and thicken the *philosophical anthropology* more or less visibly at work in contemporary bioethics. The concept of personhood in such an analysis will be connected to an understanding of such concepts as embodiment, vulnerability, dignity, and authenticity. To be a person is not only to be a rational agent; it is to be an embodied, cultural creature relying on intersubjective bonds formed through what the phenomenologist calls 'being-in-the-world' (Heidegger 1996; Merleau-Ponty 2012). Bioethicists need to deal with the gravitational points and details of this phenomenology of human being in their analyses, and this book is an attempt to present *one way* in which this could happen (for a similar attempt to bring phenomenology to contemporary moral philosophy, see Hatab 2000).

Phenomenological bioethics pursued via a study of the essential components of human personhood will bring us to the question of what it means to encounter *another* human being. The medical meeting, as it occurs between doctors and other health-care professionals and patients, is an obvious point of gravity for bioethics. As we have seen in the survey above, the encounter with the other person forms the cornerstone of several phenomenological moral philosophies

– not only the one found in Levinas, but also those in Stein and Jonas. In such a phenomenological analysis, more or less *hermeneutical* prolongations of philosophical anthropology will occur when we strive to articulate the essence and structure of good medical practice (Gadamer 1994, 1996; Ricoeur 1992; Taylor 1991). Empathy and other capabilities (virtues) needed to understand and help the suffering person are the relevant phenomena to explore here (Halpern 2001). The phenomenological perspective opens up possibilities to understand the clinical encounter as a meeting with a suffering person and not only as a scientific investigation of the diseases of his body. In cases that concern the implementation of medical technologies, in addition to the face-to-face encounter, questions regarding reification or even instrumentalization of patients and their bodies will come to the fore. In addition to this, the societal framework of health care and medical research raises issues regarding responsibility and justice that concern the actions of not only physicians but also of politicians and, indeed, of each and every one among us.

Phenomenological bioethics and wide reflective equilibrium

Rather than being seen as abandoning the idea of a reflective equilibrium, the third understanding of phenomenological bioethics – as doing philosophical anthropology – could be viewed as a needed contributor to what is called a 'wide' equilibrium (Arras 2007). As developed above, the main idea of a narrow reflective equilibrium is that the moral principles should be brought into equilibrium with (i.e. be balanced by and cohere with) the moral intuitions that we first have when confronted with the situation under ethical analysis. To judge the situation from an ethical point of view will mean going back and forth between moral intuitions and moral principles, letting them mutually enlighten each other. By way of this procedure one reaches a more complete picture of what is at stake and, ideally, also reaches a wise judgement about what to do in the situation – a judgement that is philosophically informed but still close to the situation at hand – by engaging with it emotionally in a considered sense.

This version of reflective equilibrium in bioethics might be too narrow, however, since the scrutiny of intuitions and principles will soon bring the bioethicist to more detailed theoretical considerations regarding the meaning of concepts that are brought up in the analysis. In the methodological version referred to as a wide reflective equilibrium these theoretical considerations are explicitly brought into the analysis. This is achieved by taking into consideration not only full-blown ethical theories from which principles are derived, but also theories concerning different aspects of what it means to be human, including philosophical anthropology, developmental and social psychology, sociology, and political theory. As developed above with the example of the depressed patient, such considerations will appear in the ethical analysis directly or indirectly as soon as one starts describing the situation to be dealt with and the way persons think and feel about it.

A phenomenological version of philosophical anthropology will concern not only the meaning of personhood and autonomy, but also various aspects of human suffering and the intersubjective aspects of being-in-the-world related to empathy, responsibility, and instrumentalization. It could play a fundamental role in a clinical ethics spelling out the structure of the encounters between patients and health-care professionals, but it could also be used to analyse the borderline situations of human life – coming into existence and dying – as well as various technological practices of contemporary biomedicine. Philosophical anthropology is, indeed, a core part of every type of ethical analysis, whether the philosopher acknowledges this to be the case or not, and the phenomenological tradition is a rich source in doing that type of reflective, considered moral analysis. In bioethics this means not only to tell rich and adequate stories about ethical dilemmas, but also to provide a conceptual structure in which the well-known prima facie principles can be anchored and critically transformed in a sustained way.

The third version of phenomenological bioethics – that of doing philosophical anthropology – will make use of the first version – that of adequate and rich descriptions of the situations to investigate – to end up as a form of the second, critical version of phenomenological bioethics when the standard prima facie principles of bioethics are embedded in or, if you will, transformed into richer normative concepts: human suffering versus flourishing, the possibilities of empathy and the risks of reification and instrumentalization, and the imperatives of responsibility and solidaric sharing. This will be the road travelled in this book, and I will begin the analysis in chapter two by addressing the phenomenon of human suffering and its existential predicaments.

Summary

Phenomenology has been brought to the domain of bioethics in several, and mostly indirect, ways. Phenomenology has entered bioethics via the philosophy of medicine and medical humanities in studies of themes such as embodiment, pain, and illness, or via parts of bioethics that go under names such as caring ethics, feminist ethics, and narrative ethics. In this chapter an attempt has been made to tell this history and to systematize three ways in which to think about phenomenological bioethics in the future.

Phenomenological bioethics can be carried out either as an integrated part of, or as a critical outside perspective on, principle-based bioethics. Phenomenology can be used either to inform the application of principles by way of describing the lived experiences of moral dilemmas or to criticize the contemporary set-up of bioethics and offer alternative approaches. The critical alternatives may be more or less radical in nature as concerns the way bioethics should be done: offering alternative principles or abandoning the systematic set-up of application altogether. It is typical of moral philosophers in the phenomenological tradition that they offer meta-ethical approaches rather than normative theories in their own right. Ethics in the phenomenological tradition has not been pursued as a development of rules to guide human actions but as a spelling out of the meaning of the good and the just in the first place.

The discussion about what type of perspective phenomenology is able to offer opens up a third alternative regarding the characterization of phenomenological bioethics, in addition to the two approaches just mentioned. The field may be viewed as an opportunity to scrutinize and thicken the philosophical anthropology implicitly present in contemporary bioethics. The concept of personhood in such an analysis will be substantiated in this book by an exploration of such phenomena as embodiment, suffering, empathy, responsibility, and instrumentalization.

2

THE SUFFERING PERSON

Suffering and bioethics

Illness experiences come in many different forms, more or less obviously dependent upon different diseases – least so in the cases of mental illness, an issue I will return to below in some more depth. To suffer from an intestinal cancer and to suffer from a depression are two very different things, which, in turn, are very different from suffering from a migraine or diabetes, or from countless other forms of illness experiences originating from different types of diseases (or forms of illness experiences that are not dependent upon any type of currently known disease). To make things even more complicated, different persons will experience a particular disease condition in very different ways – to acknowledge this is to have begun walking the path of phenomenology – because they embody different forms of being-in-the-world. However, one thing importantly unites all forms of illness experiences: they are examples of human *suffering*. Suffering is not something unique to illness – there are many other forms of human suffering which do not depend on any diseases or harms done to the body – but illness is a very important form of human suffering and it is the form that matters most to bioethics. Suffering is a consequence of the *vulnerability* of human life. As we will see, persons are vulnerable in many ways, but the most obvious reason for their vulnerability is that they are embodied creatures that can fall prey to different diseases or injuries of the flesh (MacIntyre 2001; Mackenzie et al. 2014).

To respond to and try to alleviate suffering is perhaps the most important ethical principle in medicine (Green and Palpant 2014). But what does suffering really consist in? This is certainly a vital question if we want to be able to understand and help people who suffer, as we do in health care. Is suffering a feeling or is it rather a matter of having one's major life goals frustrated? In what sense is the whole of a person and not only his body involved in the suffering process? Does suffering ever make life better for a person, or is it always a nuisance to be avoided? In what follows, I will try to provide answers to these and other related questions by adopting a phenomenological point of view.

Suffering is a philosophical and moral problem as old as mankind. Maybe it is the key moral and existential problem among them all. Why do we have to suffer? And why is there so little, or perhaps no, justice to be had in suffering? One of the oldest records of this question is the Book of Job in the Hebrew Scriptures, written sometime around 500 BC (Jones Pellach 2012). The torments inflicted upon the faithful disciple Job by God and Satan are debated and interpreted in various ways in the story itself and in the rich commentary literature found in Judaism and Christian theology. Satan challenges God that Job is not really pious but worships God only because he thinks it is in his best interest. God denies this, and they set out to test Job's faith. Is he God-fearing and righteous just because he is prosperous and fortunate? Suddenly all Job's possessions are destroyed: his animals are killed, his house is demolished by a storm, killing his entire family, and he falls ill with painful, itching boils covering his entire body. Despite all this, Job refuses to draw the conclusion that God has abandoned him. He will not curse God's name, as his wife suggests, or accuse God of being unfair to him. Who is he to know the purposes of the almighty, as God intervenes to tell him at the end of the story?

Job's unfailing loyalty is rewarded at the end of the story – he is cured of the carbuncles, he gets a new family, and he becomes twice as prosperous as he was before, but this is arguably not the most important message to be learned from the story – believe in God and you will be remunerated. Even more important is the message that suffering is potentially *meaningless*; it is not only hard to bear but is sometimes, maybe even most often, without any form of purpose or reward to be had at all. This is a horrifying thought that has grown even stronger in our modern, scientifically dominated age. Not only do we not understand the purpose of our sufferings because we do not know God's master plan for creation, but there is no purpose to be found in suffering whatsoever, at least not for the individual person. Suffering may be a necessary evil from the point of view of biology and the evolution of the species, but there is nothing in it for you. Or is there, perhaps? I will return to the issue of suffering and personal development later in this chapter.

The meaningless evil of suffering is also why the *relieving* of human suffering, wherever we encounter it and have a possibility to do something about it, is a major ethical calling, perhaps even a duty. Suffering afflicts not only human animals; other creatures may also be included in the ethics of suffering in various ways, but this will not be my major subject here, since, as I will try to make clear, there are ways of suffering that are open only to human beings and that we need to care especially about. Suffering is not only about physical pain and brute fear; it has many other dimensions that can make it even harder to endure. Pain and other unpleasant feelings that non-human animals may suffer from are bad enough, and I am certainly not saying that we should leave such suffering unaccounted for; what I am saying is that we need a *richer* concept of suffering for medicine and bioethics.

What is suffering? This may look like a silly question. We all know what suffering is, as we know what happiness is, maybe not in its deepest and most captivating forms, but we know. And yet the way we talk about suffering, the words we use to define it and the paths taken in conceptualizing it, can be more or less successful in *articulating* the phenomenon in question. Theories of suffering can fail to get hold of suffering because they only catch part of the phenomenon, or because they catch different parts of it but fail to connect the parts to each other in a way that explains how they are related to what we might call the *whole* of suffering. In contemporary bioethics suffering is thought about in at least three different ways: as a bodily sensation; as a failure to accomplish important life goals; and as a broken, uncompleted, life narrative (Green and Palpant 2014). There are truths to all these different positions and they are sometimes applied in combination with each other to cover a vaster territory of suffering. And yet they seem to lack a connecting thread, a conceptual pattern that can explain what a sensation like pain has to do with goals of actions and the story of my life. This is where I will attempt to show that phenomenology could be useful by providing such a conceptual pattern.

Suffering as an attuned being-in-the-world

In hedonistic theories of well-being suffering is thought of as a painful sensation. A sensation you do not want to have because it hurts at the very and only place where things do hurt in the most non-metaphorical way – that is, in your own body. Pain is the primary example of this, but there are some other forms of bodily suffering that should also be mentioned here: failure to get air, feeling too cold or hot, nausea, thirst, hunger, and inability to move, to mention the most important ones. Doctors and nurses know all these forms of physical sufferings and how important it is to try to mitigate them if the patient is to be blessed with any time and energy to devote to things in life other than coping with the bodily torments. With this I do not want to say that pain and other bodily afflictions would not be psychological experiences in addition to having a physiology; all I want to say is that some forms of bodily suffering are so severe and overwhelming that they consume almost all the attention and time there is to be had for the person who is suffering from them (Charon 2006).

Negative utilitarianism (caring about the aggregation of pain rather than happiness) is arguably right in stressing the utmost importance of such experiences for our well-being and probably also in proposing that we have a major duty to relieve them among all parties when and where we have a chance of doing so. What many utilitarians have not thought about long and hard enough is what pain in its many different forms really *is*. Pain, I would like to suggest, is not only a sensation; it is also a *mood* (Leder 2016: chapter 2; Svenaeus 2015a). That is, pain – and the other related forms of physical sufferings I have mentioned – is not only the sensing of a part of the body in a painful way but the appearance of the *whole world* of the sufferer in a painful manner. When I have a headache, am short of breath, or nauseated my whole field of attention is changed, thereby affecting the things I am able to perceive and the way they attain meaning for me. Think about the difference between seeing or smelling a delicious meal when you are very hungry, in contrast to when you have been taken ill with nausea. Think about how a beam of sunlight will catch your attention when you are shivering with cold, in contrast to when you are having a migraine. The world of the physical sufferer is totally different, in wholes as well as bits, from the world of the happy enjoyer.

That feelings (I am using this term in an all-encompassing sense here) in the form of moods are not only bodily sensations but, more importantly, make for meaningfulness by opening up a world of objects, actions, thoughts, communication, and so on, is a thematic developed by phenomenologists such as Max Scheler, Martin Heidegger, and Jean-Paul Sartre (Freeman 2014; Solomon 2006). The philosopher who is most important to my analysis in this chapter of suffering as a mood is, no doubt, Heidegger (1996), though his interest was never illness per se but, rather, the way such experiences may guide us in a phenomenology of human life and being as such (Svenaeus 2011).

Different things show up in the world because of the background mood, and they do so through a certain style of being placed there. Human animals have a much richer world than other animals because the things that show up to them through the moods in question are interwoven in patterns of meaning that have developed into what we might call a *culture*: a system of human-made significance that is articulated and communicated in and through a language. This makes humans better equipped to address and alleviate suffering than other animals, but it also makes them more prone to suffer in ways that are different and deeper. However, to have a culture – a life world – is not an *on* or *off* phenomenon. Whereas cockroaches do not live in cultural meaning patterns, chimpanzees definitely do. Whether the world of chimps is rich enough to deserve the label of culture is a hard question, but they can definitely suffer in ways that no cockroaches, and also no cats or dogs, can.

Why are the issues of mood and life world (or 'being-in-the-world', see chapter one) important from the perspective of suffering? Because they provide clues for understanding how physical suffering is connected to the other themes of suffering that have been brought up by bioethicists and which I mentioned above: frustrated life plans and broken narratives. Most bioethicists are not hedonists, since they think that things other than pain can make you suffer: to not get what you want, to get what you really do *not* want, to not become who you want to be, or to become who you really do *not* want to be, for instance. How are these forms of 'mental suffering' – if I may call them such for the time being – connected to physical suffering? Well, pain can surely stop me from doing what I want to do or becoming who I want to be, but this is only one of the potential relationships between physical and mental suffering. Many feelings other than physical pain are in play here, and, indeed, play into each other in various ways. What one focuses one's attention on and what one desires most in life can matter immensely for the ways in which the experience of physical pain can be relieved or intensified.

Wishes and strivings for certain goals in life are surely also forms of feelings, but as *emotions* they include, in contrast to pain, specific thoughts. They are ways of presenting not only the whole world but also specific states of the world as what is to be desired by the person who has them (Goldie 2000). The thoughts in question, however, can be more or less *conscious* to the person having the emotions. The ways we live and embody ideals and values are not always very well reflected upon but may be, rather, subconscious. Having said this, how are we to think about a 'life plan', or a 'life narrative', and the ways in which they can be frustrated for a person? How explicit are the goals we set for ourselves in our lives? I think the phenomenological idea of a basic 'moodedness', or attunement, of life, providing us with a way of being-in-the-world and being-with-others, worked out in detail by Heidegger (1996), provides a promising start for the philosophy of suffering in relation to the concepts of life goal and personal narrative, and to this I will return shortly.

The suffering person

But before attempting to spell out in more detail the phenomenology of suffering by way of moods and emotions, let us take into consideration a work that has been very influential in underlining the importance of a broader concept of suffering for medicine and bioethics: Eric Cassell's book *The Nature of Suffering and the Goals of Medicine*, published originally in 1991 and released in a second, extended edition in 2004. Cassell's main message is that medicine has been too preoccupied with the *causes* of pain and other bodily symptoms and too ignorant of the way the symptoms attain *meaning* for the person suffering from them. Cassell defines suffering as follows:

> Suffering occurs when an impending destruction of the person is perceived; it continues until the threat of disintegration has passed or until the integrity of the person can be restored in some manner. It follows, then, that although it often occurs in the presence of acute pain, shortness of breath, or other bodily symptoms, suffering extends beyond the physical. Most generally, suffering can be defined as the state of severe distress associated with events that threaten the intactness of the person.
>
> *(Cassell 2004: 32)*

The 'events' on which Cassell spends the most energy in his book are, for obvious reasons, severe diseases and other physical traumas, but according to his definition suffering could also be initiated by a 'mental' trauma – that is, an unwanted, catastrophic life event that hurts the person in a more indirect way than a physical wound does. The key concept here is, indeed, 'person', which for Cassell involves a great many different issues that he does not tie together neatly by means of any philosophical theory of personhood but nevertheless gives many examples of and excellent discussions about in his book. Cassell chooses the concept of 'person' instead of 'self', because he thinks issues of selfhood are somehow 'self-concerned' and exclude interpersonal and worldly issues (Cassell 2004: 33), but I do not see any reason to adopt such an impoverished notion of 'self' in my own analysis (see Carrithers et al. 1985; Zahavi 2005). If not otherwise specified, I will use the two terms of 'person' and 'self' interchangeably in this book. In any case, a person, or a self, is surely not to be thought about as a soul connected to a body, and Cassell is very careful about avoiding any charges of dualism in his books; instead he puts it as follows:

> Persons have personality and a character, a lived past, a family, a family's lived past, culture and society, roles, associations with others, a political dimension, activities, day-to-day behaviors, an existence below awareness, a body, a secret life, a believed-in future, and a transcendent spiritual dimension. The importance of these features for understanding suffering is that each can be affected by illness and become a source of suffering if the integrity of the person is thereby disrupted.
>
> *(Cassell 2004: 150)*

This line-up of dimensions of personhood involved in suffering is much richer than the philosophy language game of sensations, vital life goals, and life narratives I have presented above, but the problem here is that it is not clear to what extent Cassell's different issues overlap and how they are to be thought about in relation to each other. This might be a problem for philosophical theories of suffering and personhood, too, especially if you consider the relationships among different theories of suffering, as I have done above, but in Cassell's case the difficulties are even worse, because so many different *types* of issues are involved in his description (see also Braude 2012). What is the relationship between 'personality' and 'character'? What does it mean to 'have a body', and how is this body related to the person's 'existence below awareness'? How are the 'lived past' and the 'believed-in future' to be related to the other issues that are not temporally specified? How is the intersubjectivity implied in the mentioning of 'family' and 'associations with others' to be thought about? What is the relation between 'culture and society' and 'a political dimension'? Does every person have 'a transcendent spiritual dimension' to their life? And so on.

Perhaps even more pressing with regard to definition are the terms Cassell uses to make us understand suffering as such – that is, the threatened 'integrity' or, as he sometimes also puts it, 'intactness' of the person. These concepts are put in place by Cassell to separate cases of suffering from other unpleasant, but not equally significant, processes that a person can go through in life, but they seem to imply that we know how to think about the person as a kind of *whole*, since it is the very holding together of the person that is threatened or broken down in suffering. Do we know what such a holding together of a person consists in?

The same issue seems to come up in the talk about life plans and life narratives in bioethics, since they demand some kind of cohesiveness in order to be the life plans and life narratives of *this* person in contrast to another person. If life is a narrative, it is a whole in the sense of being stretched out in time with a beginning and an end and held together by some kind of plot. Another way of thinking about the cohesiveness of the person is to stress the experiential dimension, the holding together of a series of states of consciousness making up the self. Many issues in the philosophy of person- and selfhood are addressed here, and they are of great relevance for a number of bioethical dilemmas, not least questions about the beginning and end of the life of a person (DeGrazia 2005; Gallagher 2011). We will return to these questions in chapters six and seven, when we explore the moral status of embryos and brain-dead persons from a phenomenological point of view.

Developing a phenomenology of suffering

To aid in my struggles to make sense of suffering in this chapter I will make use of some descriptions taken from a novel by the Swedish novelist and poet Lars Gustafsson: *The Death of a Beekeeper*, published originally in 1978 (1990). The book tells the story of an early retired, former schoolteacher, Lars Lennart Westin, living in the countryside of the district of Västmanland in Sweden. Westin is about forty years old, he is divorced, has two children who visit him occasionally, and lives a quiet and rather lonely life socializing merely with his dog and the bees he keeps to earn his living. The novel is composed of texts from three notebooks claimed to have been found at his place after his death from cancer. The cancer in question is reported as having started out in the spleen and then spread to surrounding tissue in the stomach area.

The book tells the story of a slowly emerging pain and suffering gradually invading Westin's life. He decides to stay at home as long as possible, refusing to be hospitalized, even denying his death toll by not opening, but instead burning, the envelope he receives in the mail from the hospital lab containing his diagnosis. From a medical-ethical point of view one can certainly take issue with the procedure of sending such information by post – even considering that this was the 1970s – but the most interesting point here is rather that Westin does not seem to *want* to be told about his condition. Deep inside he knows that it is cancer he is suffering from, but the contents of his sufferings, in any case, develop to cover many other areas in addition to the quickly dividing cells consuming him from inside. I find Gustafsson's descriptions exemplary in covering the whole spectrum of human suffering without for a minute losing touch with its embodied roots. Westin's pain expands in invading the whole world he inhabits and the whole life he is trying to make sense of. But let us start with the body:

> I believe it really began during that night when the dog had run away, because deep in my sleep I felt, for the first time, this strange, dull tension in the kidney area, as if someone were pumping up a soccer ball which he had smuggled in there, pulsing, slowly, without the least concern whether I move or not. ... Most of the time it starts at night. I dream of it long before

it has awoken me, it exists as something threatening in my dream, and I am constantly trying to *turn away* from it, not to look at it, I literally turn my head away from it in the dream, and in spite of this it keeps coming closer and forces me to *look at it* and awakens me. Up until Christmas the pills helped pretty much – I first got them in Fagersta, when they still thought it was a kidney stone. ... Now, just a short time after Christmas, it's clear that the fairly strong pills – thank God they keep renewing my prescription – can no longer alleviate it. Not that the pain has gotten stronger, but rather the pills, e.g., my nervous system, have somehow lost their grip on it. It has given me a body again; not since puberty have I had such a strong awareness of my body. I am intensely present in it. Only: this body is the wrong one. It's a body with burning coals in it.

(Gustafsson 1990: 22–23)

Pain, and other bodily ailments, makes the body appear in a new and threatening way to the suffering person (Zaner 1981: chapter 3). The body used to be a silent friend; now it turns out to be an enemy demanding the full attention of the person who is trying to cope. The quoted passage from Gustafsson brings out this *alien* character that the body takes on in pain in a strikingly clear manner. The pain is visiting Lars in the form of something blowing him up from inside – the soccer ball – or that, as a character in his dream, he tries to turn away from and that then awakens him. Lastly, the burning coals inside present him with a body that he cannot run away from, a body that is indisputably his, but, yet, at the same time, an unwelcome stranger.

From a phenomenological point of view we could say that the 'lived body' of Lars – the body as his way of existing and doing things in the world – displays an alien character in showing up as an obstacle and a limitation instead of as an affordance and possibility for him. Drew Leder has called this the 'dys-appearance' of the body in pain and illness in contrast to the disappearance of the body enjoyed when the body stays in the background of our attentive field, which is the normal condition (Leder 1990: 69). The lived body, indeed, has a kind of background feel to it all the time, a way of being present that we can focus our attention upon by way of will. Yet this way of sensing the different parts of the body, as when we do what is called a 'body scan' in mindfulness training, is very different from the alienating force of the dys-appearing body in pain. The healthy body offers a kind of primary being-at-home for us, which is turned into a not-being-at-home in illness (Svenaeus 2009a, 2011).

So the suffering of pain is actually a way of not being at home in one's body. But pain does not stop at the *sensation* level of presenting the body as a troublesome and torturous alien; as a *mood* it also affects the person's ways of living in a world of human projects. It does this by way of presenting the world in a new, alien tonal-colour:

> I took little walks and noticed that in the last months the pain had actually coloured the landscape in a peculiar way. Here and there is a tree where it really hurt, here and there is a fence against whose post I struck my hand in passing. When I returned home during these pain-free days, the pain was, so to speak, caught hanging on the fence. Pain is a landscape. Then, of course, it came back, on Saturday evening, not all at once, but slowly, in tiny spurts, somewhat like a dog following a scent.
>
> *(Gustafsson 1990: 24–25)*

The pain-mood prevents the person from doing the things he normally does. This can be because the body hurts in trying to move, but also because the attention the body demands makes the person strangely absent, less and less present in the world of human projects and communications. Lars in the novel observes retrospectively that he had forgotten to take care of the boat and the beehives last autumn. The reason is not that, or at least not only that, he suspects he will not be around in the coming year because the cancer is likely to kill him; it is rather that his focus of attention has changed. He dwells more and more on the purpose of his life and on things that have happened in the past – his broken marriage, his childhood. One could think about these memories and meditations as a suffering brought on Lars by having his life plan frustrated, or, perhaps, his life narrative ending too soon. Yet it seems more adequate to present the happenings as Lars's *discovering* through the suffering-mood brought on him by the growing cancer that his life has been an alienated project because he has not discovered until now who he really is, or, perhaps rather, who he could have been:

> The problem with these women: they recognized that I wanted much too little. Women are ready for anything when they recognize that one wants it. I have wanted much too little. My whole life long. People never had the feeling that I had any *need* of them. The last three months have made me *real*. That is terrible.
>
> *(Gustafsson 1990: 155)*

The meaning of suffering

In her classic study, *The Body in Pain: The Making and Unmaking of the World*, Elaine Scarry discusses what pain can do to a person's life (1985). Scarry's main example is not illness but torture, so the ethical issues are with her from the very start, but in a slightly different manner than is usually the case in bioethics. To torture a person, according to Scarry, is to make not only her body but her whole *world* alien and painful, a place where everything is turned into a potential *weapon* (1985: chapter 1). Scarry describes how torturers make use of ordinary, homelike environments with things such as beds, tables, chairs, bathtubs, lamps, and so on, then turn everything into weapons to be used upon the victim. Security and rest are nowhere to be found. Everything becomes uncertain; all forms of control are taken away from the tortured person. The torture, according to Scarry, also robs the victim of the ability to express herself, since the possibility to speak on her own terms is systematically destroyed by the torturers by way of interrogations and enforced isolation (1985: chapter 3).

But the breakdown of the victim's language is also caused by the pain–mood – which includes the fear of more pain to come – leading to a collapse of all attempts to find oneself at home in the world for the one who suffers. It is hard to find words to express what one is going through in pain. And the lack of a language one can trust to make sense of one's experiences ultimately also leads to a lack of self-understanding. The pain and the fear of pain not only make the victim intensively present in her body, they also rob her of an expressed and articulated self-understanding. This is why, for sufferers of torture or life-threatening illness, the cultivation of stories in which sufferers give words to painful experiences can be important as a practice of *healing* (Frank 1995).

The example of torture makes salient a feature that is actually present in all forms of severe pain: the experience of being *acted upon*, being violated by the pain in question. To suffer is to find oneself in a situation of *passivity* in relation to feelings that hurt us. Being hurt by a weapon is the metaphor that comes to our mind when we try to describe pain, because pain is a kind of passive state in which something evil is done to us, by another person, or by the body itself. Gustafsson again:

> It begins pretty far down somewhere in the right calf, where it feels like something like liquid metal, or like something which has hooked into the musculature, a golden wire one could perhaps say. Then it radiates to the right loin, sends, along the back of the leg, a whole bundle of white radiating gold wires to the navel and the hip, and a fan of this radiating gold extends up to the diaphragm. When I lie down, it hurts twice as much; when I remain seated, it wanders up to the back, it doesn't always maintain the same pitch, the frequencies, the decibel count of this white radiating gold changes constantly, they create chords, very clean, clear chords, until they suddenly get tangled somehow and become *cutting*.
>
> *(Gustafsson 1990: 71)*

The twin concept of pain in Scarry's book is *work* (1985: chapter 4). Pain unmakes the world; work makes a world existent again through carrying out things, achieving goals imagined and then created. But work is also something *hard*, something that one can suffer under, yet this burden is manageable because work has a purpose. Pain is destructive, work is creative, so let us have less pain and more work in the world, or rather, let us have a richer world by transforming pain into work. This is Scarry's recipe. Since being in pain means being forced to perform a sort of work in order to cope and not lose control, the idea of turning this work into some kind of meaningful activity in which one tries to master the pain rather than giving in to it may be an option for some sufferers.

There are other strategies, though, that may in many cases turn out to be more successful. Accepting the pain, for instance, or trying to do other things – other work – in order to distract attention from the pain in question (Melzack and Wall 1996).

The notion of work becomes even more relevant when we approach the forms of suffering that concern relational and personal issues in addition to the bodily ones. Many philosophers and theologians have considered suffering as a *transformative* process, which could lead to a more authentic life for the one who suffers if he develops the right attitude (Frankl 1986). To approach one's suffering in this way could be considered a kind of *work* – abandoning worldly goods in order to attain a more spiritual life, for instance. There is something very important and true to the idea that development demands suffering, as everyone who has attempted to accomplish things of true significance will know (whether the thing in question consists in art, science, or sport). Such an image of suffering turns it into something worth pursuing, in contrast to the utter meaninglessness that also seems to be a forceful component of the phenomenon. Considering the fact that suffering is something we will not be able to avoid no matter how much we want to, the idea of transforming experiences of suffering into something meaningful is an attractive one. Suffering teaches a human being to know and explore his own *limits*, a theme that was developed in ancient Greek tragedy, and this can be essential to finding one's place in life, regardless of whether the matter of transcendent beings is brought into the picture or not (Chiurazzi 2012).

One can find roughly three philosophical (and theological) ways of dealing with the problem of apparently meaningless suffering since the days of Job. The first consists in insisting that the suffering in question is meaningful and does have a purpose even if we do not understand and appreciate this purpose at the time. One way of articulating this attitude makes use of an almighty God, whose ways we do not have the capabilities and resources to understand. He (or she, or it) has a purpose for us and that is what matters. Another way of articulating this position is to walk the path of asceticism; suffering will make you a wiser and morally better person, and there are no other ways of attaining these higher forms of human existence. Kierkegaard, with his claim that 'just as gold is purified in the fire, so the soul is purified in sufferings', belongs firmly to this tradition (1997: 102), and so do Nietzsche, Scheler, Heidegger, Simone Weil, and other modern purifiers of the body and soul in the interests of creativity, compassion, humbleness, spirituality, nobleness, or other virtues (Madison 2013).

A second way of dealing with suffering consists in developing an attitude of indifference or acceptance towards it. Do not fight suffering; just let it be and you will be better off, this tradition urges us. Suffering is a worldly thing and therefore it does not matter. Stoicism belongs here, and so do Buddhism and philosophers like Schopenhauer, as well as the modern mindfulness movement (Madison 2013). There appears to be an implicit dualism present in many versions of the ideal of *apatheia*, and this is also true of many of the asceticism approaches to suffering (the first alternative). An elevated stand and attitude towards suffering will make us more indifferent to the pains and appetites of the body and through this make us more of soul, so to speak. While dualism is not a popular or even tenable position in the philosophy of mind these days, in the ethics of suffering the division between bodily sufferings and the sufferings involving other, 'higher' life matters may carry some truth. Not in the way that the sufferings of the body do not really matter, though. This strikes me as an almost perverse idea, although one should consider that it may be an attitude that works *therapeutically* in making bodily suffering easier to cope with for some people. The dualistic tendency in interpretations of human suffering carries truth, rather, in the way it stresses the potential for human development in existential – *in contrast to* bodily – suffering. But how could bodily pain *not matter*? How could someone even wish to have more of it for spiritual reasons? These questions bring me to the third philosophical position regarding the problem of suffering.

The third way of understanding and approaching suffering is to deem it an evil that we should try to escape and alleviate at all costs. There is no purpose in suffering whatsoever. Most utilitarian philosophers belong in this group and so would a phenomenological philosopher, like Levinas (1998), or an existentialist, like Camus (1960). Gustafsson's Bee Keeper again:

> What's happening to me now is disgusting, horrible, and degrading, and nobody will bring me to accept it or to persuade myself that it is somehow good for me. It is disgusting to be at the mercy of an idiotic blind pain, fits of vomiting, and this entire secret inner dissolution, which is stupid and offensive, no matter what kind of an explanation there may be for it. The usual heresy consists in denying the existence of a god who has created us. It is a much more interesting heresy to imagine that possibly a god has created us and then to say that there isn't the least reason for us to be impressed by that fact. And certainly not to be thankful for it. If there is a god it is our duty to say no. If there is a god then it is the task of the human being to be his negation. We begin again. We never give up. My duty in these days, weeks or, at the worst, months which are still left, consists in saying a great, clear NO.
>
> *(Gustafsson 1990: 156)*

This strikes me as a very convincing position in the face of bodily pain. But it may be less convincing when we move to sufferings that are dependent upon the person's being-in-the-world and self-understanding rather than his bodily state. Purpose-finders for human suffering will often make the mistake of neglecting the intrinsic badness of pain, but purpose-cleansers will make the opposite mistake of neglecting the potential for growth in some human suffering. To find out what is important in life one needs not only flow but also *resistance*, and this is exactly what suffering offers us.

The moods of suffering

My idea in introducing the phenomenological concept of mood has been to build a bridge between suffering on different interacting *levels* of human life: embodiment, action, relation to others, self-understanding, and personal identity (Ricoeur 1992: 317 ff.). Provided that suffering is to be understood as a mood, what do such suffering-moods look like beyond the type of bodily pain-moods we have discussed so far? Important examples of 'mental' suffering-moods would be anxiety, fear, sadness, boredom, helplessness, despair, shame, sorrow, and self-hatred. These moods would, certainly, also be embodied – this is the reason for using the quotation marks in the preceding sentence – but the pain that is involved would be of another type than physical pain.

The moods I just mentioned are all essential ingredients in the suffering we call depression, which can be regarded as archetypal for mental suffering in gathering so many suffering-moods to the breaking point of actually falling ill with them. Other psychiatric disorders are also associated with suffering, but depression is prototypical because the moods to be found there are to such a large extent part of every human life when they appear in forms that are less severe and all encompassing (Vanheule and Devisch 2014). One may, indeed, dispute whether all of the feelings found in depression that I have mentioned really are moods, since some of them seem to involve objects, making them, rather, what philosophers call emotions (Goldie 2000). However, I do not think that this distinction is very important here, since the emotions of fear, shame, and self-hatred in depression and related mental disorders are all-encompassing emotions, affecting the whole world of the sufferer and, indeed, bringing him back to himself in a bodily manner. To be depressed affects not only one's view of oneself and the world one lives in, but also one's embodiment, making the lived body heavy and slow in a characteristic manner (Svenaeus 2013a).

Anxiety, fear, sadness, boredom, helplessness, despair, shame, sorrow, and self-hatred are not always moods of suffering in the strict and qualified sense, since they do not always, to repeat Cassell, threaten the integrity or intactness of the person suffering from them (Cassell 2004: 32). I think it is important to try to uphold some form of *severity criterion* in order not to automatically turn every negative mood into a case of suffering, or, even less so, a case of illness suffering. This issue mirrors the ongoing debates in the philosophy of medicine considering the borderline between health and disease and the driving forces of medicalization (Conrad 2007). A phenomenology of illness will help us to better understand what it means to suffer – insights that are important for bioethics in addressing dilemmas involving suffering persons and how they could best be helped. But the phenomenological characterization of suffering by means of concepts such as mood, being-in-the-world, and self-understanding will not always allow us to draw a neat line between the suffering that is the proper subject of medical interventions and the suffering that is not. Rather, it will make us see how complex the issues of medicalization are, and how other competences than being able to detect and cure diseases are involved in attaining the goals of medicine (see further chapter five).

As I have been trying to show with Gustafsson, suffering due to a painful bodily condition involves a kind of *alienation* at the bodily level, making the person no longer able to be at home in and with his own body. This easily leads to alienation at the level of the being-in-the-world and at the level of self-understanding also, because the mood affects the entire existence of the ill person. Self-understanding in these cases is linked to a *temporal* understanding of one's life, since the pain-mood and the knowledge of an impending death change the way a person approaches his past and future. There is room for positive transformations in such cases, since the seriousness of one's condition can make room for a more honest and true reflection upon what *matters* in life and *who* one wants to be. The typical illustration of that kind of rewarding suffering process is found in Leo Tolstoy's classic novel *The Death of Ivan Ilyich* (Tolstoy 2015). However, in bringing up the transformative powers of illness suffering, let us not forget the true horrors suffered by the main character of this book – not only his bodily pains but also the disappointments brought upon him by his stupid family members and unfaithful friends:

> The pain in his side oppressed him, and seemed to be constantly getting worse; it became a continuous pain, and the taste in his mouth became stranger and stranger. It seemed to him that his breath smelt disgusting, and his appetite got worse and he felt weaker all the time. He could not deceive himself: something new and terrible was happening to him, something so important that nothing that had ever happened to him in his life had been more important. And he was the only one who knew; those around him didn't understand, or didn't want to understand, and they all thought that everything was going on as before. That was what tormented Ivan Ilyich more than anything. His family – above all, his wife and daughter, who were in a positive whirl of engagements – understood nothing, as he could see; they were vexed that he was so morose and demanding, as if it was his fault. They tried to hide it, but he could see that they found him a nuisance.
> *(Tolstoy 2015: 181)*

Despite Ivan's reaching a state of relative peace towards the end in facing his destiny, this is not the way many of us would like to end up, no matter how deeply deceived we may be about our life priorities and personal identity:

> It was from that moment that the screaming began, which was to continue uninterrupted for three days, a screaming so dreadful that even through two closed doors it was impossible to hear it without horror. In that moment when he answered his wife, he realized that he was lost, there was no return, the end had come, the end of everything, and yet his doubt had still not been resolved, it still remained a doubt. 'O! O! O!' he screamed in different

intonations. He had begun by crying 'No!', and so went on, continuing with the sound 'o'.

(Tolstoy 2015: 207)

If the transformation of one's goals in life through suffering is to form an attractive alternative, we most often need more of a future in which to realize them and somewhat less of bodily pains on the way to finding them than was the case for Ivan Ilyich. Mental pains are not always easier to handle than bodily pains, but in most cases they are not as intense as the pains suffered by Ivan, who is probably dying from cancer of the intestinal tract.

Whereas bodily alienation is often hard to make sense of and benefit from, the alienation that is caused by unwanted life events (meaning things that are happening in the world rather than within one's body) is more open to work on and change for the better. This may certainly be the case with many forms of chronic bodily pains, also, but in those cases the attempts to deal with the pain in question often seem to be more about learning to cope with the pain than transforming it into a rewarding life experience (see above).

In contrast to bodily pains, mental pains – that is, moods of suffering that are not primarily of the bodily pain type – are there for a different kind of *reason*. The reason in these cases is not a bodily dysfunction, as in cancer, but a change in the being–in–the–world of the patient having to do with the person's way of life and self–understanding. Sadness or anxiousness most often *depends* upon something that has happened to a person and the way she interprets this happening in an evaluation of her life. In cases in which there is insufficient reason for an overburdening suffering-mood to occur we tend to think about such a mood as a mental disease (disorder) like depression or anxiety disorders, the reason being internal rather than external (see further chapter five).

If the reason for the suffering is external rather than internal, the prospect of transforming the suffering in question into a form of work with a purpose seems to be much more promising – at least if the hurtfulness of the external condition that brought about the suffering is dependent upon the *evaluation* the person in question makes of the situation. It is very hard to change the importance a growing cancer has to your life, whereas it may be possible to do so if we are talking about losing one's job or being cheated on by one's partner. The distinction I am after is not only about the difference between events inside my body and events that take place in the world outside my body, since some worldly occurrences – such as finding oneself in a war or being tortured – may be just as hard to change as in the case of a terminal cancer. However, many reasons for mental suffering are more like mendable diseases, in the sense that they leave scars and after-effects but nevertheless can be healed. And in this process of healing we may grow, not necessarily stronger, but at least wiser and more of ourselves in some transformative sense.

Accordingly, whereas bodily alienation is hard to make sense of and benefit from, the alienation that occurs on the level of being–in–the–world and self–understanding are more promising in these respects. Transformative processes are an option here: one may find a new job, or a new partner, and one may even change one's basic bodily ways of being-in-the-world if, for instance, one loses one's hearing or ability to move one's legs as the result of an accident. In the latter cases the transformative change in question may be more of a coping than an empowerment process, but it could nevertheless include new evaluations of one's life goals that make life bearable again.

What makes a life worth living?

Let us sum up my phenomenological characterization of suffering so far:

Suffering is an alienating mood overcoming a person and engaging her in an embodied struggle to remain at home in the face of the loss of meaning and purpose in life. It involves painful experiences at different levels of the person's being-in-the-world that hang together through the suffering-mood but are nevertheless distinguishable by being primarily about (1) my embodiment, (2) my engagements in the world together with others, and (3) my core life values enacted by way of my life narrative. The being-at-home of a person in a mood is always enacted as a being-in-the-world, which is also a being-as-a-body and a being-in-time.

The most intriguing part of the phenomenology of suffering is perhaps the way a person's suffering is both determined and potentially changeable by way of the *core life values* she embodies. What does this mean? If I am a professional musician, the sudden painful inability to move my little finger is much more important to me than if I am a philosophy professor. In the same way, finding out that my wife has been having an affair is much more devastating if I believe in lifelong faithful marriages than if I believe that the ideal of monogamy is a destructive illusion. The moods we live in embody such life priorities and evaluations by the way they make things in our life appear as more or less *significant* to us.

Charles Taylor, in his book *Sources of the Self*, analyses the way our selves, our personal beings, are built up by way of such evaluations. Most important are those priorities he calls 'strong evaluations', about the things that makes a human life worth living beyond satisfying the basic needs of food, drink, sleep, safety, sex, and so on (Taylor 1989: 4 ff.). (The well-known moral philosopher Ronald Dworkin calls the same things 'critical interests' (1994: 199 ff.).) These strong evaluations concern moral matters in a narrow sense: what responsibilities I have for the life and flourishing of other persons. They also, however, concern questions about what a *good life* means for me and how I attain *self-respect in the eyes of others*:

> To understand our moral world we have to see not only what ideas and pictures underlie our sense of respect for others but also those which underpin our notion of a full life. And as we shall see, these are not two quite separate orders of ideas. There is a substantial overlap or, rather, a complex relation in which some of the basic notions reappear in a new way. This is particularly the case for what I called above the affirmation of ordinary life. In general, one might try to single out three axes of what can be called, in the most

general sense, moral thinking. As well as the two just mentioned – our sense of respect for and obligations to others, and our understandings of what makes a full life – there is also the range of notions concerned with dignity. By this I mean the characteristics by which we think of ourselves as commanding (or failing to command) the respect of those around us.

(Taylor 1989: 14–15)

In his tracing of the origins of the modern self, Taylor, in addition to this preliminary outline of the territory of strong evaluations, spends considerable time articulating the importance of *self-expression* for our ways of being constituted as persons in the modern era. Protestantism and romanticism are his major sources in stressing the importance for the modern self of *spelling oneself out* by way of a form of creative work (Taylor 1989: 374). The artist, the genius of the Romantic era, creating her works of art and herself by making her inner nature visible to us in the form of a painting or a poem, is exemplary in this regard. This creative act can be understood as a form of suffering transformed into self-expression. From this image it is not a very long leap to a model of the self – the person – as constituted by a life narrative, a model we find in contemporary culture and bioethics (Schechtman 1996). Taylor's strong-evaluation idea about what essentially matters to us in life and how we may flourish is also consonant with research in developmental psychology about how we attain a sense and concept of selfhood together with and in the eyes of others (Rochat 2009: 86 ff.). Our feelings of who we are and what matters to us in life are to a very large extent dependent on the way we connect to others and their views on us. The story of a human life is from the very beginning a narrative that attains meaning for a person in the eyes of others (see further chapter seven).

The idea that a person (self) is a narrative obviously has to be interpreted in some metaphorical way to make sense (see many of the essays in Gallagher 2011). Human lives are not stories, written or told, in the strict sense of the word. The life of a person, however, clearly has a temporal structure including a beginning and an end, and also a kind of narrative structure in the way that the life should make sense to the person living it. When we attempt to understand things, and especially ourselves, we turn to stories. The narrative structure is where the cohesiveness of a human life comes from: it is not enough to have temporal continuity; one also needs to develop a narrative to explore and to show who one is (Goldie 2012; Ricoeur 1992). The question of personal identity in this extended sense is connected to the core life values we identify with. The most important values as regards self-identity are the ones Taylor identifies as demanding strong interpretation: values regarding the treatment of others, values regarding the content of a good life, and values regarding the identification of oneself as someone worthy of respect in the eyes of others (Taylor 1989; see also Taylor 1991). These three zones of core life values are interconnected, and they demand, at least to some extent, self-reflection. But core life-narrative values do not come about only through philosophical reflection; they become embodied by being-in-the-world with others from the very beginning of our lives. Strong evaluations are always dependent upon a life form, a horizon of attuned understanding that one has grown into through the support and influence of others, and they can thus be more or less implicit or explicit for a person. Core life values are, nevertheless, always core life-*narrative* values, because they are only possible to comprehend and/or formulate by way of stories about a person's life (Goldie 2012: chapter 6). A human life is not a narrative, but it is bestowed with reason and coherence through stories that can be more or less true to the life of the person they are about (Goldie 2012: chapter 7).

Suffering can be brought about because of events that prevent one from realizing the values that are vital for (i.e. belong to the core of) one's life and sense of self-respect. The suffering-mood in question could be related, for instance, to no longer being able to do something that has been of utmost importance to one's sense of meaning in life – such as listening to music, climbing mountains, or drinking good wine. The suffering could also be related to events depriving the person of other persons whom she loves and lives with. In all these – and similar – cases the suffering would have the quality of a mood that the person lives in, and the mood in question would be related to a particular way of being-in-the-world and being-in-time, as well as being-in-the-body, that would be *alienated* in the sense of fundamentally *unhomelike* to the person in question. This is also the point at which we could talk about broken life narratives. Such a suffering is not fundamentally a case of having certain wants in life frustrated (no matter how important they are); it is more like losing one's footing in the world and beginning to doubt that *anything* really matters anymore.

In many cases the life narrative can be fixed by way of changing one's core life values, but there are clearly limits to such possibilities, and, above all, to change is a matter not only of thinking hard and making new choices in life but of working through the suffering-mood in question and thereby finding a new way to stand up. As I stressed above, it is important to *qualify* the concept of suffering, and I have done so by way of an *alienation* criterion, which I have identified on three interconnected levels: bodily being, being-in-the-world, and matters of self-understanding. Typically, the three ways of being alienated will feed into each other in various ways through the moods of suffering, but suffering can clearly be more or less bodily in character, and also more or less about daily activities or core life values.

As a consequence of the alienation criterion, people cannot be said to really suffer when they do something painful just to achieve some other thing that they strive for and that demands the effort in question. Bodybuilding is not suffering, at least not under standard circumstances, and neither is giving birth. The latter is, indeed, called a form of *labour*, and this indicates exactly the positive outcomes that are to be expected and make the activity meaningful – remember Scarry's ideas about pain and work that I have discussed above (Scarry 1985). However, whether or not giving birth is a case of suffering will clearly depend on the individual circumstances. If the pain-mood in question is too intense and overwhelming to be tolerated and made sense of for the woman in labour, it will turn the event into a case of suffering. Likewise, giving birth when there is a bad outcome (e.g. when the woman or the child is injured in the process) will normally be a case of suffering.

Suffering-moods can be distinctively more 'mental' than 'bodily' in character and origin, especially when we move into the territory of suffering that is not an obvious issue for health-care professionals. In such cases the second and third levels of suffering will be very visibly involved, whereas the first, bodily level will be rather invisible or at least not very significant. If a parent loses her child in a car accident, the suffering will be *about* the loss in question; this suffering, as grief and mourning, will also be bodily experienced, but this bodily aspect is not very important from the point of view of understanding the suffering in question. Cases of mental illness are more interesting as regards the relationship between the worldly issues of the person and her embodiment (Ratcliffe 2008, 2015). In chapter three I will explore the territory of illness in relation to the culture and society the person is living in more thoroughly by way of the example of anorexia nervosa. This will bring up questions regarding embodiment and alienation in a rather different way than the example of Gustafsson's beekeeper has been able to do in this chapter.

Summary

In this chapter I have presented and defended a phenomenological understanding of suffering according to which suffering is an alienating mood overcoming a person and engaging her in a struggle to remain at home in the face of the loss of meaning and purpose in life. Such a mood (or combination of moods) involves painful experiences at different levels that are connected but are nevertheless distinguishable by being primarily about, firstly, my embodiment, secondly, my engagements in the world together with others, and, thirdly, my core life-narrative values. The being-at-home or not-being-at-home of a person in a mood has been interpreted via the concept of being-in-the-world, which is also a being-as-a-body and a being-in-time. Suffering, especially the sufferings brought on us by illness, is a bodily experience, but the alienating powers of suffering cover a territory that includes many kinds of life-world and self-interpretation issues.

Suffering is in essence a feeling (a mood), but as such it has implications for and involves the person's entire life: how she acts in the world, communicates with others, and understands and looks upon her priorities and life goals. It is essential for medicine and bioethics to discern these different layers of suffering and how they are connected through the suffering-mood. Suffering-moods are typically intense and painful in nature, but they may also display a rather subconscious quality in presenting things in the world and my life as a whole in an alienating way. In such situations we are not focused directly upon the suffering-mood – as in the cases of pain and other bodily ailments – but upon the things that the mood presents to us – situations in the world that prevent us from having a good enough life and being the persons we want to be. Such sufferings may in many cases be transformed or at least mitigated by a person's identifying and changing core life values, and in such a manner reinterpreting her life story to become an easier and more rewarding one to live under the present circumstances.

3

THE BODY UNCANNY

Phenomenological explorations of the body as alien

In this chapter I will continue my phenomenological analysis of illness suffering by means of exploring different ways in which the body and life of a person may show up as alien and uncanny to her. The main example will be the case of anorexia nervosa. I have selected this example to introduce the role of culture, gender, and politics in the bodily alienation process. There are many examples of bodily 'otherness' that would be fruitful to explore in this regard, and I will deal with some of them in this book: pregnancy, feeling the need for cosmetic surgery, and going through an organ transplantation, to mention just a few (see the essays in Zeiler and Käll 2014).

All the stated examples introduce the issue of living with a body that is no longer only one's own but also *other* to its owner in some way. When the body reveals such a life of its own, this is in many cases an *alienating* and also an *uncanny* experience for the person to whom the body belongs. Various forms of illness are the major examples of such uncanniness, but the experience of being at the will of the body is not *necessarily* alienating. Pregnancy is a clear example of the opposite, at least in the standard case (see further chapter six), as are other everyday situations in which we find ourselves at the will of the body but do not suffer as a result: think of cases in which the body reacts or performs on its own when we are faced with a demanding situation, such as fleeing in the face of danger. In such situations, we experience the body's taking command of the happenings, and it does so for our own good, so to speak. Similarly, we can allow the body to take over in activities that demand coordination and control which we are not able to execute by way of will and consciousness alone: think of playing tennis or driving a car.

What does it mean to be bodily alienated in addition to having an experience of my own body as something whose ways I do not fully control? It means that the body is experienced as *foreign* and *strange* to me. In my becoming bodily *alienated*, the foreignness of the body reminds me of a state of being at home with it that is no longer present and that I desire to have reinstated. Alienation is usually portrayed as an experience of becoming foreign to one's life in terms of the things one does and thinks (Guignon 2004). The body is my basic home-being, and therefore alienation within the bodily domain is a particularly *uncanny* experience, compared to other ways of being alienated (Frank 2002; Slatman 2014). A focus on action and thinking are common threads of Marxist or existentialist frameworks of the alienated life, but alienation can also be an experience of foreignness within the domains of embodiment, as I tried to show in chapter two with the examples taken from Gustafsson (1990).

The 1979 science fiction movie *Alien*, directed by Ridley Scott, offers the archetypal example of the horrors of bodily alienation through being possessed and taken over by something foreign hiding itself in the body. After landing on an unexplored planet, from which the towing spaceship *Nostromo* has received strange transmission signals, a member of the crew of gets infected by an alien, parasite creature, which lays its eggs in him by attaching itself to his face. Officer Kane is taken on board and recovers as *Nostromo* takes off from the planet to continue its journey. He is, however, far from healthy, as the crew will soon find out. The scene in which, during a meal, Officer Kane begins to choke and convulse until an alien creature bursts from his chest, killing him and escaping into the labyrinths of the ship, is famous in horror-film history. A war begins between the creature and the remaining crew members, who get killed one after the other by the alien in the creepy environment of the ship. In the last scene, Officer Ripley (Sigourney Weaver), the last survivor of the crew, has managed to flee the ship in a shuttle after blowing the creature to pieces, but she still has the crew's cat with her, and who knows what is hiding in its intestines? This alien certainly survived to be the main figure of many succeeding movies, reminding us of the severe uncanniness of bodily parasitic possession, which, in real life, is limited to smaller creatures like worms, fungi, bacteria, or viruses.

Bodily alienation is an uncanny experience. The word 'uncanny' actually hides the meaning of alien within itself, if we investigate its German etymological origins. The German word '*unheimlich*' ('uncanny') has the double meaning of something being hidden and fearful ('*heimlich*') and of not being at home – that is, alienated ('*unheimisch*'). Sigmund Freud brings this out in his essay 'The Uncanny', which rests heavily on early nineteenth-century horror fiction, such as E. T. A. Hoffmann's novel *The Sandman* (Freud 1959). Freud's main hypothesis in the essay is that we experience something as uncanny when we find ourselves in doubt about whether it is dead or alive, as in the case of encountering automata or ghosts. What is uncanny in these examples is not the experience of my own body, but the experience of the body of something that (or someone who) is other than me and whose status with regard to being alive is uncertain. However, Freud also gives a lot of other examples in the essay that describe the uncanny character of being controlled by something foreign that is nevertheless a part of oneself (the unconscious), and links this to the development of the ego and the separation from the mother and the father (Freud 1959).

The body, as I pointed out in chapter one, is not a thing that I am accidentally hooked up with and can choose to disregard, as a dualist or, indeed, materialist perspective might fool us into assuming (Gallagher 2005; Merleau-Ponty 2012). The body is *me*, my fundamental way of existing and making myself at home in the world. This is why becoming a victim of the autonomous 'will' of the body can be such an *uncanny* experience: at the heart of my home territory, foreignness now makes itself known, as Richard Zaner writes in his rich study, *The Context of Self*:

> If there is a sense in which my own-body is intimately mine, there is furthermore, an equally decisive sense in which I belong to it – in which I am at its disposal or mercy, if you will. My body, like the world in which I live, has its own nature, functions, structures, and biological conditions; since it embodies me, I thus experience myself as implicated by my body and these various conditions, functions, etc. I am exposed to whatever can influence, threaten, inhibit, alter, or benefit my biological organism. Under certain conditions, it can fail me (more or less), not be capable of fulfilling my wants or desires, or even thoughts, forcing me to turn away from what I may want to do and attend to my own body: because of fatigue, hunger, thirst, disease, injury, pain, or even itches, I am forced at times to tend and attend to it, regardless, it may be, of what may well seem more urgent at the moment.
>
> *(Zaner 1981: 52)*

Drew Leder, in the important work, *The Absent Body*, draws our attention in the same way to how the 'own-body' (lived body) might appear as something that hurts and resists the will of its owner (1990). Leder names this the 'dys-appearance' of the body, indicating that the body can sometimes lose its transparent qualities and show up as a hindrance and obstacle for the person living it (1990: 69). In contrast to this, the 'me-like' showing of the body is most often a case of the body's *not* letting itself appear to me. The body normally *disappears* to allow the things of the world that I encounter and strive for in my activities to show up (Leder 1990: 25). When I write these words on my computer, to offer a nearby example, my hands and eyes do not appear to me, and neither does the rest of my body, sitting on the chair and leaning on the table; rather, they make my thoughts appear to me on the computer screen.

But that the body disappears does not mean that it ceases to exist. Through the moods that penetrate my different ways of being-in-the-world, the body is *pre-reflectively* present to me exactly as my very way of being, a fact that has been explored not only by phenomenologists but also by brain scientists (Damasio 1999). This pre-reflective, non-thematized appearance of the body is most often non-appealing in character, but just as the body might 'dys-appear' in hurting and resisting our actions, it can also 'eu-appear' when we enjoy the things we do, as

Kristin Zeiler has pointed out (2010). The homelike being of my own body harbours processes beyond my control: notably, the autonomic functions of our visceral life that are controlled by subconscious processes of the brain stem. These processes, however, as I have pointed out, are normally not a source of uncanniness. We do not feel controlled in any foreign or bad way by the fact that we breathe air and digest food without having to think about it all the time; quite the contrary, it would be a very demanding and frightening experience to constantly have to support these life-sustaining processes by way of will and thought. Nevertheless, at the moment when the automatic functions of breathing and digestion become disturbed, the body will (dys-) appear to me. Sometimes the causes of dysfunction can be found in foreign disease agents conquering the body (bringing us back to the *Alien* example), but most often the changed appearance of the body is rather an imbalance of the lived body itself with multiple causes.

The books by Zaner and Leder are seminal on this account since, in contrast to most earlier works by phenomenologists, they display an open and penetrating interest in the otherness of the lived body that dwells at the heart of its homelike being (see also Slatman 2014). Whereas Edmund Husserl and Maurice Merleau-Ponty were busy showing how the body is first and foremost not an object encountered by the person, but the basic form of subjectivity itself, Zaner and Leder attempt to give a fuller account of how the body as this basic form of subjectivity is also other, and sometimes alien, to its subject.

Sartre on falling ill

A preamble to Zaner's and Leder's analyses is found in Jean-Paul Sartre's famous work *Being and Nothingness*, published in 1943 (1992). Sartre asks how we are to understand the process by which we gradually come to realize that we are ill and might need the attention and advice of a doctor. After having defined and explicated the dual structure of being – being-for-itself (consciousness and selfhood) and being-in-itself (thingness) – in the preceding two parts of *Being and Nothingness*, Sartre now wants to show in part three how these two forms of being are not only opposed to each other, but also necessarily conjoined in the human way of existing as a bodily being (1992: 401 ff.).

In his attempts to uncover the structure of embodied experience, Sartre turns to medical examples. When my body is examined and understood by the doctor as a malfunctioning biological organism, it is objectified, according to Sartre, in a manner analogous to when I am exposed to the gaze of the other person in everyday life (1992: 460 ff.). But in discussing the process of falling ill, Sartre also explores ways in which the lived body can be affected by feelings that interfere with activities we are engaged in before the doctor has entered the scene. His main example is the headache involved in reading a book late at night (compare with the accounts of pain offered by Gustafsson in chapter two) (Sartre 1992: 437 ff.). The headache shows itself in the very activity of reading in which the text gets harder and harder to focus upon and understand. Pain – *douleur* in French – at this pre-reflective level is a lived pain, which does not show itself as a sensation *in* one's own-body but rather as a pain belonging to the very *activity* of reading. The pain is not known – not focused upon as an in-itself – but is still *there* in my pre-reflective way of being. The pain quality is dependent upon the way I choose to focus upon things in the world in different activities. If I stop reading and start listening to the radio, the pain might stop. But the quality of the experience is also dependent upon the way the world sucks me in – the very absorption into the world of the book might make me forget the pain. Sartre's description of the nature of pain as a melody which has a life of its own that influences, and in some cases becomes the dominating melody of, a person's life, is, to my mind, very apt in understanding chronic pain (Sartre 1992: 441; see also Svenaeus 2009a, 2015a).

Sartre's analysis makes lucid the way pain is primarily suffered rather than known, and this is a very important insight for health-care professionals and bioethicists. Pain is not primarily objectified and reflected upon but, rather, lived as a melodic style of human experience, as we could also see in the analysis of suffering as mood in chapter two. This kind of illness suffering, I believe, is most adequately described as a kind of *bodily resistance and modulation* displaying itself at the heart of human experience – that is, an awareness of a body that is mine, yet alien, since it resists and disturbs, rather than supports, my ways of being conscious and directed towards things in the world. This experience is hard to conceptualize from Sartre's point of view: in his philosophical set-up only consciousness can take on the form of being of the for-itself; the body can show up only as an *object* of conscious awareness, and this happens only when the other person objectifies me. However, Sartre's analysis is ambivalent on this issue, since if the gaze of the other person carries the power to make me aware of my own body – in feelings such as shame – it must do so by making *my* body an in-itself. And so, it seems, the body shows up as mine precisely because it is *already* to a certain extent part of a pre-reflective, lived bodily awareness.

My conclusion here would be that Sartre does not need to turn exclusively to the battle between consciousnesses to localize the in-itself of my for-itself. This in-itself of my body shows itself as a kind of foreign life and force in experiences such as pain, nausea, and other aspects of illness. Thus, it is not exclusively the otherness of the other person, but the otherness of my own body – displayed in a painful way in illness – which lends concreteness to my existence. To find oneself in pain is to fall victim to a process in which the body becomes increasingly hard to tolerate and cope with in displaying its foreign and uncontrollable sides; this is why pain is an *alienating* process. For Sartre this alienation is not fully realized until the doctor has turned my body into an object: a biological organism, which is found to be out of order. This is what Sartre calls disease – in French, *maladie* – rather than illness: a process or lesion in the biological organism which comes to my knowledge through the examinations of the doctor (1992: 465–466). At the two earlier stages – the pre-reflective experience of pain and the melodic suffering of illness – the alienation is still blind; it is not experienced or, rather, not *reflected* as an in-itself of my body.

Illness makes us feel our own bodies: it reveals the body to us in different painful ways, through making it heavy, stiff, hot, nauseated, plagued by pain, twists, jerks, shivers, and so on. This facticity of the body is the result neither of the gaze of the other person, nor of a reflection adopting the outer perspective of the other person in an indirect way, but a result of the very otherness of one's own-body which *makes itself known* to us as an experience of suffering.

Suffering illness and having a disease

It is important to understand the fundamental difference between a phenomenological concept of illness and the concept of disease as it is usually understood. As we saw in the previous chapters, illness is a form of suffering that is experienced in the form of a mood related to an embodied being-in-the-world and the self-understanding of a person. The life world is usually my home territory, but in illness, this homelikeness gives way and takes on a rather *unhomelike* character, rooted in uncanny ways of being embodied. It is the mission of health-care professionals to try to understand such unhomelike being-in-the-world and bring it back to homelikeness again, or at least closer to a home-being (Svenaeus 2000). This involves, but cannot be reduced to, ways of exploring and altering the physiological organism of the person who is ill and suffering. Health-care professionals must also address matters of a patient's everyday life with a phenomenological eye, attempting to understand the being-in-the-world of the patient, which has turned unhomelike in illness suffering (see chapter four). Often, even chronic diseases, which by definition cannot be cured, allow for a more homelike life if the patient gets adequate medical assistance and is prepared to make lifestyle changes (e.g. in cases of Type 2 diabetes).

A disease is a disturbance of the biological functions of the body (or something that causes such a disturbance) that can only be detected and understood from the third-person perspective of the doctor investigating the body with the aid of her hands or medical technologies (Boorse 1997). The patient can also, by way of the doctor, or by way of medical theory, or, as often happens nowadays, by way of a website on the Internet, adopt such a third-person perspective towards his own body and speculate about diseases responsible for his suffering. But the suffering itself is an illness experience of the person who is in a world, embodied and connected to other people around him. Illness *disturbs* in an alienating way the meaning processes of being-in-the-world by which the person is leading her life (Svenaeus 2011).

The epistemic importance of the illness perspective has often been neglected in modern medicine in favour of the understanding of diseases that have been considered more scientific and real than the experiences of a suffering person (Svenaeus 2000: 38). However, the importance of the first-person perspective for medical practice has recently been stressed not only by phenomenologists but also by proponents of 'patient-centred' or 'person-centred' care aiming to re-establish the importance of knowing the patient as a person and not only the biological processes of her body (Gunnarson 2016). The tendency to neglect the patient's point of view has been criticized for being not only paternalistic but also *unjust* from an epistemological point of view (Carel and Kidd 2014). These movements and arguments are linked to the development of bioethics as such and are generally allies of the idea of promoting patient autonomy in medicine. In contrast to liberal, rights-based models of bioethics, phenomenology will insist on a thick notion of autonomy that takes into account the embodiment and life-world context of the person. Previous attempts to make autonomy thicker in bioethics have been pursued mainly by feminist scholars, sometimes under the label of 'relational autonomy' (Mackenzie and Stoljar 2000). Phenomenology, as we will see in upcoming chapters, will pursue questions of respecting and strengthening the autonomy of suffering and vulnerable parties in terms of concepts such as dignity and flourishing.

Typically, when I experience illness as an uncanniness of my bodily being, my biological organism will be diseased, but there are possibilities of being ill without any detectable diseases, or of leading a homelike life, when suddenly the doctor finds a disease (e.g. by way of a cancer screening). The phenomenologist would stress that the full importance and content of illness can be attained only if the doctor, in addition to being skilled in diagnosing diseases, also affords attention to the bodily experience, being-in-the-world, and life story of the patient. The life of the person (and not only the life of her biological organism) is, as a matter of fact, the reason diseases *matter* to us as human beings – because they can make our lives miserable and even make us perish. If this were not the case, we would not *care* so much about them. It is because we want to be at home in the world and in our own bodies that we study diseases and try to find remedies for them.

The relationship between suffering illness and having a disease is in many cases far from straightforward or even clear. This is especially so in cases of illness referred to as 'mental' or 'psychiatric' in contrast to somatic. In psychiatry, the difficulties of finding clear correlations between bodily dysfunctions (dysfunctions of the brain) and the symptoms of illness have led to the choice of the softer term 'disorder' instead of disease in diagnosing illness. Nevertheless, the last years have brought a heavy focus on the diagnosis of distinct disorders in psychiatry (the DSM movement), sadly often at the expense of any deeper phenomenological understanding of the suffering in question (Vanheule and Devisch 2014). Critics talk about an increasing 'medicalization' of everyday life as an undesired and even dangerous effect of the new diagnostic psychiatry, a topic to which we will return in chapter five of this book (Horwitz and Wakefield 2007; Rose and Abi-Rached 2013).

Mental disorders introduce many fascinating and complex issues in efforts to understand the illness experience from a phenomenological perspective. The complexities concern the possibilities of tracking down all forms of illness to cases of *bodily* alienation (the choice of terminology, indeed, seems to suggest that this kind of illness is exactly not bodily in nature) and how the forms of alienation found in different psychiatric disorders should be understood and categorized.

The analysis will encounter questions of how the borderline between the ill and the unhappy, or, perhaps, inauthentic, life is to be drawn, and this project in turn contains burning issues found in moral and political philosophy. To address some of these questions, which I think are pertinent for bioethics, I have picked one peculiar example of a psychiatric diagnosis to reflect upon in this chapter: anorexia nervosa. This example has the advantage of presenting the experience of the *body* as being uncanny, yet doing so in ways that introduce issues of alienation that are connected to matters of identity and politics – issues that are either not present, or harder to discern, in most cases of somatic illness (see also Bowden 2012; Fuchs 2003).

Anorexia nervosa

Anorexia nervosa (short: anorexia) is diagnosed in DSM-5 by three criteria: (1) a persistent energy intake restriction leading to a body mass index (BMI) of 17 kg/m^2 or less, (2) an intense fear of gaining weight or of becoming fat, or persistent behaviour which interferes with weight gain, and (3) a disturbance in self-perceived weight or shape (DSM-5 2013: 338–339). Two important things should be pointed out immediately regarding the diagnosis. The first is that anorexia is categorized as a feeding and eating disorder in DSM, so although we do not find obsession with food and strange eating habits among the three criteria, this can more or less be taken for granted as being the case if someone has anorexia. If these eating problems include binge eating and purging, the alternate eating disorder of bulimia nervosa will be diagnosed instead of (or together with) anorexia. The body-weight-controlling behaviour of the person suffering from anorexia will typically also involve intense exercise programmes taken on in order to lose weight.

The second important thing to point out is that although the suffering of anorexia is not restricted to girls, it is far more common for females than for males (the ratio is about 1 to 10) to be diagnosed with anorexia, as it is for people living in a Western society compared to a non-Western society. Anorexia typically affects adolescents, and the prevalence of the disorder is far higher today than it was only fifty or so years ago. It is common that the prevalence of psychiatric disorders varies a lot over time and with gender and culture, but anorexia is nevertheless a bit extreme in this sense: it seems almost normal for a teenage girl in upper-class New York to develop a fanatical preoccupation with avoiding food for the sake of being extremely slim, whereas it would be very strange and almost unheard of for a man in his fifties living in Congo Kinshasa to do so. Many psychiatric (and somatic) diagnoses are more common in one of the sexes, in a certain age group, or in a certain ethnic population, but most other cases of diagnostic skewedness do not seem to be tied to cultural norms in the strikingly clear manner that anorexia nervosa is. Nevertheless, it appears that eating disorders like anorexia are increasingly diagnosed and suffered by women (and men) in other cultural and social groups than the North American and European upper and middle class (Bordo 2003: xv).

Is anorexia a cultural disorder in the sense that it is *created* by a society that overtly signals to young girls that their success value is tied to bodily appearance and their ability in this and other, related ways to please the opposite sex? Many feminist scholars have argued that this is the case (e.g. Fallon et al. 1994; Malson 1998), but it is has also been pointed out that there is a genetic disposition to develop the disorder (Bulik 2005), and that the presence of a perfectionist personality type seems to be important to the tendency to fall ill with anorexia (Polivy and Herman 2002). In my phenomenological attempts to understand anorexia, I will not be able to assess the aetiology in establishing what is the most important cause of the diagnosis; rather, I will try by following some narratives of anorexia to better understand the way the experience of the own-body is involved (see also Merleau-Ponty 2012: 163–169). My main examples in this chapter are taken from Halse et al. (2008), but there are countless stories about anorexia to be found in different books, and, above all, on the Internet by entering search words such as 'stories of anorexia'.

Most narratives of anorexia appear to start with a scenario in which a young girl suddenly understands by way of comments or behaviours of others that she is too fat. These comments can be nasty and part of bullying, but they can also be rather innocent or perhaps even self-inflicted:

> Ruth is a cheerful, lively little girl with flashing eyes and a wide, captivating grin. She's got a cheeky sense of humour and can always make her family laugh with her funny impersonations of her school teachers. Until she was ten years old, Ruth had little interest in sport or exercise. She was a real 'lounge lizard' who loved eating and lazing in front of the television. All this changed when she began dance classes. Ruth looked around the class and all she could see were 'skinny' girls. Although Ruth was slim and petite, she felt fat and self-conscious, particularly in the body-hugging leotard the dance class had to wear. Ruth ached to look just like all the other girls and, in an effort to recast her figure, she embarked on a fitness campaign. She began by cutting out junk food, chocolates, and the desserts that she'd always loved, and by doing a bit more exercise – nothing significant, just practicing her dance routines and riding her bike.
>
> *(Halse et al. 2008: 127)*

Ruth's experience of her own body as unsatisfying is different from the way the body turns up as uncanny in somatic illnesses. It is, indeed, as Sartre highlighted in *Being and Nothingness*, a way of being objectified by other people in being looked upon by them (1992: 345). This being looked upon – the own-body appearing as an in-itself for consciousness in the terminology of Sartre – is readily turned into a self-objectifying gaze, as in the case of Ruth. We can imagine her in front of the mirror (maybe a mirror present already in the ballet class) introjecting the gaze on her own body as too fat for a beautiful ballet girl in filling up her 'body-hugging leotard' and resisting her efforts to display the lightness and grace of a ballet dancer in moving to the music. The *shame* Ruth is experiencing in the ballet class in being exposed to the (at least in her eyes) contemptuous looks of the other girls is no doubt a powerful and painful experience (Bowden 2012). Developmental psychologist Philippe Rochat even argues in his study *Others in Mind* that shame is the very origin of self-consciousness, experienced for the first time when children at the age of about eighteen months recognize themselves in the mirror (2009: 107). What children appear to be experiencing at this age is that they are exposed to the evaluative looks of others, and this is obviously a painful experience involving the fear of being rejected (see also Fuchs 2003).

But the shame and fear of being fat is just the starting point of anorexia. The more or less imagined, contemptuous gaze of others does not seem to lead to anorexia for every person exposed to the norms of slenderness in contemporary society. Not for most men, a fact that might be explained by other (bodily) ideals for men than for women, but also not for most women, or even for most young girls exposed to the ideals in question. There are, of course, many cases of eating habits and slenderness among women that could be claimed to border on the unhealthy, even if they are not diagnosed as anorexia nervosa; however, a more common behaviour regarding eating and exercise among women *and* men today is rather to become overweight than too thin. The 'fat epidemic' has hit more than 13 per cent of the adult population in the world (fat meaning having a BMI>30), and 39 per cent is found to be overweight (meaning having a BMI>25); but this does not stop anorexic girls from comparing themselves to a bodily ideal that is consequently becoming increasingly statistically abnormal (WHO 2016b). It seems, rather, as though the media talk of the fat epidemic has a kind of encouraging effect on anorexics in starving and exercising themselves to death, whereas the people who would benefit from cutting down on fat and sugar and trying to exercise their too-massive bodies are either unaffected or unable to profit from the message.

Ideals of beauty are tied not only to slenderness; how beautiful and sexy we are considered to be is also determined by the look of the face – the shape of the eyes, nose, and lips – along with the shape of the entire body – with different ideals for women and men. These ideals are nurtured by the fashion and movie-star industry, and they are increasingly invading the life of almost every individual on the planet by way of commercials and sponsored content in newspapers, TV shows, movies, social media, and sites on the Internet. As a consequence of this, an increasing number of people are not happy with their looks; they feel that they do not look nearly as good as they could, should, and would if they were given the opportunity to choose and change their bodies. Important players in this cultural and social movement of bodily discontent are the companies and clinics that offer cosmetic surgery by way of which it is possible to look as beautiful, young, and gorgeous as you really are (on the inside) (Elliott 2003; Slatman 2014).

To change your looks by way of the knife is becoming increasingly common in many parts of the world, especially for women, and the nose jobs and eyelid lifts performed conform to ideals that are clearly Western–European: Argentinian girls make their noses smaller and straighter, Korean girls make their eyes look less

Asian, for instance. Breast augmentations, liposuctions, and other body-shaping forms of surgery are performed all over the world where people have the money to afford them. The sheer number of beauty operations performed every year – several millions – is a clear sign that people do not feel at home with their bodies, and the reason for this suffering due to bodily alienation is not processes of nature, as in the case of somatic illness, but culture (Sullivan 2001). The easiest way to conform to the cultural ideals, however, is to eat less and exercise more – precisely the behaviour that is exaggerated to pathology in anorexia.

The uncanniness of the body in anorexia resonates with cultural norms, but it does so through a twist made by the body itself, in which our ideals of bodily beauty are stressed to the point at which we begin to see that these ideals verge on illness. The illness of anorexia thus brings out the illness of our culture in a different way than the fat epidemic does. Our disgust and fascination with the sickly thin and the sickly fat are inverted mirror images in a culture in which food and body shape have been made into obsessive projects tied to identity:

> Ruth pursued her fitness campaign and quickly lost her puppy fat. Her parents, Beth and David, were proud of her determination to get fit and healthy and saw this as a positive lifestyle move, and Ruth revelled in the flurry of compliments from family and friends. Even though other people thought she looked 'just right', Ruth didn't feel as if she could relax. The idea of easing up and possibly losing her new slender shape was intolerable. She didn't make a conscious decision to restrict her eating further or intensify her exercise routine. The shift crept up so gradually that no one realized.
>
> *(Halse et al. 2008: 127–128)*

The uncanny body of anorexia

Two striking elements in all narratives of anorexia that I have come across are weak self-confidence and an urge to control one's own (and sometime others') life in an almost manic way. It is not strange that self-confidence and identity are weak and searching for a firm ground in adolescence, but in cases of anorexia this unstable selfhood is met with strong attempts to take control of life by monitoring eating and exercise, and, by way of this, the looks of the own-body. The body that showed itself as foreign in the sense of not conforming to an ideal of slenderness (uncanny for the girl in question) now gradually becomes uncanny to others (the family) in exhibiting a skeletal look that the anorexic girl refuses to acknowledge as a problem. This changed perception and loss of judgement when it comes to issues of one's weight and shape is, as noted above, an integral part of the diagnosis of anorexia.

> Throughout the cold winter months, Beth and David had only seen Ruth warmly rugged in layers of clothes. Their illusions were shattered when summer arrived and the family went on holidays to the beach. Beth first

realized the extent of Ruth's weight loss when they went shopping for Ruth's new swimsuit. When she saw Ruth's emaciated body for the first time in the changing room, Beth was so horrified that she felt physically ill.

(Halse et al. 2008: 129)

The refusal to eat and to stop the manic exercise leads relatively quickly to a life-threatening condition:

As soon as they returned from holidays, David took Ruth to see a pediatrician specializing in eating disorders. Ruth's weight had dropped to 32 kilos, she was clinically depressed, her ankles were purple and swollen from all the exercise, and cardiac failure looked imminent. A few days after her eleventh birthday, Ruth was admitted to a hospital where she was sedated, put on bed rest, and fed through a nasogastric tube.

(Halse et al. 2008: 130)

Ruth develops anorexia before entering puberty. In this she is not typical, but a couple of years early: most girls develop anorexia after their bodies have begun to take on a more female shape and they have experienced their first menstruation (which often subsequently ceases as a result of the starvation process). To experience the body changes of puberty can be an uncanny experience in itself when the body, indeed, takes on a strange life of its own that (initially at least) might feel very foreign and disgusting to the person whose body is changing. For girls with anorexia, like Carol, this seems to be particularly true:

When I started developing I just hated it. Especially with being in ballet it was really hard because I felt really uncomfortable not wearing a bra but even having to start wearing bras was uncomfortable. I just hated the whole changing of my body. ... (My) first period arrived when the family was travelling in the car on the way to their annual holidays. ... Mom gave me this huge, thick pad and I cried the whole way to the holiday house. I cried for a whole week – just nonstop. I just couldn't handle it. I just kept thinking this is just complete hell. I don't – I can't – believe that women are putting up with this.

(Halse et al. 2008: 51–52)

Like Ruth, Carol develops an obsession with her own body, especially after being teased at school for having breasts:

Carol concedes that the insults and taunts eroded her self-confidence. Despite being fit and slender, she became increasingly uncomfortable with the womanly shape she saw emerging in front of her eyes. She loathed her maturing body and was convinced that it was ugly. Unable to control the teasing at school, Carol's thoughts focused inward on herself and on controlling her body and what she ate. She started weighing herself regularly—often dozens of times a day—and would stand in front of the bathroom mirror for hours composing long, detailed lists of imagined physical flaws she dreamed of changing.

(Halse et al. 2008: 54)

The element of *controlling* the body through restricting food and monitoring life is even stronger in other stories:

> The first obvious sign that Hannah's dieting was entangled with something more than a desire to be healthy came just before she was due to go away to camp with her school. She was anxious and agitated. What sort of food would they have at the camp? What if they didn't have the food she wanted? How would she manage? How could she stick to her current diet? The idea of varying what she ate, even for two weeks, sent her into a spin. The food at camp didn't help. It was the usual school camp fare – lots of bread, pastries, and oily, fried dinners. Confronted with this menu, Hannah either refused to eat or ate the bare minimum and ran 15 kilometres each day to offset what she'd eaten. Her teachers were so concerned that they contacted Laura and Peter (Hannah's parents). ... (Peter, collecting Hannah from camp:) I'll be honest, I didn't recognize her. She'd lost so much weight in the weeks she was away. She just looked awful. And all she talked about in the car on the way home was where she ate, what she ate. Meal by meal.
>
> *(Halse et al. 2008: 80–81)*

Maybe it is not so strange that being in control of exactly what one is eating becomes so important if your own body displays an alien nature. Food is the major foreign thing that enters into your body: if you control food you will also be able to control the body, make it more of your own, so to speak. But this routine of surveying and controlling eating soon develops into a pathology with a life of its own that the person is no longer able to control.

A common strategy for dealing with anorexia, used by health professionals, parents, and also by patients, is to view the disorder *itself* as something alien. Instead of viewing the body as something being uncanny to the anorexic girl herself, or becoming so to others, in this image it is not the body but the anorexia itself, as invading and taking control over the body, that is uncanny. We recognize this logic of bodily uncanniness from the movie *Alien* and also from the idea of somatic diseases in which the body is threatened by parasites (bacteria, viruses) or cells that are dividing beyond control (cancer diseases). The idea also resonates with the old image of mental illness as daemonic possession referred to by Freud in his paper on the uncanny (1959: 397). Hannah's parents:

> The idea is that the anorexia is separate from the person with anorexia, almost like a different, distinct individual. ... We said, 'Hannah, we love

you. We'll always love you but this person that's in you – this possessed
person that's in you – we hate her. We want her gone.' So we actually talked
about Hannah and the other person. And when we made the definition and
she made the definition, it was a lot easier to deal with. Luke (Hannah's
younger brother) christened Hannah's anorexia 'The Bitch'. Now he could
relate to his sister and he'd cuddle and console Hannah, reassuring her that
'The problem isn't you, it's the anorexia'.

(*Halse et al. 2008: 89*)

The strategy of reifying an illness by turning it into a bodily dysfunction not having
anything to do with the person's identity is common in cases of somatic illness. It
is also a strategy encouraged by contemporary medical science and practice when
illness is understood primarily in terms of medical concepts and measurements: as
diseases. As I have pointed out above, this reifying strategy can develop into a
problematic one if it is not kept in check by a perspective stressing the importance
of illness as a lived bodily experience that demands attention to life-world issues
and the self-understanding of a patient.

The view of anorexia as something separate from the person suffering from it,
which was developed by Hannah's family, is different from and more far reaching
than such a medical perspective, however, since the family views the anorexia not
only as another thing (a bodily dysfunction) but as another *person* in Hannah. Such
a view of alienation might be present in a minimal form in all cases when the body
shows up as uncanny, since the body in such cases displays a kind of life of its own
that is experienced by the person in question as a foreign *will* (a will is something
that, strictly, only a person and not a body can have). However, when the bodily
alienation turns into the image of daemonic possession ('The Bitch'), we seem to be
closer to the stories of *The Exorcist*, *Rosemary's Baby*, and *The Omen* than to the
parasitic possession of *Alien*. 'The Bitch' needs to be *exorcized* and should not be
considered a result of cultural circumstances (circumstances meaning both Hannah's
personal situation in her family and circle of friends, and the circumstances of
women in Western society and culture) that need to be interpreted and changed.

It is tempting to consider the story of 'The Bitch' as yet another move in the
discursive strategies of keeping women alienated and pacified in our society. In this
view, not only would our culture and society rest on ideals of success that make
girls starve themselves to death, but in this starving, the illness itself would be
considered an evil, female creature possessing the girl in question, a creature that
must be kept under control to prevent it from taking over. But I think a feminist
reading of that sort is a little too one-eyed, since no one would deny that cultural
norms have a lot to do with the *onset* of anorexia. It is a non-political reality,
however, that the disorder, when it has established itself, takes on a kind of life of
its own as an uncanny pattern of experiences and 'musts' that are not easily dealt
with and changed, no matter how politically informed the anorexic girl, her
parents, or her caretakers become. Sartre characterizes illness as a *melody*, in most
cases a rather disharmonic one, playing itself in the embodied life-world patterns of

my life beyond my control (1992: 441). Anorexia seems to do so too, providing the person with a style of bodily experience that is just as autonomous as the pain melody of somatic illness (see also Merleau-Ponty 2012: 163–169).

Anorexia, in most cases, is set off by cultural influences, but when the starvation and over-exercise have been brought into play, the malnourished body as a kind of self-defence inflicts moods that make its bearer strangely disembodied, increasingly apprehending the body as a thing, and a thing that is still not thin enough, despite its now uncannily meagre look to others. The moods of anorexia – anxiety, irritation, hopelessness, sadness, despair, aggression – all bear witness to problems with embodiment, the anorexic person no longer being properly present in her own body, maybe even claiming that it is gone or dead. Self-mutilation, cutting oneself in order to inflict a pain that is perceptibly *physical* in nature, in contrast to the moods making the body strangely foreign, is not uncommon, and neither is suicide (Halse et al. 2008: 100). The stories of anorexia bear clear witness to the double experience of being plagued and depressed by the anorexia but still being unable to give it up because it provides the only security, control, and identity that there is to have. Depression and anxiety disorders are commonly co-diagnosed in anorexia, but depressed, irritated, and anxious moods are always present, sometimes as a starting point, and most often as an effect of the anorexia behaviour (Halse et al. 2008: 74–75).

The body uncanny and bioethics

Anorexia nervosa displays several forms of being alienated from one's own-body in an uncanny way. These include the ways of the body uncanny that we have identified in somatic illness, but they also concern ways of being objectified in an everyday manner in the social world by the gazes of others. However, the objectification by way of the gazes of others in anorexia is not primarily a battle between consciousnesses à la Sartre, but a finding oneself in a cultural pattern of norms regarding the feminine, the beautiful, and the successful. The gazes of others are soon made by the anorexic girl into a self-surveying gaze, in the process of which the image of the own-body is gradually made increasingly unrealistic and self-punishing.

The different ways of becoming bodily alienated interact in anorexia in establishing an uncanniness of the body that is both conspicuous (to people around the ill person) and hard to escape (for the person herself). First comes the objectifying gaze of the other, making the girl experience her own body as foreign and ugly in being too fat to be at home with. This uncanniness is reinforced by the way the body changes rapidly in puberty, bringing new ways of being embodied, which can be hard to identify with for the girl who is not yet a woman but also no longer only a girl. Second comes the attempt to deal with this uncanniness by taking control over the body, making it slender, which can mean both remaining girl-like and becoming a beautiful woman (these two looks are, indeed, fairly close to each other in contemporary fashion culture). This behaviour of dieting and exercising is often initially rewarded by peers and family, something that sets the girl off into the project of doing even better, cutting down on food and increasing exercise. In this starvation and over-exercising process, which is often accompanied by lying about food and training habits in order not to generate attention and prohibitions from parents, the illness begins to take on a life of its own as an alien (non)presence of the body in which it appears as truly uncanny to spectators, but not to the subject herself, who increasingly feels disembodied in a kind of combination of the dis- and dys-appearance processes focused upon by Leder (1990).

The diagnosis of anorexia can itself be both a relief and a shock to the patient and her family. A relief, because it defines the problem as medical and thus not personal, even if the characterization of feeding and eating disorders as mental disorders makes this depersonalization of the illness less convincing than in cases of somatic illness. A shock, because the diagnosis means that the problems experienced with refusing to eat are serious, and, as the family will learn, potentially life threatening as well as hard to treat. Getting the diagnosis is often linked to the person's becoming hospitalized for the first time and being subjected to mistrust, surveillance, and coercion, a tough treatment regime that many find hard to accept. Treatment for anorexia may mean many more things in addition to surveillance and coercive treatment, and my phenomenological analysis of the body uncanny stresses the importance of measures beyond the acute treatment of the life-threatening starvation behaviour. To focus upon the body *experience* of the anorexic person will mean to try to understand and help the person affected by anorexia with the ways she finds her body alien and uncanny, involving the pre-reflective experience of embodiment, in which the body may show up as absent and foreign to her, and also the ways in which the body becomes objectified by cultural and medical norms that need to be made conscious and criticized in the process of finding a personal identity that is possible to live and be at home with (Russon 2003).

Bioethics could learn at least two things from the phenomenological approach to the body in anorexia. The first is that bodily problems are far more complex than just a reflection of biological dysfunctions – diseases – in the practice of medicine. In order to understand how anorexia can compromise a person's autonomy and integrity, a focus upon the body as an alien force hijacking the wills and desires of the person is helpful, not least for health-care professionals treating persons with feeding and eating disorders. The second thing is that embodiment carries meaning that can be deciphered on different levels: lived embodiment, being-in-the-world, and narrative identity. Anorexia is extreme in this regard, as it relates explicitly not only to pain or other bodily discomforts alienating the life of an ill person, but to cultural and political patterns of meaning that set up norms of bodily beauty which are harder to live by for women than for men (although the latter also increasingly fall prey to ideals of slenderness or training and eating regimes which make them suffer). In this chapter I have focused upon bodily phenomenology proceeding from philosophers such as Sartre and Merleau-Ponty, but such a phenomenological analysis could be further developed as concerns the (bio)political with the help of Foucault (1990) or feminist scholars working in this tradition, such as Susanne Bordo (2003) or Sara Ahmed (2006).

In turning to the hermeneutics of medical practice in chapter four, we do well to remember the way the meeting between health-care professional and patient is always embedded in a society upholding certain cultural norms about how people should look and behave to lead successful lives. In order to understand the experiences and life-world situations of patients, doctors and other health-care personnel need to be empathic. They need to see things from the point of view of the *sufferer* of illness. How do they accomplish or fail to accomplish this, and how is empathy in medicine related to dialogue and interpretation in the clinical encounter? To these questions we now turn.

Summary

According to phenomenological philosophers the body is exactly the centre and vehicle of my whole existence: I am *as* a body which feels, acts, and thinks in my different ways of making myself at home in the world. The lived body, however, is not only my most fundamental home; it is also a creature with a life of its own that harbours autonomous powers. Sometimes this autonomy of the body turns alien in the sense that it changes my basic being at home with it (as it) into an experience of bodily alienation: the body becomes not only mine, but also *other* to me in an uncanny way. In this chapter some such forms of bodily uncanniness have been identified and related to the example of anorexia nervosa. This analysis helps us to discern different ways in which our bodies can turn up as alien to us and what types of processes (e.g. biological, emotional-cognitive, social-cultural) the forms of otherness in question are tied to.

Anorexia nervosa displays several ways of being alienated from one's body in an uncanny way. These include forms of alienation that can be found in somatic illness, but they also concern ways of being objectified in an everyday manner in the social world by the gazes of others, finding oneself in a cultural pattern of norms regarding the feminine, the beautiful, and the successful. The alienating gazes of others are soon made into a self-surveying gaze by the anorexic girl, in the process of which the image of her own body is made increasingly unrealistic and self-punishing. Anorexia, in most cases, is set off by cultural influences, but when the starvation and over-exercise have been brought into play, the malnourished body as a kind of self-defence inflicts moods that make its bearer strangely disembodied, increasingly apprehending the body as a thing, and a thing that is still not thin enough, despite its now uncannily meagre look to others.

The mission of health care is to help persons who are suffering from bodily alienation. Illness-moods can be powerful in nature and hard to change – anorexia is a clear example of this – and in many cases a biomedical approach to the problem is not sufficient. Illness is a matter not only of diseased body states but of a person's being-in-the-world and self-understanding. In some cases a medical examination and a prescribed drug or other bodily intervention will be sufficient to make the mood of a patient homelike again — say, if he needs antibiotics to fight off pneumonia or an operation to remove an infected appendix. But in other cases a focus upon the *experience* of suffering and the life-world circumstances of the patient is necessary to understand the nature of the problem and to be able to do something about it.

4

EMPATHY AND THE HERMENEUTICS OF MEDICINE

Empathy and moral philosophy

To be a good doctor or a good nurse (or other good health-care professional) one needs to be empathic – one needs to be able to feel and understand the fears, thoughts, and wishes of patients in order to help them in the best possible way. The first-person perspective of the patient must be acknowledged and understood from the point of view of the professional, making it into a second-person perspective, empathically and dialogically explored. To this second-person perspective a third- (or rather non-) person, medical-scientific perspective is added when exploring the biological functions of the potentially diseased body and the ways they are related to the illness experiences of the patient.

The clinical encounter is an ethical event to the extent that a suffering person presents her ailments and the health-care professional is under the obligation to help. Empathy is a central and necessary capability in this endeavour, together with virtues such as friendliness, trustworthiness, truthfulness, courage, and integrity (Pellegrino and Thomasma 1993). Ethical dilemmas in health care therefore need to be analysed from the point of view of the *encounter* with the suffering person, not merely as a set of moral choice situations in which health-care professionals inform patients and respect their wishes or distribute medical services in just ways (Welie 1999). However, it is far from clear how empathy fits into the standard picture of biomedical ethics and the framework of moral principles that are most often stressed there, such as respect for autonomy, beneficence, non-maleficence, and justice (Beauchamp and Childress 2013). How are we to look upon the role and importance of empathy in bioethics? How does empathy attain moral importance in health care? These are questions I will aim to answer in this chapter.

There are lower-level definitions of empathy, making it essentially a kind of automatic mirroring process of a bodily feeling type, and there are higher-level definitions of empathy, expanding the emotional component to include cognitive and imaginative processes of mind (for overviews of empathy research, see Coplan and Goldie 2011; Decety 2012; Stueber 2006). However, most empathy researchers would agree that a low-level definition of empathy only, transforming the phenomenon into a sort of reflex, is not sufficient to get hold of what we are to mean by empathy in any full-blown sense – at least not if the understanding of the lower-level bodily processes in question are not tied to some version of what the phenomenologist calls *intentionality* (Zahavi and Overgaard 2012). The discovery of mirror neurons in the early 1990s was an important step in the research on empathy, but the fact that we are unconsciously affected by the emotional expressions of other people by mirroring them does not by itself make us more or less empathic (Rizzolatti et al. 1996). In order for an emotion to qualify as empathic it must be a feeling *about* the other person, not only a feeling that has been *caused* by the other person's emotional expressions.

What is being discussed in the empathy literature is not whether or not the higher levels of empathy exist – in the sense that they should be included in what we are to mean by empathy; what is being discussed is what the higher levels look like, and whether and how they are *dependent upon* lower, bodily levels of more or less automatic mirroring. A more controversial issue concerns whether empathy also includes a *caring* for the other person, in the sense that an impulse to relieve her suffering, and perhaps also a reflected judgement that one *ought to* help her, is built into the empathy process from the start (Slote 2007). In an everyday understanding of the concept, being empathic most often means to be morally good, whereas lacking empathy is a moral defect (Battaly 2011). Professional researchers of empathy, in contrast to this, typically want to keep the empathic and the moral realm separate (Prinz 2011). Empathy is not the same thing as *sympathy*, they point out. And getting to know the predicament of the other is not the same thing as coming to the conclusion that one *ought* to help her, or, even less, automatically taking *action* in order to help her.

It is true, of course, that having empathy is not enough to be morally excellent. Many other things influence what moral conclusions we form in situations when we are faced with the misery of other people, *and* whether we will transform these conclusions into morally righteous actions. Nevertheless, I think that in performing conceptual moves to restrict the meaning of empathy from expanding into the moral sphere, empathy researchers often pay the price of losing some of the true experiential content of the phenomenon in question. It is possible to demonstrate that empathy has a central moral significance and still explain why having empathy is not enough to be morally wise. I will come back precisely to this issue, but I first need to say a bit more about what Aristotle means by moral wisdom, *phronesis*, since this is the concept I will now bring into the analysis of empathy and medical ethics (Aristotle 2002).

Aristotelian ethics

Phronesis is thematized in the sixth chapter (or book) of the *Nicomachean Ethics* as one of the excellences, *arête*, found in the five different forms of human activities Aristotle associates with seeking and having knowledge: *episteme* (scientific knowledge), *techne* (technical expertise), *phronesis* (practical wisdom), *sophia* (philosophical wisdom), and *nous* (intellectual insight) (Aristotle 2002: 1139b). Practical wisdom is characterized by Aristotle as a kind of knowledge of how to act in situations that cannot be judged by applying algorithms (rules of action), but only by thoroughly understanding the concrete situation at hand and judging what to aim for in this *particular* case. This, certainly, appears to fit the structure of medical understanding and therapeutic action in relation to the individual patient and her ailments, a matter to which we will return. *Phronesis* is not identical to scientific knowledge, in which general truths are found which can be applied, or to technical expertise, in which case the goal of the activity is given beforehand, since the technician aims to produce a certain *thing* – for example, good wine, shoes, or a house, and so forth. Nor is practical wisdom the same thing as philosophical wisdom, which is not directly focused on taking action in human matters, nor is it the same thing as *nous*, intellectual insight, the exact meaning of which is notoriously hard to explicate from Aristotle's writings. *Phronesis* is, for Aristotle, essentially something you need to govern a state and take wise political decisions, but, as we shall see, this does not mean that practical wisdom is not at work in other activities in which persons are faced with hard moral choices, such as in medicine (Dunne 1997; MacIntyre 1985).

Phronesis is, according to Aristotle, an *intellectual* ability which is perfected by experience – actually, he claims that only old men can have it – but this does not mean that practical wisdom is concerned only with thinking in contrast to feeling or acting. In the passage preceding the definition of the five different forms of knowledge-excellences that humans can have, Aristotle discusses how good actions (*eupraxia*) are dependent not only on intellect but on a drive and desire to do the right thing (*orexis*) (Aristotle 2002: 1139a). Practical thinking is therefore rooted in feelings that guide the deliberation in question, and, as I mentioned, the territory of *phronesis* is exactly the realm of human interaction. Aristotle uses the expression 'intellectual excellence' (*aretai dianoetikai*) to distinguish practical wisdom from what he calls the moral excellences: temperance, courage, generosity, friendliness, righteousness, and the like. They are all *arête* ('excellences', sometimes also translated as 'virtues'), but practical wisdom involves a kind of *moral deliberation* that one does not find in the case of the moral excellences, which guide one's action in a more direct and unreflected way. The morally virtuous (excellent) person not only needs to embody and cultivate the different moral excellences, he also needs practical wisdom to understand and judge the situation in which he is to take action. Without practical wisdom he will not be able to act in a good way even though he is courageous, friendly, generous, and moderate, to mention some of the most important moral virtues underlined by Aristotle, or caring, trustworthy, and truthful, to mention some of the virtues added by modern medical-virtue ethicists (Pellegrino and Thomasma 1993).

I will not go into the question of how, exactly, practical wisdom and the different moral excellences relate to each other, but I think it is clear that they are mutually reinforcing and necessary for each other in Aristotle's understanding. Not only does the person who has the particular excellences Aristotle names moral (*arête ethike*) need *phronesis* to act well, but the *phronetic* person (having *arête* of the intellect, *dianoia*) must necessarily embody moral excellences, since without them it would not be possible for him to see, understand, and judge the situation at hand in the appropriate way. If I am ungenerous, unjust, a coward, or intemperate, I will not see what is at stake in a precarious situation – what we usually refer to as a moral dilemma. I will perhaps even not understand why – and that – it is a moral dilemma, because I am unable to understand the conflict at hand in a situation – for instance, in which I am tempted to lie rather than telling a truth that will make a person unhappy. Perhaps I will not even understand that telling the truth will cause the other person to suffer, because I do not understand what things are like from her perspective in the first place.

The phenomenology of empathy

My idea in introducing *phronesis* into the investigation of the role of empathy in medicine and bioethics is not to further complicate the issue by bringing all the questions and distinctions of Aristotelian practical philosophy and virtue theory onstage. Ideally, the concept of *phronesis* should make us able to see more clearly what empathy is, not hiding it behind clouds of further distinctions and problems regarding the essence of human nature, knowledge, and the good. How so? A minimal notion of empathy is that it consists in feeling and knowing the state and predicament of another person. Empathy in this sense is a kind of *discernment*, a way of seeing what is going on in a world that we share with other human beings. In a way, I think, this is exactly what Aristotle means by *phronesis*. Martha Nussbaum has shown how the Aristotelian notion of practical wisdom rests on an understanding of emotions as containing knowledge about the world we share with other human beings (1990a). *Phronesis* is not devoid of feelings; rather, it is based on feelings that help the wise person to see and judge what is at stake in the situation. In Aristotle's famous, but also notoriously vacuous, formulation it is about 'feeling at the right times, about the right things, towards the right people, for the right end, and in the right way' (2002: 1106b). *Phronesis* must therefore be *rooted* in empathy; it must take its starting point in being able to feel and know the state and predicament of the other person in the situation in which we strive to seek the best solution for the people involved. This discernment aims to map out what I earlier referred to as a moral dilemma, or, perhaps better, a situation that calls for action, but in which it is hard to know what the best thing to do is.

In Edith Stein's seminal study *The Problem of Empathy*, published in 1917, we find a phenomenological theory of empathy that manages to combine different aspects of the phenomenon in a rich and coherent way (Stein 1989; Svenaeus 2016a). Stein's suggestion for how to envisage empathy takes its starting point in the idea that empathy is a way of *feeling* oneself *into* the experiences of the other person (*sich einfühlen*). This is worth pointing out since some of the most influential ideas in the contemporary empathy debate seem to have lost track of this basic idea, which is more obvious when we proceed from the German term that was translated as 'empathy' at the beginning of the twentieth century, namely '*Einfühlung*' (Coplan and Goldie 2011).

Stein takes empathy to be a three-step process in which the experiences of the other person (1) emerge to me as meaningful in my perception of her in bodily presence, and I then (2) fulfil an explication of these experiences by following them through in an imaginative account guided by her, in order to (3) return to a more comprehensive understanding of the experiences of the other person (Stein 1989: 10). The steps that Stein discerns in the empathy process could possibly be reiterated – step three could serve as a new step one and so on – but they could also be supplemented by other ways of engaging with the other, such as talking to her or starting to do something for/to her or together with her. These ways of human interaction transform empathy as a perceptual and imaginative endeavour into hermeneutically and morally reflected forms of understanding and dealing with the other. However, even though Stein restricts the empathy process to the three-step model specified above – steps that do not include conversation and coordinated actions between the parties – a form of tacit communication is arguably already present in the empathy process as such, provided the target recognizes that she is being empathized with and therefore directs her expressive behaviour towards the empathizer in the process. And the empathic feeling-oneself-into the experiences of the other person will be at work also in many 'empathy-plus' forms of human interactions, which, in addition to perception and imagination, also involve talking, listening, and acting together in the world of persons.

Empathy and the virtues

Although it is crucial to *phronesis*, empathy cannot be put among other moral virtues as being of the same type as, for instance, courage, temperance, friendliness, trustworthiness, and integrity. A proof that is often brought up for this is the example of the psychopath. The psychopath understands exactly how the other person is suffering, but he does not feel any urge to help her, or at least he does not transform any such urge into helpful actions; rather, he acts in ways that utilize the suffering of the other for his own gain, or perhaps even to feel raw pleasure, if he is a sadist as well. Typical for the moral excellences, according to Aristotle, is that one acts upon them directly and in an unreflected way. If one is a courageous person one will act in a courageous way when faced with a situation demanding courage (Aristotle 2002: 1115a). This does not seem to be the case with empathy, as the psychopath example shows, and therefore, so this argument goes, empathy is not a moral virtue.

Perhaps one could claim that the different moral virtues always work in combination with each other and that it is the total lack of some *other* essential moral virtue that makes the psychopath's feelings and actions morally defective even though he embodies the virtue (excellence) of empathy. A more elaborate way of putting empathy into the context of Aristotelian moral philosophy is to view it not as one of the moral virtues but as an integrated part of *phronesis*. This is my suggestion. *Phronesis*, as I have pointed out, is not a moral but an intellectual virtue in Aristotle's theory, although, of course, importantly related to the moral virtues. Empathy would then be the *feeling component of phronesis*. Let us now attempt this interpretation in more detail.

The reason the psychopath does not feel the urge to help or come to the moral conclusion that he ought to help is, indeed, that he is lacking in other moral virtues, such as friendliness or righteousness, if we are to stay with Aristotle's list of virtues, or compassion and carefulness, if we expand the list of moral excellences to accommodate other considerations than those at play in Aristotle's practical philosophy. What remains for the psychopath is the feeling-understanding component of empathy unguided by the disposition to act in a morally good way provided by the other, *moral* virtues which furnish the means for *phronetic* discernment *together* with empathy. In this way it is possible to be empathic without exercising *phronesis*, even though empathy is the starting point of *phronesis* without which it cannot be performed. The wise deliberation of *phronesis* must be guided by an emotional discernment of the ways other people feel and think, *and* by other, moral virtues.

This pattern explains why empathy is most often looked upon as a moral virtue even though closer philosophical exploration makes us sceptical about its having a moral content in itself. *Phronesis* cannot be exercised without having the moral virtues, but it also cannot be exercised – indeed, even be initiated – without having empathy. *Phronesis* partly *consists* in empathic capacities. Typically, persons embody the basic moral virtues to some extent, and they also have empathy. The psychopath has empathy but lacks basic moral virtues. Other people may embody most moral virtues to a large extent but lack empathic skills, which makes them come to unwise decisions about what to do in ethically precarious situations, even though they are virtuous in the sense of being moderate, generous, brave, friendly, righteous, and the like.

Are empathy and *phronesis* then, after all, not only related but also identical things? No, they are not. The psychopath example makes this obvious, but I think it is possible, and perhaps even common, to have at least robust forms of all moral capacities (virtues), be skilled in empathic matters, and yet not be a *phronetic* person. What would be lacking in these cases are the kinds of life experiences in moral matters that make Aristotle say that only old men can have *phronesis*. What Aristotle is wrong about when he says this is his restriction of the *kinds* of experiences that will count as cultivating *phronesis*. It is not just the political life of the *polis* but also experiences from professions other than career politics and from everyday private life that will make persons wiser in ethical matters. The example of the experienced doctor who has met and helped a large number of patients, and the example of the doctor who has grown wiser through falling seriously ill and temporarily occupying the position of the patient himself, make this point obvious. Other sources of *phronesis* are the imaginative exercises of art and literature, as Martha Nussbaum suggests in her writings (e.g. 1990b). These matters bring us to how the relationship between empathy and *phronesis* I have suggested could be of significance for the way we look upon the role of empathy in bioethics.

Empathy and bioethics

As Jodi Halpern has pointed out in her important study *From Detached Concern to Empathy*, to exercise empathy in the clinical encounter is not merely a kind of ethical icing on the cake that makes health-care professionals nicer and kinder to patients in addition to being skilled in medical matters (2001). Empathy is actually a capacity that makes the doctor more able to make a correct diagnosis, and it is also a skill and attitude that contributes to empowering patients and improving their recovery by installing hope (Halpern 2001: 94). This is because empathy is not only about being influenced by the feelings patients display – emotional contagion – or feeling sorry for them – pity. Empathy is one of the basic capacities that makes the doctor able to understand what the reasons for complaints and suffering are about and what can and ought to be done to help the patient in the best possible way. In this process of clinical understanding the very fact that the patient feels that the doctor is interested in her problems and wants to help her will contribute to making the patient more able to deal with her health problems, and it will also improve recovery (what is often referred to as placebo effects). Doctors should allow themselves to be moved by patients and the feelings they display – they should not be detached – but in being moved by the patient it is crucial for the doctor to not conflate the feelings of the patient with her own feelings, or to forget that she is actually there to help the patient and not to feel sorry for her. The reason empathy is sometimes looked upon as a faulty or risky strategy for the doctor, leading to non-objective judgements or burnout on the doctor's part, is that it is confused with an emotional merging with the patient's experiences or with feeling sorry for her (Pedersen 2010; Svenaeus 2015b). Halpern notes:

> Writers on empathy either base empathy in detached reason or sympathetic immersion. Against these models I describe empathy in terms of a listener using her emotional associations to provide a context for imagining the distinct experiences of another person. Therefore, empathy is a form of emotional reasoning, with the risks of error that such reasoning involves. To empathize more accurately physicians need to strive to be self-aware, thus avoiding projecting their own unacknowledged emotions onto patients.
>
> *(Halpern 2001: xxiii)*

Emotional reasoning in the form of imagining what the patient is experiencing and what these experiences are caused by and are about is the best way of forming a good clinical judgement that at the same time displays a caring for the patient. This way of phrasing the role of empathy in the clinical encounter comes very close to the Aristotelian concept of *phronesis* that I have been investigating. Maybe Halpern's model of empathy is essentially a model of *phronesis*? I think this is the case, but I would be quick to point out that in her model of empathy Halpern points towards how empathy is a necessary *part* of good clinical judgement, rather than covering the whole ground of clinical understanding. This is exactly the point I have endeavoured to make about empathy in relation to *phronesis* in this chapter. Empathy does not guarantee that the doctor will develop an adequate understanding of the patient's problems and find the best way to help her, but without empathy the doctor is in many cases bound to fail, because she will not even see – be perceptive of – what the problem really consists in. As soon as life-world issues have some kind of bearing upon what a patient presents to the doctor, and how she presents it, the capacity for and attitude of empathy will be necessary to ensure that the doctor forms a perspective that goes deep and wide enough to address the real reasons for illness suffering and to suggest ways out of misery.

If we acknowledge this dynamic we can see how empathy forms an important part of medical ethics as a vital capacity and attitude of health-care professionals. Empathy does not enter the scene *after* the medical problems have been understood and addressed in order to guarantee that patients are treated humanely in addition to being helped with their medical problems. Empathy is a *core part* of clinical understanding, and this understanding is itself morally significant because of the duty on the part of the professional to understand and help. In order to act in a responsible way, the physician (or other health-care professional) needs to know in what ways the patient is suffering and for what reasons (compare the analysis of suffering in chapters two and three).

Medical hermeneutics

I will now address the essence of the clinical encounter in a slightly different way – not by exploring the phenomenon of empathy but by stressing its *interpretative* character. As will become obvious through this exploration, being an empathic doctor and being a good medical interpreter are two aspects of the same thing. Empathy and hermeneutics belong together in medical practice, and the easiest way to show this is by stressing their *phronetic* character. Medical practice is not merely a question of applying medical science and making use of medical technologies and therapies, since the core of medical practice is the meeting with a suffering person, not merely with her potentially diseased body. When applied and made use of in various ways, medical theories about the workings of the human body need to be enveloped in a professional, empathic *understanding* of the patient's being-in-the-world.

In what way can medicine be considered a form of hermeneutics? Even if we assume doctors and other health-care professionals to be interpreting what patients say and how the body looks and feels, as well as the results of diagnostic investigations, are these interpretations not fundamentally different from those we find in the humanities? Can medical practice be claimed to be a form of hermeneutics in a way that is similar to how the reading of a literary or historical text is interpretative? I will explore these questions pertaining to medical hermeneutics with the help of Hans-Georg Gadamer's philosophy, paying particular attention to his late publication *The Enigma of Health* (1996). In this collection of essays, the earliest of which date back to the 1960s, Gadamer develops a kind of outline of how to think about the subject of medicine and hermeneutics, and I will try to fill in his arguments and make them more explicit and comprehensive as we go along.

The idea of hermeneutics as a method peculiar to the humanities in contrast to the natural sciences has been used as a theoretical basis to develop interpretive manuals for uncovering the meanings of texts and other kinds of artefacts for a long time. The term 'hermeneutics' has consequently been used to refer to collections of *methodological principles*. Before we go any further, let me say that this is *not* the kind of hermeneutics I will claim is essential to medical practice. Patients are not works of literature – although, as we will see, they share some important ontological characteristics with texts (Leder 2016: chapter 6). This similarity is, in fact, the reason doctors can learn and hone their clinical skills through the reading of novels and poetry (Ahlzén 2002). However, the knowledge they gain from such reading is not primarily knowledge of how texts work, but knowledge about how human beings work in their efforts to make themselves at home in the world (Downie and Macnaughton 2007).

The kind of hermeneutics I will claim is essential to medicine is the *phenomenological* hermeneutics that Martin Heidegger first developed in his main work, *Being and Time* (1996), and which, as we will see, Gadamer has developed further (Svenaeus 2000: part 3). According to such a hermeneutic view, medical practice is a particular form of understanding activity which is identical neither with explanation in the sciences nor with interpretation in the humanities. Medical knowledge includes applied biology – scientific explanations of what happens in the diseased body – but is not limited to this scientific approach. The hub of medical hermeneutics is the dialogue between health-care professional and patient that represents a particular form of understanding in and by which all forms of particular scientific investigations are guided (or, at least, should be guided). I will now try to make this hermeneutics of medicine visible with the aid of Heidegger and Gadamer.

Phenomenological hermeneutics, as we find it in Heidegger, is an ontological endeavour, not the application of a method, since hermeneutics in phenomenology is taken to be a basic aspect of human life. Human beings, according to Heidegger, understand themselves through the way they are situated in a context of meaning-relations referred to as their 'being-in-the-world' (1996: 53 ff.) (see also chapter one). This being-in-the-world of human existence (or '*Dasein*', as Heidegger calls it) is primarily constituted by our practical doings, but our understanding activities also include the processes of articulation, according to Heidegger (1996: 61). When we are building a house together, for example, I will hand you the hammer or ask for it by showing you my open hand in a situation calling for a hammer to strike nails. Articulation in its more explicit form then takes on the mode of being of language: 'give me the hammer'. Yet a step is taken when dialogues (and monologues) are fixed by way of signs as texts, which may then be read and interpreted in various ways, as spelled out in the hermeneutics of Friedrich Schleiermacher and Wilhelm Dilthey in the nineteenth century (Palmer 1969). Understanding in these cases takes on a rather indirect form compared to the more immediate understanding of everyday practical activities, but the activity of reading is still tied to the same kind of worldly meaning-relations (hammers used to build houses, etc.) as those found in other practices. Hermeneutics is thus not only and not primarily a methodology for text reading, but a basic aspect of life. To be – to exist as a human being – means to understand (Wierciński 2005).

Gadamer and the hermeneutics of medicine

At first sight Gadamer's magnum opus *Truth and Method*, published originally in 1960 (1994), might seem rather remote from the phenomenology of being-in-the-world that Heidegger presents in *Being and Time* (1996). Gadamer's book is divided into three parts; the first and second parts, which are by far the most extensive, deal with the work of art and with interpretation in the humanities, respectively. The third part of the book deals with the ontology of language and can be read as an articulation of the special pattern of understanding which Gadamer has found to be present in the humanities. As Gadamer acknowledges himself, however, and as I will attempt to elucidate further, *Truth and Method* is most accurately read as an extension of the phenomenological hermeneutics of *Being and Time* (Gadamer 1994: 254 ff.).

As many readers have remarked, the title of Gadamer's book should properly read 'Truth *or* Method' and not 'Truth and Method', since it is precisely the methodological conceptualization of hermeneutics, formulated by Schleiermacher and Dilthey, that Gadamer is trying to go beyond. Truth in *Truth and Method* is meant as a basic experience of being together with others in and through language and not as a criterion for the correct interpretation of texts. This conception of truth is completely in line with Heidegger's interpretation of the concept as '*a-letheia*' in *Being and Time* – that is, truth as the openness or disclosedness of *Dasein* to the world of meaning in which things can be found and articulated *as* such-and-such things (as hammers, for instance) (Heidegger 1996: 213 ff.). Thus, for a sentence to describe, to correspond to, a state of the world – as, for example, in 'the hammer is heavy' – this prior unveiling of the world as meaningful – a place where hammers can be too heavy – is necessary. Truth in Gadamer's philosophy, however, is to be understood primarily as openness to *the other* and *his* world and not only to *my own* world. The difference, from Heidegger's point of view, would not be decisive, because the world of the other is also mine – we share the same world in our being-together. Still, human understanding is to a much greater extent a shared experience in Gadamer's hermeneutics than in Heidegger's philosophy.

Language is emphasized by Gadamer as the key mode of human existence in being together with others. The form of language he concentrates his analysis upon in *Truth and Method* is not spoken dialogue, however, but rather the reading of literature and other texts of the past. Historical texts are separated from us by a temporal distance, which makes the meaning incarnated in them more difficult to disclose. Indeed, what does it mean to uncover the meaning of such a text? When we try to understand a historical document, our world – our horizon of meaning – is not identical with the world of the author of the document. Nevertheless, our horizons are not totally separated, but distantly united through the '*Wirkungsgeschichte*' – the history of effects – of the document (Gadamer 1994: 300 ff.). It is consequently possible to bring the horizons closer together and reach an understanding of the document through what Gadamer here calls a 'merging of horizons'.

The medical encounter can be viewed as such a coming together of the two different attitudes and worlds of health-care professional and patient – in the language of Gadamer, of their different horizons of understanding – aimed at establishing a mutual understanding which can benefit the health of the ill party (Svenaeus 2000). Doctors (as well as representatives of other health-care professions) are thus not first and foremost scientists who apply biological knowledge but, rather, interpreters – hermeneuts of health and illness. Biomedical explanations and therapies can only be applied *within* the dialogical meeting, guided by the clinical understanding attained in service of the patient and his health. Gadamer's philosophy of hermeneutical understanding, which has mainly been taken to be a general description of the pattern of knowledge found in the humanities, might thus be expanded to cover the activities of health care.

Gadamer's late work, *The Enigma of Health*, supports this interpretation, addressing the areas of medicine and health care in a more direct way than the philosopher's earlier works (1996). Medicine is here characterized as a dialogue and discussion (*Gespräch*) by which the doctor and patient together try to reach an understanding of why the patient is ill:

> It is the disruption of health that necessitates treatment by a doctor. An important part of the treatment is that the patient actually discusses his or her illness with the doctor. This element of discussion is vital to all the different areas of medical competence, not just that of the psychiatrist. Dialogue and discussion serve to humanize the fundamentally unequal relationship that prevails between doctor and patient.
>
> *(Gadamer 1996: 112)*

What is particularly obvious in the medical meeting is the *asymmetrical* relation between the parties. The patient is ill and seeks help, whereas the doctor (Gadamer's main and only example of health-care professional) is at home – in control by virtue of her knowledge and experience of disease and illness. As developed above, this asymmetry necessitates empathy on the part of the doctor. She must try to understand the patient, not exclusively from her own point of view, but by trying to put herself in the patient's situation. Consequently, that the doctor attempts to reach a new, productive understanding of the patient's illness in no way implies that she should avoid empathy. It is only through empathy that the doctor can reach an independent understanding that is truly productive, in the sense of shared *and* novel, in offering new perspectives on the patient's health problems.

At this point we may return to Gadamer's model of textual interpretation in *Truth and Method* (something Gadamer does not do himself in *The Enigma of Health*) to understand in more detail how the clinical understanding is developed. It is first and foremost the doctor who is the 'reader' and the patient who is the 'text'. But since the meeting is dialogic, the reading is also a reciprocal process of questions and answers. The distance between the two parties is not a time-related distance as in the case of the reading of a historical text; it is, rather, a distance between two *life-world* horizons – the doctor's medical expertise of diseases and the patient's lived experience of illness – which can be narrowed down through the dialogue. This narrowing down, this 'merging of the horizons' of doctor and patient in the medical meeting, means that the horizons are brought into contact with each other but nevertheless preserve their identities as the separate horizons of two different attitudes and life worlds (Svenaeus 2000: part 3).

Hermeneutics and bioethics

As several commentators have pointed out, Gadamer's project in *Truth and Method* is deeply indebted to the practical philosophy of Aristotle (Berti 2003). Indeed, a discussion of 'The Hermeneutic Relevance of Aristotle' is at the centre of the chapter devoted to the problem of application (*Anwendung*) in the second part of the book (Gadamer 1994: 312 ff.). When Gadamer chooses to continue his analysis of hermeneutic practice by turning to Aristotle and the *Nicomachean Ethics* (2002), he does so in order to underline the *normative* aspect of hermeneutics:

> To summarize, if we relate Aristotle's description of the ethical phenomenon and especially the virtue of moral knowledge (*phronesis*) to our own investigation, we find that his analysis in fact offers a kind of *model of the problems of hermeneutics*. We too determined that application is neither a subsequent nor merely an occasional part of the phenomenon of understanding, but codetermines it as a whole from the beginning.
>
> *(Gadamer 1994: 324)*

The Greek concept rendered as 'the virtue of moral knowledge' by Gadamer in the quote above is *phronesis*, the word we have translated as 'practical wisdom' above. Among the last books to be published by Gadamer before his death in

2002 was his own annotated translation of Book VI of the *Nicomachean Ethics* – that is, precisely the book that deals with *phronesis* (Gadamer 1998). This fact is yet another sign of the importance of the concept for Gadamer's philosophy. It is thus clear that Gadamer intended his hermeneutics to be a practical philosophy in the Aristotelian sense, and it is also clear that practical, *phronetic* wisdom is to be considered a hermeneutical virtue (Figal 1995). Accordingly, *phronesis* is the mark of the good hermeneut, and maybe, in particular, the good medical hermeneut – the doctor (and other health-care professionals in charge of patients, we should add).

Let us now connect the concept of *phronesis* to hermeneutics in the way that Gadamer envisages, and by extension to medical hermeneutics. The first thing worth noting is that the reference to *phronesis* by Gadamer makes clear that applied hermeneutics does not mean application of universal rules. Medical hermeneutics is thus not applicative in the sense that universal, methodological rules are applied to the concrete situation. Rather, the hermeneutics of medicine is grounded in the *meeting* between health-care professional and patient – a meeting in which the two different horizons of medical knowledge and lived illness are brought together in an interpretative dialogue for the purpose of determining why the patient is ill and how he can be treated. This was one of the main points above: medical practice is not applied science but, rather, interpretation through dialogue in service of the patient's health. Within this interpretative pattern science is made use of in various ways, but the pattern itself is not deductively (or inductively) nomological in the natural-scientific sense.

The appropriation of *phronesis* at the heart of (medical) hermeneutics can also be viewed as a critique of the way applied (medical) ethics is often presented. The idea that ethical principles could somehow be directly applied to the clinical situation without having a firm and deep understanding of what is going on there is strongly countered by the reference to *phronesis*, since Aristotle's main purpose in developing this concept is that the application of abstract principles in the field of practical, ethical knowledge is insufficient (Svenaeus 2003). As we discussed in chapter one, the equilibrium between the empathic understanding of a situation at hand and moral theories advocating various principles as essential to doing good or being just in the world must be widened to include a philosophical analysis of what it means to be a human person.

How does Gadamer himself address the issues of bioethics in *The Enigma of Health* (1996)? I would say that he does so in at least two interconnected ways, neither of which bears much resemblance to mainstream work on the contemporary medical ethics scene. The first of these approaches consists precisely in going back to ancient philosophy and Aristotle. His discussions of Aristotelian themes and concepts are very similar to those we find in *Truth and Method* and other works of his, except for one thing: he now explicitly addresses *medical* practice (*Heilkunst*), and not only practice in general. Gadamer makes the point that medical practice – in its ancient as well as in its contemporary form – never 'makes' anything but, rather, helps to *re-establish* a healthy balance which has been lost. Health, according to Gadamer, is a self-restoring balance, and what the doctor does is to provide the means by which a state of equilibrium can re-establish itself by its own powers.

Gadamer's strategy in *The Enigma of Health* is to investigate the ancient philosophy of medicine in order to find guidance for contemporary medical practice. This is not (only) a nostalgic appeal for a pre-modern, 'humane' medicine which was not dominated and controlled by technoscience but, rather, a strategy that rests on Gadamer's insistence upon the importance of Greek philosophy for our contemporary thinking and our contemporary way of life. We need to address and make this influence explicit in order to elucidate the structure and goals of contemporary medical practice, just as we need to do the same in order to elucidate the structure and goals of the humanities, according to Gadamer. The second way Gadamer chooses to address matters of bioethics in *The Enigma of Health* is the way of philosophical anthropology and is very much in line with the one I have chosen in this book, although in his essays on topics central to clinical practice, such as death, life, the body, the soul, anxiety, and freedom, its development is rather cursory (Gadamer 1996).

Since the phenomenological hermeneutics of Heidegger and Gadamer is itself firmly rooted in Aristotelian patterns of thought, the marriage between the historical, philological approach and the phenomenological analysis of self/personhood in *The Enigma of Health* should come as no surprise (Gadamer 1996). What might be more surprising is that Gadamer relies to such a small extent on the pattern of understanding developed in *Truth and Method* when he analyses the dialogue essential to medical practice. Instead, he focuses upon the phenomenon that is central to the *goal* of medical practice: health. However, since this goal is what distinguishes medicine from other hermeneutical activities, which have other goals, it seems in many respects a promising way to go. It is also an original way to approach questions of medical ethics, which are seldom related to health theory in any substantive way. We will return to phenomenological health theory in the next chapter in the context of technology and medicalization. Phenomenology of health and illness is very obviously related to the phenomenology of suffering I developed in chapter two, and we will reconnect with that as well in this setting.

In what way does a phenomenological analysis of health bring us closer to *phronesis* as a key concept for bioethics? In other words, in what way do the two roads travelled by Gadamer in *The Enigma of Health* meet? Precisely by defining the goal of clinical practice as something dependent on the *individual* patient. If health is to be understood in terms of embodied being-in-the-world, and not only in terms of biomedical data, then the doctor needs to develop an understanding of the patient's thoughts, feelings, and life-world predicaments in order to carry out her profession. She needs to address the questions of the good (enough) life and the meaning of life for this particular person. This is food for thought for medical ethics. To emphasize the hermeneutic structure and essence of medical practice will bring a focus upon narratives to excavate the embodied suffering of individuals (Charon 2006; Frank 1995; Zaner 2004).

As we have seen in chapter one, Gadamer is hardly the first philosopher in the phenomenological-hermeneutic tradition to approach issues of health and illness. But other attempts at developing theories of health on a phenomenological basis have most often been restricted to the areas of psychiatry and psychology; somatic ailments have either been seen as the territory of biology and physiology, or they have been treated as psychosomatic symptoms by the phenomenologically inspired psychiatrists. That the University of Heidelberg, the place where Gadamer spent the second half of his long life, has hosted some of the most prominent figures in this tradition of phenomenological psychiatry, such as Karl Jaspers, Viktor von Weizsäcker, and Wolfgang Blankenburg, is no doubt one of the reasons Gadamer began approaching the themes of medicine and health in the 1960s (see Gadamer 1977). Jaspers, Weizsäcker, and Blankenburg are mentioned by Gadamer in *The Enigma of Health*, but without doubt he also knew the works of Ludwig Binswanger, Medard Boss, and other key figures of this tradition, such as F. J. J. Buytendijk and Erwin Straus, who are not mentioned in his book (Spiegelberg 1972).

The thesis that medical practice is a hermeneutical activity in the Gadamerian sense of a dialogic encounter between reader (doctor or other health-care professional) and text (patient) on the way to truth (about the person and his lack of health) tends to expose itself to exactly the same of kind of critical questions that were put to Gadamer by Jürgen Habermas and others following the publication of *Truth and Method* in the 1960s (Habermas 1971). How does medical hermeneutics take into account the embeddedness of medicine and health care in a political context? That critical analysis would have to be carried out by studying the interconnections among the more specific meaning patterns of medical practice and the sociopolitical pattern of, for example, the organization of health care and medical science. Interestingly, as we will see, Gadamer nurtures such a critical perspective through his roots in a Heideggerian phenomenology, which can be (and has been) developed as a critique of modern technology. To this topic we will return in chapter five.

Empathy with the dying

We have characterized clinical empathy and medical hermeneutics as integrated ways of understanding the embodied being-in-the-world of the patient in attempting to help him back to a healthier life. This will mean understanding major causes and reasons for the patient's sufferings, including those beyond the potentially disturbed biological functions of his body, especially in cases that are not amenable to merely discovering and curing diseases. But what about the situation in which the patient is not only chronically diseased – in such cases his life could still be made less painful and more at home by various medical interventions and/or lifestyle changes – but also dying? In such cases the disease(s) cannot be cured, but even so, there is no doubt a case for understanding such clinical scenarios as driven by the aim to mitigate the *suffering* of the patient, even though he will die in the end. What do we intend by such wording, and in what ways will a phenomenological understanding of suffering have implications for how we view physician-assisted suicide and/or euthanasia in such settings? This appears to be an interesting domain in which to test the essence of medical *phronesis*.

Let us return to the case of Ivan Ilyich introduced in chapter two (Tolstoy 2015). Ivan is a fairly successful lawyer living a seemingly happy life with his family and friends in Saint Petersburg when illness suddenly hits him. The doctors of this time – the 1880s – were not able to do much about cancer, especially not if it had metastasized, but the worst thing for Ivan is not that he suspects they do not have a clue about what causes his abdominal pain (a virtual line-up of famous and expensive physicians are consulted as his condition deteriorates). The worst thing is that they neither see nor understand *him* and his suffering:

> The doctor said: such-and-such and so-and-so indicate that within your body you have such-and-such and so-and-so; but if the investigations of such-and-such and so-and-so fail to confirm this, then we still have to conclude the presence of such-and-such and so-and-so instead. But if we suppose such-and-such, then, etc. Ivan Ilyich was only interested in one thing: was his condition dangerous or not? But the doctor ignored this improper question. From the doctor's point of view, such a question was pointless and could not be discussed; the only thing that mattered was to weigh up alternative probabilities – a wandering kidney and a disorder of the blind gut ... From the doctor's summing up, Ivan Ilyich came to the conclusion that things were bad; that the doctor didn't care, and probably nobody else did either, but for him they were bad. And this conclusion struck Ivan Ilyich painfully, making him feel very sorry for himself and angry with this doctor who was so indifferent to a matter of such importance. But he said nothing. He stood up, laid his money on the table, and sighed.
>
> *(Tolstoy 2015: 178)*

The medical-scientific abilities and skills involved in understanding such-and-such and so-and-so have advanced immensely since the times of Ivan Ilyich, but despite this, many patients and physicians testify that the tendency to neglect the suffering and dying person for all his diseases is still in place (Bishop 2011; Carel 2008; Cassell 2004; Frank 1995; Gawande 2014; Kaufman 2006). This is so for several reasons: the dominance of the third-person scientific perspective in contemporary medicine; the tendency to divide the investigation and treatment of a patient among different medical specialities and professionals; the unwillingness to address matters concerning impendent death in a discussion with the patient because this will involve anguish and terror; the wish to focus on curing diseases, or at least keeping the patient alive, since for a physician death is the ultimate disaster and failure to be avoided.

Doctors are supposed to save lives, not end them, but in some situations they are faced with the choice of treating a disease that is killing the patient or attempting to mitigate his suffering. Currently, in such cases, when further treatment of the disease will only prolong life marginally and it will actually mean increased suffering for the patient, the recommendation by experts is increasingly to focus on palliation rather than fighting disease. Patients have the right to choose among various options that doctors judge to be medically feasible and advisable, but before presenting such choices the professionals should take care to empathically understand the suffering persons they are facing and what their main issues are (Gawande 2014). The heroic imperative of 'doing everything possible' in all situations, and putting one's faith in a medical science that will soon be able to treat every disease, has vanished as it has become obvious that, in some situations, advanced treatment possibilities and technologies can intensify and prolong a patient's suffering rather than the other way around.

Doctors have become incomparably more successful in mitigating the kind of bodily pains that Ivan Ilyich suffers from in the novel, not least the pain he endures the last three terrible days of his life (see chapter two). Are they also better at understanding the core life-narrative values of their patients than Ivan's doctors (as well as family members and friends) were? Not necessarily; the skills of empathy, dialogue, and narrative understanding have not been focused upon in modern medicine until fairly recently, and in many settings they are still more or less absent, overshadowed by the focus upon medical science and the diseases of the living body. To some extent, the medical-scientific successes of the last century have even ignored 'the art of medicine', a tradition which some doctors in the times of Ivan Ilyich knew and practised (not the ones he encountered, though) (Svenaeus 2000: part 1).

Palliative care is a speciality that is increasingly focused upon in modern medicine, and we can hope that doctors will become even better at treating the pains we often suffer towards the end of our lives. However, as I have tried to argue in preceding chapters, suffering is not only about physical pain but also about what we are able to do in the world and who we are able to be there in the company of others. All the researchers I have referred to above stress these additional suffering domains in their attempts to understand the pains and hardships of dying persons (Bishop 2011; Carel 2008; Cassell 2004; Frank 1995; Gawande 2014; Kaufman 2006). Human life is a 'being-towards-death', as Heidegger puts it in *Being and Time*, and this means that death is not only a physiological event at the end of our life but a relationship to our own ending that we potentially face all the time (Aho 2016; Heidegger 1996: 235 ff.). The meaning of my life narrative and the core life values I more or less consciously embody are inseparable from the beginning and end of my life. A story always has a beginning and an ending; this is part of what makes it a story with a certain plot. And a miserable ending can change the meaning of the whole life story if a person becomes severely alienated concerning the ways she lives and looks upon herself in the more or less imagined eyes of others (Dworkin 1994: 199 ff.).

When we become old our bodies inevitably display the kind of vulnerability we have actually been suffering from ever since we were born (MacIntyre 2001).

'Trans humanists' dream of an age when we will no longer have to die, because doctors and other scientists will be able to fix or replace our ageing body (parts) (see chapters five and seven). However, for a foreseeable future we will have to live with our vulnerable condition, which means that ageing inevitably comes with more illness suffering and the kinds of alienation that follow in its track. We adapt to this increasingly vulnerable and weak condition with the more or less spontaneous changes of lifestyle that often commence in growing old. Old people live slower and more cautious lives; they become less focused upon doing new things and treasure relationships with people they already know (Gawande 2014). To become older means embodying a life narrative that is coming to a close, and this is not necessarily a bad or sad thing.

In using the expression 'embodying a life narrative' I literally mean a person's lived embodiment as the central aspect and way of existing in a life world. Ways of embodiment change with age, and this is also the reason persons modulate or change the preferred life projects from which they derive their core life-narrative values (see chapter two). We generally become less physically active and more thoughtful as we grow older; we often care less about our shortcomings and appreciate the things we are still able to do (Gawande 2014). In this manner we can escape alienation and even become more at home with ourselves in getting closer to the end of our life. But in some cases, the changes brought on us by diseases and other sad life events are possibly too severe or tragic to allow for changed life priorities. We feel the suffering is too much to bear and live with, and we would rather die than survive in this condition and situation if nothing can be done about it.

Questions of physician-assisted suicide and euthanasia are complicated, not only because they involve a health-care professional doing something that is apparently opposite to what she is normally supposed to do – helping to kill or killing in contrast to curing diseases and saving lives. These questions are complicated because it can sometimes be very hard to judge whether a life situation is truly hopeless and undignified – meaning there is nothing that can be done about the severe suffering – or whether there are still solutions to be found that would lead to a life worth living for the person who wants to die.

If faced by the choice of either living the last three days of our lives as Ivan Ilyich did or receiving a lethal injection at the beginning of day one that would kill us painlessly, I am sure a vast majority would choose the second alternative. But doctors are better at treating pain today than they were in the 1880s, and many argue that we do not need the option of the lethal injection to live tolerable and dignified lives to our very end. This is probably so in almost every case, but there still seem to be some cases in which palliation does not work to a sufficient degree, thus leaving the patient in intolerable pain (Dworkin 1994: 179 ff.). Even trickier, though, are the cases in which the perceived intolerable suffering consists not in physical pain but in being unable to do what is seen as the things that bestow meaning on one's life – such as having a good meal, going for a walk, reading the newspaper, or joining in a discussion with friends. Is it always possible to adapt by changing one's fundamental goals in life, or are some changes beyond what is reasonable to expect, especially in consideration of persons who will soon die and do not have a large number of years in which to realize their changed life priorities?

If we return to the third level of suffering surveyed in chapter two we find the strongest arguments for, as well as against, allowing euthanasia or physician-assisted suicide by law, as has happened in a number of Western countries during the last twenty-five years (e.g. the Netherlands, Belgium, Luxemburg, some states in the United States, and Canada) (Birnbacher and Dahl 2008; Cholbi and Varelius 2015). The third level of suffering concerns the ways a person becomes alienated from the core life values that constitute her view of what makes a life worth living, how we should treat each other morally, and who she is in the eyes of others (Taylor 1989: 4 ff.). Such fundamental values become articulated by a narrative that holds together and bestows meaning on the whole life and identity of the person in question (Baker 2000; Ricoeur 1992; Schechtman 1996). If, in view of a chronic medical condition that plagues her and will soon lead to her inevitable death, a person finds her current situation incompatible with being the kind of person she has become and wants to be in and through her life narrative, this is a very strong argument for allowing her to die (Dworkin 1994: 235–236). Such cases could also include situations of advance directives, as they are called, in which persons have stated that they do not want to be kept alive by means of feeding tubes or ventilators should they end up severely demented or enter a vegetative state. However, allowing someone to die is not the same thing as assisting a person in taking her life, much less killing her; if the latter two actions are to be allowed we minimally need the person to be able to assess her present condition in a rational way and ask for this help. How to arrange this practically and legally is a matter I will not deal with here, but I think it is important to notice that the phenomenological perspective on personhood and suffering in medicine does not rule out that some measures taken to mitigate or avoid severe suffering for a patient may include at least assisting him in taking his life.

The reason the third level of suffering also involves the strongest arguments against allowing assisted suicide or euthanasia is that the narrative identity which can be felt to be impossible to live with in what is perceived as an undignified condition is a self-respect *in the eyes of others* (Taylor 1989: 14–15). This is the way human persons constitute their value and worth, and if – as is often the case when persons became unable to take care of themselves in advanced age – they feel they *should* wish they were dead, they might say so to doctors. Increased patient autonomy has undoubtedly been one of the most important developments in late modern medicine – inter-nested with the rise of bioethics in the 1960s and 1970s – but a too-narrow view of the person as a rational decision maker devoid of context and narrative is an easy and dangerous way out of taking professional responsibility for the patient and his well-being (Halpern 2001; Jonsen 1998). Clinical empathy and medical hermeneutics – *phronesis* – demand an attempt to understand the whole life situation and identity of the patient, especially in cases of severe, chronic, and terminal suffering. What does the patient's life look like and what makes it worth or not worth living? What does he fear the most, and why is this the case? Only through empathically asking such questions and interpreting the responses can doctors help patients to die well in end-of-life care (Gawande 2014: chapters 7 and 8).

Summary

To be a morally wise physician or other health-care professional one needs empathic abilities, but in the process of developing a more substantial understanding of the patient and her health problems the practical wisdom takes on a hermeneutical character. Empathic understanding develops into interpretative understanding of the other person's being-in-the-world. Within the pattern and limits of such a hermeneutical framework, medical knowledge about the human body and its functions are applied and used to detect and fight diseases responsible for the illness. The total medical understanding itself is richer than and different from explanations of bodily dysfunctions only, since it is about a person and her life world, about the way she embodies core life values by way of a narrative.

Having empathy and developing an understanding of the condition of dying patients make it evident that the final goal of the hermeneutics of medicine is to relieve or alleviate human suffering. Such suffering takes place on three interrelated levels dealing with embodiment, being-in-the-world, and the core life-narrative values of a person, respectively. Questions of physician-assisted suicide and euthanasia are complicated, not only because they involve a health-care professional doing something that is apparently opposite to what he is normally supposed to do – helping to kill or killing in contrast to curing diseases and saving lives. These questions are complicated because it can sometimes be very hard to judge whether a person's life situation is truly hopeless and undignified – meaning there is nothing that can be done about the severe suffering – or whether there are still solutions to be found that would lead to a life worth living for the person involved.

The third level of suffering concerns the ways a person becomes alienated from the core life values that constitute her view of what makes a life worth living, how we should treat each other morally, and who she is in the eyes of others. If, in view of a chronic medical condition that plagues her and will soon lead to her inevitable death, a person finds her current situation incompatible with being the kind of person she has become and wants to be in and through her life narrative, this is a very strong argument for allowing her to die. However, our analysis of alienation by way of life story also delivers the strongest arguments against allowing assisted suicide or euthanasia, since what is perceived as an undignified condition is so from the imagined perspective of others. This is the way human persons constitute their value and self-worth, and if – as is often the case when persons became unable to take care of themselves in advanced age – they feel they are supposed to wish they were dead, they might say so to doctors.

5

MEDICAL TECHNOLOGIES AND THE LIFE WORLD

Phenomenology and medical technology

New medical technologies are increasingly transforming the meaning patterns of everyday life. The new diagnostic and therapeutic possibilities that medicine offers challenge borders between life and death and what is normal versus abnormal in direct and indirect ways. Technologies of assisted reproduction and prenatal diagnosis change the way we have and choose our children. Life-supporting technologies and tissue transfer procedures make it possible to postpone death and to share cells and organs between bodies. Genetics and stem cell research play major roles at both ends of life in developing the knowledge and techniques of starting, predicting, and prolonging life. Brain science and psychiatry offer us ways of understanding and changing persons and their personalities by means of imaging technologies, implants, prostheses, and pharmaceuticals.

This development has only begun, and bioethicists are presently examining the ethical challenges that future 'medical enhancement' technologies will bring (Gordijn and Chadwick 2008; Habermas 2003; Hauskeller 2013; Malmqvist 2007; Mills 2011; Parens 2015; Savulescu et al. 2011). This is important work: our abilities to handle new technologies – and not let the technologies handle us – will be decisive for the society to come. However, in these ethical analyses of challenges that new medical technologies bring, phenomenology is too rarely brought into play in any substantive manner. In the present chapter I will attempt to do so by introducing and discussing the most well-known contribution to philosophy of technology made by a phenomenologist – namely, Martin Heidegger's critique of modern technoscience (Heidegger 1977). Is it possible to make Heidegger's critique productive for contemporary phenomenological bioethics, and if so, how? In answering these questions the phenomenon of *health* will be brought to our attention, and especially the tendency of modern technology to *medicalize* various life-world issues. Human suffering in the twenty-first century is increasingly explained in terms of diseases and other bodily dysfunctions preventing our flourishing (Conrad 2007). However, an increasingly sophisticated medical science and the new possibilities it brings appear, rather, to make us *less healthy* than before, a paradox that I think a phenomenological analysis of medical technologies can help us to better understand and possibly undo.

Heidegger's philosophy of technology

Heidegger's suggestion that the essence of modern technology is a way of comprehending nature in making it useful for human purposes has gained much attention in the philosophy of science and technology (Ihde 2010) and in environmental ethics (Foltz 1995), but it has remained, if not unheard of then at least under-researched in biomedical ethics (but see Brassington 2007; Fielding 2001; Krakauer 1998; Malmqvist 2007). The reason for this may be that Heidegger's examples of modern technology are either devices that intervene in our environment (e.g. power plants, technologies of modern farming and mining) or devices that intervene in human language and communication (e.g. television, typewriters, and information technologies), not in the human body. Heidegger did not foresee, or else was not interested in, the breakthroughs in medical science and practice that began at the same time his own thoughts on modern technology were first published (in the 1950s), and he did not (with a couple of minor exceptions) later supplement his analysis with examples taken from disciplines such as molecular biology and brain science, or with technologies such as the dialysis machine, organ transplantation, ventilators, assisted reproduction, genetic diagnosis, or computer tomography. For this he may be partly excused, being sixty-four in 1953, when Watson and Crick first presented the structure of the DNA molecule, and ending his life in 1976, before most of the technologies that are scrutinized by bioethicists today were on the public agenda. This should not stop us, however, from trying to extend his analysis to biomedical technologies and, in this endeavour, also critically reviewing his arguments about the status and impact of modern technology as a whole.

In the essay 'The Question Concerning Technology', published in 1954, Heidegger sets himself the aim of articulating what he calls the 'essence' of modern technology (1977). Modern technology means technology guided and made possible by natural science; but nevertheless, Heidegger claims, modern technology has priority over science in the sense of determining the essence of our age, what Heidegger calls our historical 'sending of being' (*Seinsgeschick*). This means, according to Heidegger, that although the scientific revolution of the seventeenth century articulated a physical and mathematical theory that was necessary for the development of modern technology, the essence of this modern scientific way of viewing the world only comes to *expression* in the technologies of the nineteenth and twentieth centuries: through factories, trains, cars, aircraft, telephones, radios, television sets, machines of modern agriculture and mining, weapons, power plants, and so on. According to Heidegger, modern technology has allied itself with science in such a way that the character of modern technology must be seen as fundamentally different from the character of traditional technologies based on craftsmanship. To implement modern technology is not only a matter of shaping nature in order to satisfy human goals; modern technology also entails an 'enframing' world view (in Heidegger's German: *Gestell*) whereby nature is viewed purely as an energy resource in a scientific-economic calculus. *Gestell* literally means rack or frame, but it also alludes to different German words formed with the verb *stellen* (putting in place): *vorstellen* (representing), *einstellen* (adjusting, shelving), *aufstellen* (erecting, establishing), *bestellen* (ordering), and *herstellen* (producing).

Historians and philosophers of science and technology have been sceptical about Heidegger's claims in many ways. A major point of scepticism concerns the existence of any shared essence of modern technology. Modern technology, according to this view, is merely applied science that can be used to do many different things. Heidegger says explicitly in the essay that the essence of technology he is trying to articulate is not the instrumental use of a piece of technology in the sense of goals that might be different depending upon the occasion. He finds the idea that human beings could simply choose to do whatever they want with new technological inventions a bit naïve, and in this I think that many contemporary historians and philosophers of technology would give him right. New technologies not only open up new spaces of possibilities for our doings; they also make us see things in new ways. Heidegger's way of putting this is to say that modern technology 'reveals' the world in a certain way; it makes the world appear as a 'resource' (*Bestand*). This might appear to be an idea quite close to the standard instrumental view of technology, but it is not, really, since the instrumental essence in Heidegger's version considers not only the way technology becomes a means in human projects, but also the way technology dominates the *goals* of human projects, changing our views on what is worth pursuing in the first place. The modern hydroelectric power station straddling the river Rhine is Heidegger's main example in the essay. The power plant makes the river a 'water-power supplier' in contrast to the old wooden bridge over the Rhine, which allows the river to be a river and not just a source of energy (Heidegger 1977).

Many commentators have accused Heidegger of a romantic view of old technologies, failing to see how pre-modern man put stress on his environment and used nature up in ways that were not very mindful towards animals, plants, rivers, and oceans (Riis 2011). Modern technologies can sometimes be much more respectful of nature than old ones in the sense of being more ecologically sustainable; think of solar energy in contrast to traditional heating with wood or coal, for instance. This criticism, however, misses Heidegger's main point: namely, that modern scientific technologies change our way of viewing and understanding the world when we take action in it. Such a change might apply to contemporary solar energy also, if it leads to a way of life in which the sun is comprehended as an energy resource only, regardless of whether the solar cells have a negative impact on the environment in making it dirty or ugly. Heidegger's idea can be brought home by quoting the only mention he makes in 'The Question Concerning Technology' of modern medicine:

> Only to the extent that man for his part is already challenged (by modern technology) to exploit the energies of nature can this ordering revealing happen. If man is challenged, ordered, to do this, then does not man himself belong even more originally than nature within the standing-reserve? The current talk about human resources, about the supply of patients for a clinic, gives evidence of this … Yet precisely because man is challenged more originally than are the energies of nature, i.e., into the process of ordering, he never is transformed into mere standing-reserve. Since man drives technology forward, he takes part in ordering as a way of revealing. But the unconcealment itself, within which ordering unfolds, is never a human handiwork, any more than is the realm through which man is already passing every time he as a subject relates to an object.
>
> *(Heidegger 1977: 18)*

'Ordering revealing' (*Entbergen*), 'standing reserve' (*Bestand*), 'unconcealment' (*Unverborgenheit*), and, a couple of pages later in the essay, 'framework' (*Gestell*) are all related to what Heidegger in his first major philosophical work, *Being and Time*, published in 1927, calls 'being-in-the-world' (1996) (see chapters one and four). These terms are attempts to name and characterize the basic meaning pattern through which things appear as such-and-such things for us. Heidegger's point is that modern technology has decisively changed the meaning pattern of the world, which has traditionally involved a number of different natural and cultural features constitutive of human practices. His point is also that modern technology has done so in a way that we should find problematic and strive to move beyond because it severely limits what we are able to see, think, and do in the world. His point is not that we should abstain from all use of scientific technology and try to live a pre-modern life (he was quite fond of watching football on television himself). He knows more than well that this would be not only undesirable, but also impossible. His point is that the essence of technology has developed into a danger in becoming the *dominating* and, most often also taken for granted and therefore *barely visible*, world view of the modern age. We must live within the 'framework' of modern technology, since there is no other way to live today, but we can strive to make this meaning pattern of modern technology and science visible through a philosophical analysis and take measures to prevent it from becoming the all-encompassing pattern of our being-in-the-world (Borgmann 2005; Ruin 2010).

Heidegger and medical technologies

Reflecting upon the meaning and significance of medical technology (something that Heidegger never did himself) is actually a good way to save Heidegger's analysis from falling into traps of romantic anti-scientism. Heidegger could hardly deny that inventions such as X-ray, the medical laboratory, the artificial kidney, or antibiotics do more and better things to us than exposing us to a life in the technological 'framework'. Therefore, it would be wrong, I think, to forge a necessary and immediate link in Heidegger's writings between the use of modern technology and the domination of a technological world view. The essence of modern technology is not something technological, as Heidegger says several times in his essay, and this we can see even more clearly if we turn to a couple of lines from another text by Heidegger, published for the first time in 1958 but conceived as early as 1939, 'On the Essence and Concept of *Physis*':

> Medical practice and technology (*techne*) can only cooperate with nature (*physis*), can more or less facilitate the health (of the patient), but as technology it can never replace nature and in its place become the principle of health as such. This could only happen if life in itself became a 'technically' producible artefact, but if this were to become the case there would no longer be any health, any more than being born or dying would exist.
>
> *(Heidegger 1978: 255, my translation)*

To facilitate the health of a patient with the help of medical technology need not be identical to enforcing a 'framework' of technology on him – a new way of defining, shaping, and producing health and life under the reign of medical science. But it is a constant *risk*. Hans-Georg Gadamer articulates this risk in his collection of essays *The Enigma of Health*, which we encountered in the preceding chapter of this book – a philosophy of health and medicine which is deeply indebted to Heidegger's philosophy of technology:

> In medical science we encounter the dissolution of personhood when the patient is objectified in terms of a mere multiplicity of data. In a clinical investigation all the information about a person is treated as if it could be adequately collated on a card index. If this is done in a correct way, then the data (*Werte*) all belong to the person. But the question is nevertheless whether the unique value of the individual (*Eigenwert*) is properly recognized in this process.
>
> *(Gadamer 1996: 81, translation has been altered)*

The enframing of a human being through medical science and technology takes place when the embodied complaints of the patient are taken out of the life-world context of human dialogue and replaced by a medical-scientific analysis only. This, I think, is the core relevance of Heidegger's philosophy of medical technology for bioethics. In order to see this more clearly, let us now turn to the only work in which Heidegger approaches the nature and problems of medical practice.

Heidegger among the doctors

During the 1960s Heidegger held several lectures in the little Swiss town of Zollikon at the invitation of the psychiatrist Medard Boss, who was trying to make use of Heidegger's philosophy in the version of psychotherapy he was developing: *Daseinsanalyse* (the 'analytic of Dasein' is Heidegger's own name for the philosophy of being-in-the-world he had developed in *Being and Time*). Heidegger and Boss had been good friends since 1947, and in the seminars Heidegger meets with Boss's colleagues and students, attempting to give them an introduction to the phenomenological way of thinking he has been pursuing from the very start of his career (Heidegger 2001). The seminars, for obvious reasons, have a special emphasis on themes that will be relevant to doctors, but they also dwell on basic metaphysical questions such as the nature of space and time. A prominent theme is Heidegger's criticism of Freud and psychoanalysis, and the alternative form of therapy Boss is trying to develop with the help of Heidegger's philosophy. These parts of the seminars are not, however, the ones that are most relevant for our purposes; rather, we will focus on the parts dealing with medical practice in general.

Heidegger thinks that phenomenological philosophy is very important to doctors for the very reason that they should not fall under the spell of technology: 'It is of utmost importance that we have *thinking* doctors, doctors who do not rest content with abandoning the field of medicine to scientific technicians' (2001: 134). Heidegger approaches this importance (*Not*) in the seminars by focusing upon two themes: the problem of *method*, and the problem of *embodiment*. He takes these themes, or problems, to be identical in medicine, since the problem of embodiment (*Leiblichkeit*) is first and foremost a problem of method (Heidegger 2001: 122). Heidegger characterizes the scientific method by going back to the scientific revolution in the seventeenth century – to Galileo and Descartes and the ways of thinking they inaugurated.

Science, according to Heidegger, presents nature as a collection of entities and energies that can be understood and controlled by articulating causal laws in a formalized language assigning mathematical values to variables in formulas. These laws are tested in controlled experiments, which, in turn, make use of technologies that rest on scientific theories. This is the method common to all natural scientific disciplines, such as physics and chemistry, and the physiology and biochemistry found in scientific medicine are no exceptions. Heidegger claims that an essential split between the human subject (self, person) and the objects of nature was put in place by the scientific revolution, and he also claims that this split robs human beings of their own nature, since the human subject itself becomes an object: 'Engaged in such a modern science is a dictatorship of mind, that degrades the mind itself to a handling of calculable operators' (Heidegger 2001: 139). This reification of human being becomes a central part of modern scientific medicine when the body is viewed as a machine, a metaphor used by Descartes and since then dominating the medical field. But the human body is not only a biological object; it is also a way of being:

Everything that we refer to as our lived body (*unsere Leiblichkeit*), including the most minute muscle fibre and the most imperceptible hormone molecule, belongs essentially to our mode of existence. This body is consequently *not* to be understood as lifeless matter, but is part of that domain that cannot be objectified or seen, a being able to encounter significance, which our entire being-there (*Da-sein*) consists in. This lived body (*dieses Leibliche*) forms itself in a way appropriate for using the lifeless and living material objects that it encounters. In contrast to a tool, however, the living domains of existence cannot be released from the human being. They cannot be stored separately in a tool-box. Rather they remain pervaded by a human being, kept in a human being, belonging to a human being, as long as he or she lives.

(Heidegger 2001: 293, translation has been altered)

The important thing here is not that Heidegger appears to be unaware of the medical technology of organ transplantation, rapidly developing at the same time he is speaking (with organs being carried around in tool-boxes) (Svenaeus 2010); the important thing is the fundamental difference he makes between the body as a biological object (*Körper*) and the body as a way of being-in-the-world (lived body: *Leib*). That 'the body is pervaded by human being', as Heidegger says, means that the body understands and inhabits the world. Heidegger expresses this in his late talks to Boss and to the latter's medical students through the neologism 'Das Leiben des Leibes': human existence is a 'bodying forth' in the meaning-structures of the world, and this is something that must not be missed by the doctor if he is going to be able to help his patients (2001: 113). Psychosomatic medicine is the most obvious example of this, but Heidegger's remarks are not restricted to instances in which the body displays physiological signs of stress and unresolved unconscious conflicts. As a matter of fact, he is very sceptical about the very concept of 'psycho-somatic', which he shows to be imprisoned in a scientific, causal model that does not acknowledge the primary belonging together of mind and body in a being-there in the world as a lived body (Heidegger 2001: 99 ff.).

As a contrast to the scientific method, Heidegger articulates the phenomenological method as a means of philosophizing in which the ways of the lived body can be articulated and understood. Examples he gives are the understanding of the meaning of a blush, the feeling of a pain, or the experience of sorrow, phenomena that cannot be measured and made intelligible by medical physiology, but which can nevertheless be essential for the doctor to understand in meeting with the patient (Heidegger 2001: 106). These are bodily phenomena, but they are nevertheless pregnant with meaning that cannot be articulated by the scientific, but only by the phenomenological, method. The same goes for the effects that pharmaceuticals may have on a person's thoughts and behaviour:

From the fact that something can be brought about in bodily being through chemical interventions the conclusion is drawn that the origin and cause of the mental in human beings is physiological chemistry. This is wrong, for something that is a requirement for an existential relation between human beings is not its cause, not its yielding cause, and consequently not its origin. The existential relation does not consist of molecules, does not come into being through molecules, but is also not without that which can be reinterpreted as a physiological–molecular happening.

(Heidegger 2001: 200, translation has been altered)

Doctors, according to Heidegger, should by no means be hostile to science, but they should learn to see the limitations and dangers of acting *only* as scientists in their profession when they are meeting patients with bodily problems, since this could, as Heidegger drastically puts it, 'lead to the self annihilation (*Selbstzerstörung*) of human being' (2001: 124). The annihilation of human being – not as a biological being, of course, but as a being-in-the-world – is therefore a problem and danger that stems from choosing the scientific method as the only one relevant in medicine. This is also the danger that Heidegger sees in using medical technology in attempting to help patients. The greatest danger is not that the pieces of modern technology would by themselves dominate or make the patient as a person disappear from the attention of the doctor, although this may happen in the individual case; the danger is that the scientific attitude finds a dominating *hold* by way of the technology that makes the attitude in question harder to critically scrutinize and complement with the phenomenological point of view.

The two brief examples Heidegger gives of medical technologies in *Zollikon Seminars* confirm this interpretation, since they portray the technology in question not as an installation of the 'framework' of modern technology but rather as a danger in facilitating the domination of the scientific method (at the expense of the phenomenological method) in medicine. Both examples concern the brain, which is obviously central to Heidegger's concerns, not only because he is speaking with psychiatrists, but also because we are talking about the 'organ of thinking'. The first example is EEG:

We do not have any possibilities to know how the brain bodies forth in thinking. What we see in an EEG picture has nothing to do with the bodying forth of the brain, but with the fact that the brain can also be thought about and visualized as a chemical-physical piece of matter.

(Heidegger 2001: 245, translation has been altered)

The second example of a medical technology mentioned by Heidegger is even more interesting, since it concerns a form of treatment that was highly disputed – one might even say demonized – in the 1960s: electroconvulsive therapy (2001: 244). But Heidegger does not make any comments about punishment and control being enacted through the therapy in question; his main concern is instead to show that the machine can only release moods, not produce them, since moods derive their meaning from human being as a being-in-the-world. To articulate the meaning of such moods of suffering was the main concern of chapter two in this book. In my phenomenological articulation of suffering in terms of mood and being-in-the-world Heidegger was obviously a main source of inspiration, and it is interesting to notice that the philosopher himself was on the way to articulating the significance of his phenomenology for medicine in a late phase of his work.

Implications of phenomenology of technology for bioethics

The main lesson Heidegger taught to the doctors in Zollikon seems to be that they should be wary of letting the scientific attitude dominate their encounters with patients. Medical science has to find its proper place in relation to the phenomenological method of interpreting the being-in-the-world of the patient in medical practice. As we noted in chapter four in investigating the hermeneutics of medicine with Gadamer, phenomenology or hermeneutics (Heidegger talked about phenomenological hermeneutics and/or hermeneutic phenomenology) is not a method in the sense of following algorithmic rule procedures; it is a way of addressing the patient and understanding his life-world predicaments.

Heidegger's main concern in the seminars is with pinpointing the origin and nature of the scientific method, in combination with introducing phenomenology as an alternative perspective in medicine. But medical science, as we all know, does not just represent the threat of reifying the suffering of patients; it has also led to major breakthroughs in helping patients with diseases that could not be treated by pre-modern doctors. These breakthroughs have come to the fore in the form of different medical technologies making diagnosis, prevention, and treatment of diseases possible (Reiser 2009). The technologies in question may well harbour the risk of 'dissolving' the person, as Gadamer says in the quote above, or 'annihilating' her, as Heidegger puts it, but they can also mitigate suffering and save a person's life – a service I think few would like to abstain from if they were severely ill.

Given the fact that Heidegger does not provide us with this analysis himself, do we have any ways of distinguishing among the medical technologies that we could use without being swallowed up by the scientific-technological framework and the ones we should abstain from using because they will make us inhuman? Some Heidegger scholars would protest that this question is wrongly put. Heidegger's concern is not to distinguish good technologies from bad ones but to put his finger on the price we have to pay for already being enframed by the essence of technology, and, also, that we should search for better ways to live through acknowledging the world-saving power of art and philosophy: what Heidegger calls *Dichten* and *Denken*. It is true that Heidegger's concern is not with individual examples of technologies but rather with what he calls their essence. The *Gestell* is not more or less present in an individual piece of modern technology; it is the framework of meaning that puts the different pieces together, making us view nature as a product with utility value only.

Acknowledging this clarification, I think it still makes sense to ask about the effect or risk an individual technological invention may harbour in putting us on a track to a form of life in which the essence of modern technology comes to dominate our world view and actions. The individual instantiations of modern technology are not just like *any* part of the world. If they were, why would Heidegger concern himself with *technology* in the first place in spelling out the dangers of the *Gestell* in his writings? Modern technology, in contrast to other pieces of nature or culture, has a tendency to enchant us in blocking out other aspects of our being-in-the-world. Heidegger's way of putting this, as I mentioned above, is to say that modern technology 'reveals' the world in a certain way; it makes the world appear as a resource. Heidegger considers not just the way technology becomes a means in human projects, but also the way technology dominates the *goals* of human projects, changing our views on what is worth pursuing in the first place. This instrumentalizing tendency is surely enhanced and could perhaps also be taken beyond our control by particular technological inventions, and therefore I think it makes sense to inquire into the difference between 'good' and 'bad' medical technologies.

In evaluating the risks a type of technology will harbour in making us see and think about things only as resources, we could pick up on Heidegger's analysis in the *Zollikon Seminars* of the importance of human embodiment for our being-in-the-world (Heidegger 2001). We could argue that medical technologies that divorce us from our current embodied life form also tend to rob us of our personhood and all the human values that go with it (Hauskeller 2013; Parens 2015). The *lived body* is our fundamental contact with nature, not only as something that we make use of, but as something that we *are* and must *respond* to rather than trying to dominate and install new standards for. The old medical advice of helping nature to heal itself can sit well with modern technological inventions for the diagnosis, prevention, and cure of diseases, like computer tomography, lab tests, vaccines, pharmaceuticals, dialysis, surgery techniques, and so on, but the measure of the *lived body* would also make us wary of the technologies that tend to block life-world concerns in order to prolong or even produce life as a goal in itself. Such a criterion would square well with some attempts to draw a line between medical technologies that help us to improve the human life form and technologies that make us leave it in order to proceed to the post-human (Agar 2013). Heidegger's early emphasis on finitude ('being-towards-death') as the source of meaning for human existence (see chapter four), and his attempts to analyse this form of life through the significance of different forms of attunement that make us present with others in the world and for ourselves (as embodied), plotted already in *Being and Time*, would fit well with such attempts to find a human measure for medical technologies (Heidegger 1996).

Admittedly, the criterion would have to be developed and refined in order to solve the hard cases. It is easy to make an argument with the help of such a criterion that we should refrain from uploading our brains to computers in order to live forever, or from cloning babies to be grown in artificial wombs, but what about the borders of assisted reproduction and the limits of organ transplantation? In many cases the same technology will have 'good' and 'bad' uses – think of the current use of ventilators or genetic diagnosis. And the impact of medical technologies should not be thought about only through the drastic examples of making human life radically different by 'producing' human life, as Heidegger himself puts it in the quote from 'On the Essence and Concept of *Physis*' above (1978: 255), but also through examples of technologies that tend to narrow the scope of health by inventing new diseases, or by expanding the boundaries of the diseases that we currently treat (Conrad 2007; Stempsey 2006; Svenaeus 2007a). *Medicalization* – the expansion of medical concepts and treatment methods beyond the borders of health and illness in redefining other forms of human suffering and morally deviant behaviours in terms of diseases – is a major bioethical issue that we have touched upon in previous chapters and will soon return to below.

Indeed, the phenomenon of health itself could be looked upon as a particularly urgent theme to study and explicate for a contemporary medicine that tries to answer to the dangers of modern technology that Heidegger spells out in his writings. As Heidegger writes, if life were to become a technically producible artefact 'there would no longer be any health, any more than being born or dying would exist' (1978: 255). Heidegger himself never carried out such an analysis of the meaning of health and illness in his works, but I think it is obvious from what we find in *Zollikon Seminars* that it would have to proceed from a position giving priority to the lived body and the life world (being-in-the-world) of human being, rather than from a position giving priority to applied medical science.

I have tried, myself, in other books and papers, to show with the aid of Heidegger's philosophy how the healthy versus the ill life can be explicated as *homelike* versus *unhomelike* being-in-the-world (e.g. Svenaeus 2000, 2011). These concepts were also central to the analysis of suffering carried out in chapter two of this book. Suffering was found to be an alienating mood overcoming a person and engaging her in a struggle to remain at home in the face of the loss of meaning and purpose in life. Homelikeness and unhomelikeness in a phenomenology of health would refer to two contrasting features of the being-in-the-world of human beings. To be ill means to be not at home in one's being-in-the-world, to find oneself in a pattern of disorientedness, resistance, helplessness, and perhaps even despair, instead of in the familiar transparency of healthy life. It is important to repeat the fundamental difference between a phenomenological illness concept in a theory such as this and the concept of disease in its biomedical sense (see chapter three). A disease is a disturbance of the biological functions of the body (or something that causes such a disturbance), which can only be detected and understood from the perspective of the doctor investigating the body with the aid of her hands or medical technologies. The patient can also adopt such a scientific perspective towards his own body and speculate about diseases responsible for his suffering. But the suffering itself is an illness experience of the person who is in a world, embodied and connected to other people around him. Illness has meaning, or, perhaps rather, *disturbs* the meaning processes of being-in-the-world in which one is leading one's life and understanding one's personal identity by way of a life narrative.

Gadamer, in his late work *The Enigma of Health*, which I quoted from above, points out, in the spirit of Heidegger, that health cannot be produced by the doctor with the use of technical and scientific skills; rather, health must be *re-established*, as something that has been lost, by helping the patient to heal himself. Health, according to Gadamer, is a kind of self-restoring balance, and the doctor provides the means by which a state of equilibrium can re-establish itself on its own power:

> Without doubt it is part of our nature as living beings that the conscious awareness of health conceals itself. Despite its hidden character, health nonetheless manifests itself in a kind of feeling of well-being. It shows itself above all where such a feeling of well-being means that we are open to new things, ready to embark on new enterprises and, forgetful of ourselves, scarcely notice the demands and strains which are put upon us. ... Health is not a condition that one introspectively feels in oneself. Rather it is a condition of being-there, of being-in-the-world, of being together with other people, of being taken in by an active and rewarding engagement with the things that matter in life. ... It is the rhythm of life, a permanent process in which equilibrium re-establishes itself.
>
> *(Gadamer 1996: 112–114, translation has been altered)*

The conceptual backdrop for Gadamer's analysis of health in the quote above is undoubtedly Heidegger's phenomenology of everyday human being-in-the-world, found in *Being and Time*, which is also the starting point for my own analysis of suffering and illness in this book (Heidegger 1996). Despite the fact that Heidegger did not address and develop any phenomenology of health himself in approaching technology and medicine, his philosophy offers a promising starting point in such endeavours.

Heidegger's and Gadamer's philosophies can help us to see how the scientific attitude in medicine must always be balanced by and integrated into a phenomenological way of understanding the life-world concerns of patients (Taylor 1991: 106). The difference between the scientific and the phenomenological method in medicine is articulated by Heidegger in distinguishing two different ways of studying the human body: as biological organism and as lived body. Medicine needs to acknowledge the priority of the lived body in addressing health as a way of being-in-the-world and not as the absence of diseases only. One important consequence of this explication of Heidegger's philosophy of technology is that the philosophy in question is by no means hostile to technology when it comes to medical practice, but the perspective of the lived body as a way of being-in-the-world will also make us wary of the technologies that tend to block life-world concerns in order to prolong or even produce life as a goal in itself (more about this in chapters six and seven).

Psychopharmacology and medicalization

Let us continue our efforts to analyse health and its relationship to diseases, medical technologies, and the driving forces of medicalization. The main focus of the enhancement and post-humanism debates in bioethics so far have been future technologies that will make it possible to genetically design persons in vitro or radically transform them by way of prostheses that are surgically grafted to the body and the brain in a cyborg manner (More and Vitra-More 2013). In contrast to science fiction technologies, which may make it possible to develop creatures with an intelligence, moral capacity, physical strength, and lifespan beyond the human, cosmetic surgery and various pharmaceuticals currently prescribed show us what medical enhancement already looks like today. Cosmetic surgery is by definition in the business of changing our looks according to cultural norms rather than repairing injuries or congenital defects, and it is often criticized for reinforcing sexist, ageist, and racist aesthetic ideals (Sullivan 2001). According to such a critique, the enforcement of these ideals by way of surgery not only prohibits rather than supports the flourishing of the persons who are operated on but also makes life worse for *other* individuals, who do not satisfy the norms (and who cannot afford or do not wish for surgery). In addition to cosmetic surgery, medications for sexual dysfunction, baldness, menopause, premenstrual syndrome, and a whole flora of steroids and anti-ageing pills are all examples of contemporary enhancement drugs. However, the most challenging cases of enhancement today are found within psychopharmacology.

Pharmaceuticals are clearly examples of biomedical technology, and in the case of psychopharmacology the targets of the chemicals are the functions of neurons of the brain, making the drugs into 'neurotechnologies' (Rose and Abi-Rached 2013). The advent of Prozac in the late 1980s inaugurated a debate about what it meant to be put in a state that was 'better than well' by means of psychiatric medication (Elliott and Chambers 2004; Healy 1999; Kramer 1994; Svenaeus 2007a, 2009b). The new antidepressants (SSRIs, SNRIs, and others) transformed the treatment of mood disorders – depression as well as anxiety disorders – in the 1990s and sold in numbers beyond imagination. The rapidly increased use of Ritalin and other drugs to treat ADHD (attention-deficit/ hyperactivity disorder) during the same period of time proved to be a parallel example of how psychopharmacological drugs have effects on the mood and personality traits of millions of people (Conrad 2007; Saul 2014). What is striking in surveying these two examples, as well as many of today's other pharmacological enhancement technologies, is the way the technologies are implemented: not by directly subscribing to enhancement but instead by expanding the domain of the diseased and disordered. In a way this is the inevitable consequence of how pharmaceuticals are tested, approved, and sold according to a system of clinical trials developed in the 1960s (Healy 1999). In order to get a drug into the system the pharmaceutical company developing and eventually selling it needs to get the drug approved for the treatment of a diagnosed disease or mental disorder (the latter is the preferred term for diseased states of the brain and soul in psychiatry). Consequently, the enhancement of moods and personality of patients must always take place as the curing or relieving of an unhealthy state of being. Naturally, pharmaceutical companies try, by means of marketing, sponsoring, and other interactions with doctors and patient groups, to push the inclusiveness of the diagnoses they are developing drugs to treat (Elliott 2010).

As the French historian and philosopher of medicine Georges Canguilhem remarks, the meaning of the Latin and Greek roots of the word 'normal' are 'to make geometrically square' and 'to enforce grammatical order', respectively (1991: 239, 244). Canguilhem was Michel Foucault's teacher, and in these etymologies we already discern the latter philosopher's analysis of 'biopolitics' as a dominating practice and discourse in modern Western societies (Foucault 1990). According to the theory of biopolitics, the successes of the new antidepressants and ADHD medications are both examples of *normalization* in the sense that the norms for feeling and behaving well in contemporary Western culture and societies are made tighter and less inclusive with the help of the drugs. In tandem with this narrowing tendency of the healthy, the cultural ideals influencing what we may term human flourishing in contrast to human suffering also change in our society. Antidepressants and ADHD medications foster the ideal of a positive, in-control, energetic, and socially competent personality that it is now possible to achieve by way of taking medication. There are no more excuses for staying melancholic and neurotic or disorganized and impulsive if this can be fixed with the help of a drug.

When the new pharmaceuticals have been introduced, the old ways of life are no longer viewed as cases of unhappiness or socially cumbersome behaviour; they are viewed as states of mental disorder. Normalization by way of pharmaceuticals is consequently typically a process of *medicalization* that expands the domains of the unhealthy at the expense of parts of the previously healthy and/or socially deviant behaviour, previously likewise considered abnormal, but in a moral sense relating to cultural ideals and not to theories of mental disorder. Medical enhancement, which in the standard bioethical definition is that which takes us *beyond* the curing of diseases, is currently argued for and propagated in terms of achieving health, *not* in terms of making people better than well. This is clearly a medicalization process in the descriptive sense of the word; the numbers of diagnoses of ADHD, depression, and anxiety disorders *have* skyrocketed, and in all three cases involve 5 to 10 per cent of the population each year in the United States and many other Western countries (Svenaeus 2013a). The important question is whether the rise of diagnoses is also a process of medicalization in the *normative* sense, meaning that a large number of the newly diagnosed patients are actually healthy and not ill in spite of what the doctors claim. In order to answer this question we need a definition of health, and I now turn to explore whether phenomenology is able to provide such a thing.

Might Prozac and Ritalin be neurotechnological examples of *producing* health rather than reinstating it – by means of producing newly diagnosed individuals who are treated with the drugs – in the way that Heidegger and Gadamer put it in their critique of modern technology (Gadamer 1996: 81; Heidegger 1978: 255)? Since some of the patients treated with antidepressants and ADHD medicines describe their experiences as having never before felt the way they now feel, and some of them even have the experience of 'being themselves' for the first time on the drug (Kramer 1994), the answer to this question seems to be yes: health is not brought back by helping the body to reinstate its lost norms; it is produced as a novel state of being. Gadamer actually criticizes modern psychiatry for exactly this reason:

> I am thinking of the world of modern psychiatric drugs. I cannot separate this development entirely from the general instrumentalization of the living body which also occurs in the world of modern agriculture, in the economy and in industrial research. What does it signify that such developments now defines what we are and what we are capable of achieving? Does this not also open up a new threat to human life? Is there not a terrifying challenge involved in the fact that through psychiatric drugs doctors are able not only to eliminate and relieve various organic disturbances, but also to take away from a person her deepest distress and distraught?
>
> *(Gadamer 1996: 77, translation has been changed)*

The keyword to understanding the instrumentalization–medicalization process of psychopharmacology from a phenomenological point of view is, I think, the concept of *alienation*. Psychiatric drugs (when they are effective) relieve patients of their suffering as they become more at home in their life on the interconnected levels we discerned in chapter two: lived body, everyday engagement in the world with others, and life narrative. The fear Gadamer harbours is that by doing this – by relieving symptoms such as feelings of hopelessness, anxiety, and restlessness – the drugs also may separate the person from her true self. When the pills flatten the life moods of the patient he is no longer forced to challenge himself on the true meaning of his life: what he wants to accomplish and who he wants to be (what we called core life-narrative values in chapter two). By producing health the drugs would therefore – at least in some cases – alienate the patient from his true self.

The phenomenology of health and human flourishing

This line of thinking seems to clash with my previous efforts to understand health as a homelike being-in-the-world. How could the pharmaceuticals make the being-in-the-world of the patients homelike – assuming their life was previously unhomelike due to stressful moods – and simultaneously alienate them by blocking access to strong-value exploration (Taylor 1989, 1991)? In order to stay clear of this potential confusion and contradiction we need to distinguish four different things in the phenomenological analysis: suffering, illness, health, and flourishing (the good life). We have already made clear (in chapters two and three) that not all suffering is of the illness type; there is suffering due to forms of alienation other than illness: political suffering and existential suffering are the two main examples. By political suffering I intend a broad category that includes suffering due to poverty, political injustice, war, and exploitative labour. By existential suffering I intend exactly the kind of fundamental life quest that Gadamer fears Prozac and Ritalin will eradicate: exploring who one wants to be and what to accomplish in life. In addition to these two kinds of suffering we may add the suffering brought to us simply by bad luck in life matters (remember the example I gave in chapter two of a parent's losing a child in a car accident).

Illness consists of the type of suffering that typically occurs simultaneously with disease, injury, congenital defect, or mental disorder. In biologically based theories, health is defined as the absence of such maladies in the body and brain of the patient (Boorse 1997). Maladies are defined as disturbances in biological functionality that make it harder and eventually impossible for a living creature to survive and reproduce. For the phenomenologist, biological functionality cannot have the final word when it comes to defining health; this would mean giving in to naturalism and abandoning lived experience as the starting point for philosophical analysis (see my discussion in chapter one). Biological-statistical health theories have their own problems when it comes to defining and delimiting the concept of disease and other maladies (Nordenfelt 1995; Svenaeus 2013b). It appears that lived-experience evaluations will inevitably haunt the biological-statistical health theory, since clinical encounters with patients *suffering* from their maladies are needed to encircle and delimit the interval of biological functionality that should be considered normal in contrast to abnormal (e.g. the interval between too-low and too-high blood pressure). This means that attempts to find an objective-scientific concept of health (via disease) as a basis for medicine will always connect back to the sphere of human values: how persons feel, think, and act together in the life world (Canguilhem 1991: 223).

In the same way that the phenomenology of suffering proceeds from the mood, life world, and narrative of a person, a phenomenological theory of illness and health will use human experience and understanding as its springboard. Illness does not equal presence of disease even though the standard reason for this type of human suffering will be exactly diseases and other disordered conditions of the body, including the brain (mental disorders). As pointed out in chapter two, the main difference between illness suffering and other types of suffering is that the alienation in question is experienced in a *bodily manner*. Certainly, every human experience involves the lived body subconsciously performing in the background to offer us a focus of attention in the world, but in cases of illness the pain, resistance, disorientation, and helplessness make themselves *known* on this bodily level. The body 'dys-appears' instead of disappearing, to repeat the characterization coined by Drew Leder that I introduced in chapter three (Leder 1990: 69).

What about mental (psychiatric) illness? The point of using the adjective 'mental' for this type of illness and, likewise, referring to 'disorders' instead of diseases seems to be precisely that mental illness does *not* manifest itself by way of bodily symptoms. However, as I have tried to make clear from the beginning of this book, every experience has both a bodily and a mental dimension; meaning is ingrained in the patterns of lived bodily intentionality, and thinking has a bodily element in the way it is experienced and carried out by persons living in a world. The feelings and actions of a person are the mediating and connecting avenues between body and thought in phenomenological theory (Colombetti 2014; Ratcliffe 2008). Moods are experienced bodily and open up the life world as a meaningful territory in which thoughts can be formed. Actions depend on the lived body's preconscious capacity to carry out meaningful undertakings in the world that can be extended to thoughtful plans and projects in the life of a person. How a person feels and what she is able to do are therefore the crucial things to explore in a phenomenological analysis of illness, whether 'somatic' or 'mental' in nature.

Mental illness, like somatic illness, is standardly connected to agonizing feelings and difficulties in carrying out everyday actions. These feelings of suffering and difficulties in following everyday patterns of meaningfulness clearly also have bodily features in cases in which the pains and difficulties are commonly referred to as mental in character and the illness in question as psychiatric. Anxiety disorders and depression are connected to having panic attacks and experiencing moods of sadness and boredom, which make themselves known in making the body painful, immobile, and paralyzed, the lived body being unable to make itself at home in the world (Svenaeus 2013a). ADHD is defined by patterns of inattention and hyperactivity that are visible through the actions of persons and surely also experienced as moods which 'fill up' the body when the persons struggle to concentrate or stay calm.

Similar cases could be made for other mental disorders manifesting themselves as alienating processes within the domains of the lived body and the everyday being-in-the-world of the patient (Fuchs 2000; Fulford 1989). But what about the existential domains of suffering – that is, the difficulties in making oneself at home with one's own life purposes and life story that we found to be present in some cases of somatic illness in chapter two? Lars Westin and Ivan Ilyich both suffered immensely from being faced with an impending death which revealed to them that they would not be able to end their lives in a way that would cohere with having been the persons they wanted to be. At a certain point in their illness history they queried whether the life they had led was true to who they really were and what they should have done. These are signs of fundamental existential alienation, which adds to the suffering already in place within the domains of the lived body and the everyday world of actions in these two cases. Yet this type of suffering related to self-quest and experienced inauthenticity is exactly what Gadamer fears will be eradicated by Prozac and Ritalin. The reason for his fear is that existential suffering in situations that are possible to endure and survive will often lead to a fuller life *in the long run*, because the suffering person will come to know herself through the life crisis and will change her life goals in this process (Madison 2013). Somatic illness typically involves existential suffering only in severe cases, whereas mental illness involves existential suffering in most cases, including the cases referred to as mild and looked upon as bordering on unhappiness (e.g. mild cases of depression). Accordingly, while somatic illness can (in severe cases) give rise to existential suffering, in the case of mental illness it is standardly present.

Political suffering, in which the features that prevent flourishing are found in the world of the person rather than in her body, and existential suffering tied to self-searching and self-realization, as well as other cases of unhappiness due to sheer bad luck, are all experienced by way of feelings of alienation. Political suffering may lead to illness suffering and so may existential suffering or sheer bad luck. But they need not, and it is important to point out the differences between illness and these other types of human suffering – differences that appear as well on the other end of the spectrum in distinguishing between health- and non-health-related well-being. Health is experienced, or rather, *not* experienced, as the founding mood of everyday action in the life world. Health is a disappearing mood of familiarity that makes it possible for us to concentrate on the things we are usually doing and to embark on new projects, open to the possibilities of life, as Gadamer puts it (1996: 112–114). Health is the opposite of bodily and everyday-activity alienation, but it is not the same thing as well-being, if the latter means to feel happy (the German expression Gadamer uses in talking about health – *sich wohl fühlen* – does not have the connotation of happiness that we find in 'well-being'). Health is not the same thing as human *flourishing* (a concept which is not mixed up with health as easily as 'well-being'), which consists in ways of examining and fulfilling one's individual capacities and life goals – a definition of the good life that we find at work already in the philosophies of Plato and Aristotle (Madison 2013). To be at home with oneself in the existential sense is therefore not the same as being healthy; human flourishing is typically made possible through health, but it could also be absent in health or, indeed, be present in severe illness if the sufferer has managed to make peace with his life story despite being in pain and bodily incapacitated (compare the discussion of palliative care in chapter four). A flourishing life rests on *authentic* self-understanding, according to most phenomenological thinkers, since the core life-narrative values that a person honours have been attained through some sort of critical and honest self-scrutiny (Heidegger 1996; Taylor 1991).

DSM and the *Gestell*

That existential suffering is typically involved in a different and more constitutive way in mental illness than in somatic illness – actually, from the phenomenological point of view, 'mental' and 'somatic' illness both involve the lived body – means that we should be even more cautious in subjecting the field of psychiatry to technologies that bring medicalization in their wake. We have concentrated on the prescription of certain types of pharmaceuticals, but an even greater danger from the phenomenological viewpoint lies in the standardization brought by the increasing use of diagnostic manuals. These are surely pieces of technology that may subject us to the *Gestell*, the enframing world view that Heidegger held to be at work in modern technology and science.

DSM-5, published in 2013 by the American Psychiatric Association, includes over three hundred psychiatric diagnoses described and defined on 950 pages (DSM-5 2013). ADHD has evolved historically from diagnoses such as minimal brain damage, minimal brain dysfunction, hyperactive syndrome, and attention deficit disorder; and over the five versions of DSM, starting 1952, it has successively been defined in an ever more inclusive way (Conrad 2007: 49). The label ADHD (in place of the predecessors) entered the DSM in the 1987 revision of DSM-III, and it was preserved as well as expanded diagnostically in DSM-IV, published in 1994, and in DSM-5. In the most recent version of the manual it is viewed as a mental disorder that displays its symptoms in childhood (before the age of twelve) and in many cases lasts for life (this is a novelty compared with earlier versions of DSM in which ADHD was viewed as a health problem of childhood and adolescence that would typically vanish as the patient grew older). ADHD, like all other disorders in DSM-5, is diagnosed by way of symptoms and behaviour of the person in question; there are no biomedical tests in use to display the presence of genes or functional defects of the brain tied to ADHD specifically (there are actually no such clinical tests for any mental disorder at the present time).

To make the diagnosis, the doctor or medical team is to check for behavioural signs and symptoms in two categories describing problems with inattention and hyperactivity, respectively. If the person has five out of nine typical signs in either of the two categories, or both, and the behaviour is present in at least two settings – social, academic, or occupational – and these types of behaviour have been present before the age of twelve, the person is likely to be suffering from ADHD (DSM-5 2013: 59–66). The following are the typical signs. For inattention: fails to pay close attention to details; has difficulty sustaining attention in tasks; does not seem to listen when spoken to directly; does not follow through on instructions; has difficulty organizing tasks/activities; avoids, dislikes, or is reluctant to engage in tasks requiring sustained mental effort; loses things necessary for specific tasks; easily distracted by external stimuli; and forgetful in daily activities. For hyperactivity: fidgets with hands/feet; leaves seat in situations where remaining seated is expected; runs about or is restless; has difficulties engaging in leisure activities quietly; acts as if driven by a motor; talks excessively; blurts out answers; has difficulty awaiting turns; and interrupts or intrudes on others.

It goes without saying that many of these behavioural signs can be the effects of things other than a disordered brain; they could be personality traits or the effects of a stressful environment. The criteria are also highly amenable to interpretation: How disorganized or forgetful is too much? How impulsive and restless is over the top? There are no measurements by number to be found here, as is the case when one measures blood pressure or insulin in the blood. The scale is at best nominal – the behaviour is present or not present – not ordinal- and interval-based as in the case of biological functions.

The risk with using diagnostic manuals in psychiatry is not only overdiagnosis and the medicalization of healthy behaviours and feelings, which are cases of political or existential suffering rather than illness suffering by the phenomenological characterizations given above. The risk is also that persons are stereotyped – made into their diagnoses instead of being approached and understood in the empathic and hermeneutic manner, addressing life-world concerns, that I described in chapter four. Psychiatry carried out predominantly by way of DSM clearly harbours precisely the instrumentalizing tendency that Heidegger saw at work in power plants and coal mines; what is being enframed in this case is not only (human) nature but also personhood and ways of life. The effects of Ritalin may have a stereotyping effect as concerns moods and ways of being-in-the-world, but even more so does the tendency to map and sort persons into diagnostic categories such as ADHD.

Diagnosis is a necessary and important instrument of medical practice, but when it is used to categorize human experiences and behaviours rather than to explain what has gone amiss in the body, the technology in question blocks the view of what should be the real concern of the doctor and health-care team: the patient's being-in-the-world. DSM wants to create the impression that doctors can explain and cure the sufferings of the soul in the same manner as they explain and cure the sufferings of the body; but, of course, they cannot, since life-world matters and existential questions are not amenable to biological analysis in the way the functions of the body are. Diseases can be detected with the help of medical technology, and the way they cause illness suffering can be explained by medical science. Mental disorders can at best be described in everyday language and understood by way of good psychiatric practice. In both cases medical drugs, surgery, or other technological interventions may help in relieving the suffering, but in the case of diseases the doctors are also often able to *cure* the diseases, whereas mental disorders heal through the work of time or remain for the entire life of the patient.

The reason for these differences between mental and somatic illness is not only that the brain is the most complex organ of the body; it is also that existential and political suffering are enmeshed in mental illness in a manner that often makes it hard to discern the most important *reason* for the suffering in question. Did the poverty and family-related problems of a person lead to depression, or was it the other way around? No brain scans can answer this question; only the life story of the patient told in a meeting with a psychiatrist (or other health-care professional) can. From the phenomenological point of view, the differences between illness suffering and other forms of human suffering cannot be defined by way of brain-disease findings, even though abnormalities in biological functions of the body (including the brain) could be taken to *indicate* that the suffering is medical in nature. However, when it comes to the functions of the brain, the challenge of defining normal intervals is even harder than in the cases of somatic illness, inevitably leading us back to the *experiences* of potentially diseased/disordered people. Even the brain 'bodies forth', as Heidegger puts it, and this means that it belongs to a person and her meaningful way of inhabiting the world (Heidegger 2001: 245).

Consequently, to refer to the functions of the brain in attempts to distinguish illness from other forms of human suffering will not work as a cure for medicalization. Instead, the demarcation and difference between mental illness and political, existential, and sheer bad-luck suffering will have to be made on the phenomenological level of being-in-the-world. Alienation in terms of embodiment and everyday doings are major signs of *illness* suffering; other forms of suffering tied to core life values could *lead* to illness, but they should not be considered medical in character from the start. In cases of *mental* illness – not denying the symptom-relieving effects of psychopharmacological drugs – diagnosis and treatment should primarily address the everyday realms of the person's life rather than her brain chemistry.

In trying to see the relevance of Heidegger's philosophy of technology for medical ethics, it should finally be pointed out that Heidegger himself always resisted the name 'ethics' for what he was doing. This does not, however, preclude his philosophy's having very clear normative implications (Hodge 1995). The reason Heidegger resisted the label of ethics for his philosophy can, indeed, be illustrated by pointing towards the risks bioethics is running by becoming an institutionalized field and activity for experts naming themselves ethicists. Ethics can very easily become pure procedure, a game of applying pre-made principles to situations in which moral guidance is asked for (or, at least, pretended to be asked for). Applied ethics in such versions hides itself behind an image of neutrality, pretending not to advocate any specific image of the good human life but instead providing the medics with objective advice.

Bioethics should be well informed about the practice it is studying, and this includes learning a lot about medical science and technology. But it should also keep a critical outsider's eye on medical practice, and, above all, it should be critically aware of why philosophy is not a scientific method, in precisely the way that Heidegger and other phenomenologists illustrate through their writings. When bioethics pretends to be a science, or when it becomes a mere servant of science in providing an ethical excuse for doing things that would have been done anyway, it runs the risk of becoming the perfect example of what Heidegger named *Gestell*: a business that serves the use of something whose point is not questioned or, even worse, is covered up by the ethics in question (Elliott 1999, 2010).

Summary

The main relevance of Heidegger's philosophy of technology for bioethics is that bioethics itself needs to keep a broad focus on what medicine and health care are really about in the first place. Ethics in medicine needs to address ontological questions (what is health?) as well as epistemological questions (what kind of knowledge should doctors have?) if it is to be able to properly address and understand the dilemmas it is trying to solve. Bioethics could profit from Heidegger's philosophy of technology also in cases in which the dilemmas do not directly involve the use of medical technologies. Heidegger himself gives such an example when he says that the technological framework is revealed in the current talk about human resources, about the supply of patients for a clinic. This scientific and economic manner of reifying and resourcifying ill persons relies on economics and information technology rather than medical technology, but the effects are the same.

A phenomenology of health and illness must be related to and distinguished from human flourishing and suffering in a broader sense. Health is experienced as homelike being-in-the-world and illness as unhomelike being-in-the-world, but the ways human beings flourish and suffer also include the areas I have called political and existential (and cases of sheer good or bad luck). Mental illness is different from somatic illness in having a closer and enmeshed relation to these other forms of suffering, and this makes psychiatry even more at risk of the medicalizing and instrumentalizing tendencies we find at work in contemporary medical diagnosis and treatment. In this chapter I have described and analysed these risks by exploring diagnoses such as depression and ADHD and the way they may be produced through diagnostic manuals and treated by drugs such as Prozac and Ritalin.

What is striking in these cases – and will probably also be true in cases of future medical 'enhancement' technologies – is, firstly, that the technology is presented as curing or relieving diseases/disorders and *not* in terms of an enhancement project, and, secondly, that the experiences and capabilities that are medicalized were previously cases of types of human suffering and deviant behaviour other than illness. However, the phenomenological critique of overuse and abuse of medical technology should not make us blind to the great opportunities technologies of various forms hold in making life more homelike for suffering persons. In addition to the treatment options opened up by biomedical diagnostics, the knowledge of what type of process in the body is responsible for illness suffering can be a relief in itself, reifying illness in a healthy manner by naming a disease. Mental illness, however, has a far more complicated relationship to the processes of the body (brain), and this means that to the extent that the behaviours and feelings of a person cannot be separated from cultural norms and existential quests, reification runs the risks of becoming speculative and unhealthy.

6

THE BEGINNING OF LIFE

Medical science and human reproduction

In the previous chapters of this book, we have focused on what the phenomenological perspective can achieve in providing accounts of the suffering endured by ill persons, and how such suffering of illness can be approached and understood in the clinical encounter. We have also initiated an analysis of the way medical technologies impact medical practice as well as our views on health. The last two chapters of this book will be focused not only on the experiences and self-understanding of ill persons but on what it means to *be* a person from the phenomenological perspective. Medical technology has, at least in some circumstances, fundamentally changed the way human beings come into life and end their lives. In this chapter we will, for the most part, deal with the beginning of human life. The subsequent chapter will address the medico-ethical challenges that concern death and dying.

Women and men have tried since the dawn of human history to prevent pregnancy as a result of sexual intercourse. Likewise, the termination of pregnancy by way of what are, more or less, medical methods emerged in proportion to the failure of prevention. In the 1960s and 1970s, new contraceptive methods (the pill) and more permissive abortion laws in (some) Western countries initiated more effective and safer ways to either avoid or terminate pregnancy for women who wished to do so. Regardless of how we view these contraceptive methods and more permissive views on abortion from an ethical point of view, they have no doubt changed the ways we have sex and form relationships.

Only half a century later – now – we are witnesses to scientific developments bestowing upon humans true command over conception by means of assisted reproductive technologies (ART). *In vitro* fertilization (IVF) in combination with many different technologies such as surrogacy, sperm/egg donation, and pre-implantation genetic diagnosis (PGD) procedures make it possible to choose not only when (contraceptives) and if (abortion) children are brought to life, but also *what type of* children should be brought to life (Buchanan et al. 2000; DeGrazia 2012; Habermas 2003; Malmqvist 2007, 2014). Future reproductive medicine may also include various ways of manipulating embryo DNA and/or bypassing pregnancy altogether by way of artificial wombs in which it would be possible for embryos/foetuses to mature. Such manoeuvres are the topic of well-known science fiction books and films – for example, *Brave New World* and *The Matrix* – and it remains to be seen if the future they evoke will come true. Recent landmarks that make such developments look more realistic are the transplanting of uteruses (Gallagher 2014) and the editing of DNA by means of CRISPR/Cas9 technology (Liang et al. 2015). However, as Michael Hauskeller convincingly argues in his book *Better Humans? Understanding the Enhancement Project*, the question of what personal characteristics in addition to health will make a human life better is not only up for philosophical debate but is also very hard to answer in advance as well as out of context (2013). The reason for this is that all, or at least most, of the desirable traits suggested by enhancement enthusiasts – physical strength, intelligence, emotional stability, a long lifespan, predispositions to feel happy, and so forth – are complex traits that interact with other traits of a person in unforeseeable ways.

In association with the new practices of human reproduction, medical science and technology are making the boundary between embryonic cells – so-called stem cells – and other types of human cells increasingly diffuse. Intense bioethical debate was initiated twenty years ago when the transfer of DNA from an adult cell to the nucleus of an oocyte led to the birth of the first cloned mammal: Dolly the sheep (Nussbaum and Sunstein 1999). Cloned embryos can be used not only to produce offspring, but also to produce cells used in medical research and/or for treatment, which is known as therapeutic cloning. Stem cells multiply in the laboratory to form stem cell lines, and they can also be turned into various types of differentiated somatic cells by making them divide together with cells of the desired tissue type. Although the world community of scientists and ethicists has been rather unified on the ban on human reproductive cloning so far, the predicates of embryonic stem cell research have given rise to massive debate, which has generated considerably different guidelines and laws in different countries. Should use of spare embryos from IVFs be permitted to produce embryonic stem cell lines, or should such activities be forbidden (Devolder 2015)? Should we allow human embryos to be cloned in a similar manner for the purpose of research and medical treatment? Because stem cell research holds possibilities for curing severe diseases and prolonging life for millions of people, it is clear that both the medical and economic stakes are high (Waldby and Mitchell 2006). Does it matter that human beings in the very early stage of first-week embryos (discounting the time spent in the freezer) are destroyed in the process of making stem cells?

Researchers have recently presented methods through which *in vitro* embryos may be harvested for stem cells without destroying them in the process (Rodin et al. 2014). Embryonic stem cells (the origin of all other types of cells in the body) may also be obtained by means other than harvesting IVF or cloned embryos, by 'reprogramming' differentiated cells of various tissue types (e.g. skin, muscle, heart, etc.), which makes them turn 'backwards' into stem cells (so-called induced pluripotent stem cells) (OHSU 2013). In the future cells from an embryo may be used not only to produce differentiated somatic cells but also to obtain germ cells (ova, sperms). These two techniques in combination – a procedure that has been shown to work in experiments with mice – could change the forms of human reproduction altogether, making it possible for biological children to be reared by an individual, by same-sex couples, or in kinship constellations that involve more than two people – so-called 'multiplex parenting' (Palacios-González et al. 2014).

Phenomenology and early forms of human life

What do all these stunning procedures mean for philosophical and ethical debates about the nature of human being? How do they affect our views on personhood and human interrelatedness, particularly the bonds that are created by way of reproduction? Some of the breathtaking possibilities invoked by medical scientists and bioethicists may very well never turn out, not only because of legal obstacles but because they will not prove to be feasible in practice. However, even though some or most of the hypothetical technologies will not be implemented, the bioethical imperative is, arguably, that they nonetheless should be taken into consideration. Philosophical thought experiments are problematic, however, insofar as we lack live access to the things being explored. For instance, it is not currently possible to know what it would feel like to be cloned in relation to a 'parent' or to be the result of a 'pregnancy' in an artificial womb. Nevertheless, science undoubtedly has an important say in ontological questions, particularly when the scientific breakthroughs have already occurred and are in the process of changing human practices and forms of life in thoroughgoing ways (Rose 2007). A phenomenology of suffering cannot proceed in ignorance of the science of diseases. Correspondingly, a phenomenology of personhood cannot disregard the (soon) available biotechnologies used to engineer human life.

The ethical questions raised by ART and stem cell research are different in that they concern two different human practices – reproduction versus science. Yet questions arise precisely because these two practices are increasingly being brought into contact with each other in the domain of the hospital. Research on IVF embryos is performed not only in order to produce stem cells but also to improve the methods of IVF itself. And the possibilities of reproducing in new ways are the result of scientific methods: the birth of the first IVF baby in 1978 was announced as a *scientific* breakthrough, as were the more recent births made possible by way of sperm injection in 1992 and uterus transplantation in 2014.

The discussion in the previous chapter made us aware of a certain danger in allowing human life issues to become dominated by scientific models. The misuse of medical science may lead to *instrumentalization* of existential issues, as in the cases of medicalization of human suffering by way of psychiatric diagnoses. The instrumentalization of reproduction presents a similar threat, perhaps even more deep-going, since it is not only the good life, but human life as such, that risks being turned into a scientific object or even a commodity on a market when germ cells, embryos, and surrogacies are for sale (Cooper and Waldby 2014; Mills 2011). That human embryos are definitely not persons – lacking not only self-reflective abilities but also the ability to feel – does not mean that they do not deserve some kind of respect on the strength of being the kind of entities they are. The forms of respect that we arguably owe to things that are not yet persons (embryos), no longer persons (corpses), or not persons but still having a value beyond the dimension of utility (most animals, plants, or landscape formations that we treasure, etc.) are often put in terms of these things being 'sacred' or 'dignified'. This terminology does not necessarily reflect a religious attitude; it is simply a way of voicing the intuition that some things are inherently valuable even though they are not persons (Dworkin 1994).

Adopting a phenomenological point of view, what can we say about the respect human embryos or foetuses in their different developmental stages deserve, and what we may accordingly allow ourselves to do with them? These questions will be the topics of the following three sections of this chapter, which are devoted to the ethics of embryo research and abortion. In the final two sections of the chapter I will return to the possibilities of making embryos in novel ways and selecting as well as editing them in IVF treatments to choose or design types of babies. The phenomenology of pregnancy will be the thread that connects the ethical understanding of embryo research, abortion, and the genetic design of babies. In the next and final chapter of this book, I will enter more deeply into the type of relationship we have with parts of our bodies and, subsequently, how we should understand the possibilities that enable us to make them gifts, resources, or commodities, such that they may serve other persons in need.

Are embryos potential persons?

In order to make sense of the different positions in embryo ethics and consider how phenomenology may contribute to the bioethical discussion we first need to provide some basic biological facts. In the first two weeks after fertilization the human embryo, or 'pre-embryo' as it is sometimes called, goes through several developmental stages (Brevini and Pennarossa 2013). The fertilized oocyte is called a *zygote*, and this cell, already containing the complete DNA of a human being, further divides into a ball of cells called the *morula*. After about three days, the *blastocystic* stage begins as the cells of the embryo begin to form a hollow cavity. At this stage, the embryonic cells divide into two types: cells that will form the foetus, and cells that will form the placenta. Stem cells that are obtained in the zygote–morula stage are *totipotent*, since they can give rise to a new embryo, including a placenta, whereas stem cells that are obtained in the blastocystic state or later are merely *pluripotent*, since they can develop into any type of tissue but cannot form a new embryo with a placenta of its own. In addition to these, we have the *multipotent* stem cells, which may develop into one or more, but not all, of the cell types found in the human body and which are found in the bodies of all human beings (also called adult stem cells).

At around one week the embryo 'hatches', and the trophectoderm cells – which will form the placenta – attach to the endometrial cells of the uterus. The embryo then becomes embedded in the endometrium through the process known as *implantation*. Rapid growth now occurs, and after about one more week the cells of the embryo begin to differentiate into the cell types that will form the tissues and organs of the foetus, a stage known as *gastrulation*. This is the last stage of the pre-embryo phase, after which the 'primitive streak' will appear, which is the structure that will develop into the spine of the embryo.

The embryo continues to grow and develop the various cell types that will later form the baby's organs. After eight weeks, precursors of all organs in the body have been formed and the embryo is now referred to as a *foetus*. The weeks standardly referred to when stating how far a pregnancy has matured – the so-called gestational time – are calculated by starting from the week of the last menstruation, which occurs around two weeks before fertilization. (The embryo becomes a foetus in week 9 after fertilization, which corresponds to week 11 of gestational time.) This is potentially confusing, and in what follows I will always try to make clear whether I am referring to gestational time or the age of the embryo/foetus calculated from fertilization. I will return to the stages of embryonic and foetal development in more detail in the ethics of abortion section below.

Embryo research is performed on *in vitro* embryos that are not older than fourteen days. Among countries that allow research on human embryos, this limit is stipulated in a worldwide agreement. The limit squares roughly with the process of gastrulation and the formation of the primitive streak. It also reflects the practical difficulties of bringing *in vitro* embryos to develop beyond two weeks of age if they are not implanted. However, it appears that embryo researchers have recently developed methods to extend the life of embryos *in vitro* beyond fourteen days, and as a consequence the limit is currently being questioned (Hyun et al. 2016). This development is in line with many of the scientific breakthroughs in embryo research described above, and it underlines the fact that circumscribing limits for this type of research according to practical concerns, as opposed to ethical concerns, is insufficient. Stem cell lines are presently harvested at the morula or blastocyst stage of the embryo, but detailed knowledge about how the embryo develops beyond these phases would nevertheless be of great value for stem cell research as well as for the purpose of developing better IVF technologies, and therefore such research will likely be pursued if it is not stopped by a ban.

That embryos are destroyed in medical research need not be a problem if one does not believe that this timeline of human life involves anything significant in addition to cellular biology. The only ethical issue if one holds such a view would be the need to obtain informed consent from the persons who are donating the embryos being harvested for stem cells. The extreme opposite view in embryo ethics is the view that the zygote is understood to already possess characteristics that assign it equal ethical standing to a person. Persons are generally defined as creatures possessing self-consciousness, language, memory, and an ability to plan their actions, so this is hardly a coherent view if you do not want to change the understanding of personhood altogether (DeGrazia 2005: 3–7).

A much more interesting argument, often invoked in embryo ethics, claims that the zygote – the first-cell stage of the embryo – needs to be protected because it is a *potential* person (Gómez-Lobo 2004). Gametes, in contrast, do not deserve this kind of respect, since they do not possess the complete DNA of an individual human being. Gametes are not human beings; they represent only pre-stages to human being, since they have only half of the number of chromosomes necessary to make the embryo–foetus–child develop into a person. The genetic make-up of the zygote, however, so the argument goes, directs the development of the embryo from day one, if the embryo is given the opportunity to mature in its *natural* environment (meaning the uterus of a woman).

The main difficulty with this view is the fact that a single embryo may divide into two or more separate embryos during the first two weeks of its life (there are also occasions when human chimeras or Siamese twins are formed through two embryos fusing or conjoining in the womb) (Brown 2007). How could I be identical to, let us say, a sixteen-cell embryo, if this embryo could have split and given rise to two or more separate embryos with identical DNA ending up as different persons? The embryo-being-me ethicist may reply that as a matter of fact this splitting did not occur (if she has no identical twins), or that she was admittedly never identical to this sixteen-cell embryo, but that she is identical to one of these cells that 'left' her identical twin behind and developed into the person that she now is (she may also be identical to the remaining fifteen-cell cluster).

The arguments exploring the nature and significance of potential being and personhood get increasingly complicated at this point, making it hard to reach consensus on what embryos are and why this matters (Mahowald 2004; Wilkins 2016). Although it is hard to deny that all embryos, through their biology, are human beings, the question of whether they are also *persons* in being depends on the way one defines identity and potentiality. If one is generally suspicious about the ethical significance of potential being it is tempting to claim ethical status for actual persons only, leaving the embryo out of the picture. However, the problem with this view is that it must, in consequence, deny ethical status to foetuses and newborn babies also (since they are not yet persons), and this does not look like an attractive alternative (but see Singer (2011) in defence of such a utilitarian view).

All arguments that explore the ethical status of the embryo by way of its potentiality for personhood will have to specify *under what circumstances* and *in what context* this potentiality is supposed to hold (Svenaeus 2007b). An embryo can develop into a person only if it is surrounded and supported in the 'natural way', which means being implanted in the uterus of a woman and provided with the appropriate support by her bodily being. This, of course, may change should we witness the development of artificial wombs in such a way that *in vitro* embryos were able to mature into babies in them. We find a restricted version of this possibility with the nursing care in incubators of foetuses born as early as the twenty-second week of gestation. The remaining time gap between the use of incubators for present embryo research (maximum fourth week of gestation) and the use of incubators in neonatal care units is about eighteen weeks. Considering the complex biology constituting the necessary conditions for embryo and foetus growth, not to mention the ethical issues involved, the artificial womb will be hard to achieve, but such a medical scientific breakthrough is, nevertheless, possible in the future.

Another possibility would be to implant human embryos in the uterus of a mammal species other than *Homo sapiens*. This way of 'baby making' would probably be easier to achieve than the method of artificial incubation. The risks for the babies involved would nevertheless be very high – the lifestyle and health of the pregnant woman has increasingly proved to be very important to the health and characteristics of a baby – and this, together with the ethical issues of species crossing per se, will probably stop such experiments for a foreseeable future.

It could be argued that the circumstances of IVF and embryo research have already changed the natural circumstances and context of the embryo by *producing* it *in vitro*. Such a view seems particularly tenable when the embryo has been (will be) produced by means of procedures such as somatic cell nucleus transfer or induced stem cell technology, plus germ cell production (Palacios-González et al. 2014). Are such embryos the potential children of potential parents even if the parent(s) have not contributed their germ cells (but rather their somatic cells)? Proponents of novel approaches to biological parenting will have to argue that they are, although the technologically engineered embryos do not necessarily have this potentiality *in contrast to* the potentiality to become research material.

Perhaps cloned and multiplex embryos could be considered to have the potentiality for personhood *in addition* to being a potential object of research, should they remain within the laboratory. In any case, to claim that the circumstances owed to these embryos is the womb of a woman appears to be problematic, since these *types* of embryos would never have existed if medical technology had not reached its present (or future) stage. In contrast, the type of embryos fertilized in the old-fashioned way have been brought into being long before the practices of IVF and stem cell technology were introduced. Indeed, IVF is referred to as a part of *assisted* reproduction, a fact indicating that the aim was originally to support rather than change the ways of human reproduction altogether. It could equally be claimed that the current forms of maternity, birth, and neonatal care presently taking place in hospitals (with the assistance of modern technology) have developed as supportive functions in response to pre-modern birthing practices that took place in a home environment with the aid of (at best) a midwife. The original intention in changing the circumstances for birthing situations was hardly to make babies in new ways; the goal was to make pregnancy and birth less painful and more safe for mothers and babies.

Before the advent of IVF in the late 1970s, the potentiality of human embryos was unproblematic, if considered. They were future children of future parents *only*, even though this potentiality was not to be realized in every case (e.g. miscarriage) and did not protect the embryo from being aborted under certain circumstances. The purpose of Judith Jarvis Thomson's classic paper of 1971, 'A Defence of Abortion', is exactly to argue that *even though* the embryo/foetus is a potential person it may rightfully be aborted if the woman who carries it views its continued life inside her as interfering with her life goals (Thomson 2006).

When embryos began to be produced *in vitro* their potential being became more challenging, even though this was never the original intent. The standard procedure in IVF treatment, since the 1980s, has been to produce far more embryos than will ever be used in treatment. Following ovarian hyperstimulation, somewhere between five to fifteen eggs are retrieved from the woman, and these are then fertilized and screened in the laboratory. Presently, in most cases, only one or two of these embryos will be implanted. The surplus embryos are cryopreserved (deep frozen) and can be used in future treatment by the couple (woman) or for other couples (women). Since embryos may be stored only for a certain period of years – how long varies with the laws and regulations of different countries – this process has inevitably led to a large number of surplus 'waste bin' embryos. Many bioethicists claim that this surplus ought to be used for research, given that even if they are not used they will eventually be destroyed at their expiration date.

It could be argued that rather than being an unintended surplus of IVF treatments, embryos, under the current set-up, are actually being *produced* for research. The ethical concern is then that the surplus production of embryos for research is part of an *instrumentalizing* process that will affect our views on human life, as such, in the long run. To nurture such a concern does not equal a view of embryos as persons that are killed by the researchers in harvesting them for stem cells. The concern is not about the life or death of individual embryos but about the way medical technologies affect our everyday being-in-the-world and attitudes towards life. This concern with instrumentalization, which we scrutinized in the previous chapter, is a way of spelling out the common intuition that some things, even though they are not persons, have a dignified character that demands respect (Dworkin 1994). In the case of embryos, this respect-commanding quality is connected to the embryo–foetus–child's potential to become a person according to its successive stages.

Embryo ethics and the instrumentalization argument

The standard reference in embryo ethics regarding worries about instrumentalization is not Heidegger's ontological critique of modern technology but Kant's moral philosophy (Mauron and Baertschi 2004). According to Kant's categorical imperative of practical reason, no person may be treated as merely a means to an end, in contrast to as an end in herself. Embryos, however, are not persons but potential persons. Kant, for obvious reasons, did not feel any need to apply his argument to potential persons such as embryos, but if we extend it accordingly we obtain: no potential person may be treated as merely a means to an end but only as an end in her/itself.

A strict application of the categorical imperative would not only deem embryo research unethical, but would view IVF treatment as equally unethical, unless the latter were to change its procedures in such a way that no embryos would be deprived of an opportunity for implantation. However, the ethical judgement appears to hinge on the way we interpret *implantation opportunity*. The strictest interpretation will demand that every embryo that has a chance of developing into a not-too-diseased baby should be implanted. The only embryos without implantation obligation would be those that are predicted to spontaneously abort, or that will develop into babies with severe diseases.

A less strict interpretation of the Kantian dictum would interpret 'implantation opportunity' as having a *fair chance* for implantation in competition with other embryos fertilized during the same cycle of IVF treatment. However, even the less strict interpretation of the categorical imperative concerning embryos would forbid some being produced for research, and consequently, the ethical question will turn on the issue of whether surplus embryos are being produced with research intent or not (Devolder 2015). Although it could be successfully argued, I think, that no person – health-care professional or parent – purposely fertilizes particular embryos for research, the system does nevertheless have the foreseeable effect of producing surplus embryos, so that the argument that the embryos will be wasted anyway and could therefore be used for research will fail in the eyes of the Kantian.

'The system' in this case captures the way practices of IVF and embryo research are set up in contemporary society. The phenomenological worry is consequently that embryos – and other human cells, tissues, and organs – become reduced to *pure material* used in medical research and treatment, or even to *commodities* on a market (Cooper and Waldby 2014; Svenaeus 2016b). This worry reflects a Heideggerian sensibility rather than one derived from Kant, since the concern is about a potential change in the way we perceive and understand human life in general, not about a number of embryonic potential-person lives being lost in the process of medical research. The biopolitical critique of (late) modern medicine and society found in Foucault (1990) and Agamben (1998) belong to this tradition of phenomenological analysis. Their analyses of how human bodies are disciplined and made use of in modern prisons, schools, hospitals, and even concentration camps, could easily be applied to the question concerning embryo use in research labs.

A phenomenologist who has relentlessly criticized instrumentalizing tendencies in modern medicine is Hans Jonas (1984, 1987). The arguments in his critique of the 'technological civilization' are clearly indebted to the philosophy of Heidegger. According to Jonas, the duty of preserving the possibility of a life worth living for future generations means not only to avoid the extinction of the human race but also to avoid turning human life into a commodity. We will return to Jonas's scepticism and worries regarding IVF as baby production, and brain-dead bodies as organ banks later. But first we need to settle the ethical issue of embryos as potential research material.

If Jonas and Heidegger had lived long enough to pass ethical judgement on our contemporary situation, they would predictably have sided with the Kantians: embryos should never be produced for the purpose of research, and this would include the foreseeable surplus of embryos from IVF treatments (see also Habermas 2003). Research on stem cells, they would claim, should therefore be limited to so-called adult stem cells, which are neither totipotent nor pluripotent, but merely multipotent, and which can be retrieved from living human research subjects after they have consented. It could perhaps be argued that induced stem cells are also non-embryonic in nature, despite their pluripotency, since they cannot give rise to an embryo in the way a fertilized, cloned, or multiplexed embryonic stem cell can (the difference between the zygote–morula and the blastocyst-implantation stages of the embryo surveyed above).

But such a harsh judgement on embryo research is not the inevitable outcome of a phenomenological instrumentalization critique of the intersecting domains of IVF and stem cell research. It could be argued from a phenomenological point of view that the possibilities of producing embryos and stem cells in new ways in the laboratory make the potential of the early *in vitro* embryo ambivalent. The cell cluster that constitutes the zygote–morula–blastocyst pre-embryo throughout its successive stages is about 0.1 to 0.2 millimetres in diameter and does not, at any stage, look like a living being when viewed under a microscope (not counting creatures such as amoebas or bacteria). The implanted and/or gastrulated embryo, in contrast, changes significantly in size and shape, soon taking on the form of a vertebrate creature measuring 1 to 2 millimetres. After four weeks it has doubled this size, and what will develop into the head and limbs become visible. Taking into account the character of the different stages that the early embryo goes through, the fourteen-day rule of embryo research appears to be an attractive alternative in determining the ethically significant beginning of human life, at least when embryos are made and kept *in vitro*.

It would be short-sighted to pretend that phenomenology can provide us with ultimate or exact answers regarding the ethically significant beginning of human life, including the ethical status of embryos in their successive developmental stages. However, phenomenology can offer viewpoints and arguments that take the person-experiential perspective into account in addition to the perspectives from science and logic. The two views on instrumentalization in the case of embryo research presented above are both consistent with a phenomenological understanding of the nature of medical technology and human reproduction. Elsewhere, I have defended the view that cloned embryos, in contrast to fertilized embryos, would be legitimate sources for embryo research and the production of stem cell lines (Svenaeus 2007b). Fertilized *in vitro* embryos, in contrast to cloned embryos, would belong strictly to the practice of IVF treatment. My reason for arguing that the potential of these two different types of embryos belong in different realms – science versus reproduction – was taken from the concern that instrumentalizing tendencies would take hold of the latter if embryos in general were considered to be a supply from which to produce things as opposed to being gifts of life to be received and treasured (Parens 2015). I still maintain that this concern is legitimate, and I will return to it below during the discussion of ways of choosing children. Having said that, I have become increasingly sceptical about the possibility of separating 'natural' embryos from 'artificial' embryos in the laboratory. After all, the techniques of IVF are developed to make oocytes and sperms fuse in exactly those cases when they will not do so in nature (in the body of a woman). To what extent can it then be claimed that these embryos would be nature-made in contrast to other artificially made embryos? Fertilization by way of sperm injection, for instance, is definitely not natural in any feasible sense of the word. Why, then, would such embryos deserve the respect that cloned embryos do not?

My present view is that already by bringing embryo making out of the woman's body, the practice of IVF changes the ethical status of the pre-implanted, non-gastrulated embryo. The technologies used to facilitate fertilization and make embryos in new ways *in vitro* underline that we are dealing with objects of a new type: embryos brought out of the environment that previously determined their form of potential being in a one-way manner. If we want to resist the conclusion that the appropriate environment of an embryo can in some cases be a research lab rather than a woman's body, we need to abstain from the practice of IVF treatment altogether (or, at least, change it in a way that does not result in surplus embryos that will as a matter of routine be wasted or used for research). The phenomenological judgement that the *in vitro* embryo is a different type of entity than the embryo formed by fusion of egg and sperm in the Fallopian tubes of a woman does not mean that we can treat *in vitro* embryos like any kind of stock – using them to make soap, for instance (the analogy with Auschwitz is deliberate). *In vitro* embryos, however they are made, still have a significant *symbolic* standing that demands respect on the strength of their biological potentiality (compare my remarks on the dignity and protection-worthiness of non-person entities above). Such a standing could be reflected in practice by limiting the use of IVF embryos to fields of research that seek cures for severe human diseases and that cannot be pursued by other means (in the way experiments with animals should be regulated) and by forbidding the buying and selling of human embryos.

The ethical standing of the embryo will become more powerful and demanding as it develops beyond the stage of implantation and gastrulation and is in place in the uterus of a woman. To perform research on aborted embryos or to use parts of them in order to produce stem cells (or other medically valuable outcomes) may still be ethically admissible, depending on the exact circumstances. However, to produce them for this purpose, or to use abortion as a form of contraception by arguing that it produces valuable research material as a side effect, is not compatible with the phenomenological concern about instrumentalization in any interpretation. For the phenomenologist, the difference in ethical standing between the *in vitro* embryo, which has not been implanted or gastrulated, and the embryo that has been implanted or gastrulated would be contingent on the different developmental stages of an embryo, thus making the embryo more and more subject-like in addition to object-like when we perceive and judge its being. As the embryo–foetus develops in the womb, it will increasingly demand ethical attention as *a particular* human being in the process of possibly becoming a person, not just as an instance of human life in general.

The ethics of abortion

If an embryo has been implanted in the uterus of a woman, whether assisted by medical techniques or not, purposeful ending of its life becomes a matter of terminating pregnancy by way of abortion. As we have seen, the fact that the cells of the embryo carry the complete DNA of a human being from day one does not, by itself, settle the ethical questions of embryo research. Even less does it settle the issue of abortion. Abortion ethics, however, is not built to the same extent as embryo ethics on a set of worries regarding the dangers of instrumentalization. The instrumentalization critique is certainly still valid – if embryos were aborted for the reason of obtaining research material merely or mainly, we would be greatly concerned – but since such practices appear abhorrent to a vast majority they are not presently being considered and debated the way research practices on *in vitro* embryos are. Abortion ethics, in addition to the instrumentalization worries, includes the questions of under what circumstances and within what gestation-time limits it is acceptable to end the life of an embryo/foetus granted that this is not done for utility purposes.

From the phenomenological point of view, questions concerning if, when, and on what indications abortion may be performed must be answered by way of reference to the condition and situation of the pregnant woman, as well as the different developmental stages of the embryo/foetus as they are revealed through the pregnant woman's experiences and by means of medical investigations. These are the ways in which the embryo/foetus *shows up* in human experiences before it reaches a stage of development in which we can assume that it has experiences of its own, even though we cannot gain any direct phenomenological access to such foetal experiences. The main difference between the phenomenological and most pro-choice views on abortion in such an analysis will be that the body of the woman is not considered as her property but as an embodied way of *being* that goes through drastic and significant changes in the process of pregnancy (Mumford 2013). The main difference between the phenomenological and most pro-life views on abortion will be that the being of the embryo/foetus must be considered from the perspective of the pregnant woman's life as soon as implanted and not simply as a person-in-being taking residence in her body (Mackenzie 1992).

At least two different questions have to be dealt with in a phenomenological–ethical investigation of abortion. First, under what circumstances and possible time limits should it be permitted by law and made medically available for a woman to abort her embryo/foetus simply because she wishes to do so? Second, what other circumstances concerning the pregnancy (e.g. brought about by rape, fear for the woman's life if continued) and the state of the foetus (medical defects) would make it reasonable to extend an established time limit, and in these cases, how far should the benchmark be moved? It should be underlined that the moral–philosophical analysis of abortion cannot be directly translated into political decisions (laws, policy documents). Considerations beyond ethical arguments may play into political decision-making in this and many other bioethical areas, and legitimately so (Dworkin 1994; van der Burg 2009). As in the case of embryo ethics, phenomenology is equipped to provide a *point of view* that can contribute to informing political decision-making more than it can provide detailed regulations on its own. Nevertheless, as in the case of embryo ethics, rather than retreating to the ivory tower, I will aim for an ethical analysis that stays close to lived experience and the essential aspects of pregnancy and embryo/foetus development.

Let us begin with the question of legal abortion, the right of a pregnant woman to abort a foetus on non-medical grounds. The conditions and limits to qualify for such opportunities vary significantly in the laws of different countries. And the standards have often changed over time due to shifts in political majorities. Countries in Africa, South America, and South East Asia generally do not allow abortion, with the exception of rape or on medical grounds. On the other hand, abortion is most often permissible by law in the countries of North America, Europe, North and West Asia, and Australia and New Zealand. However, among the countries that allow legal abortion, the circumstances concerning the procedure for a woman's informed consent may differ. And as it stands, the upper time limit of legal abortion varies significantly from country to country, from ten to twenty-four weeks of gestational time.

What circumstances have been taken into consideration in the political process of deciding how late a woman may decide upon abortion? Generally, countries that have a considerably wide time frame – the United States, Great Britain, Singapore, Sweden, The Netherlands – refer to the *rights* of the individual woman to do as she pleases with her own body. Whereas countries that adopt stricter limitations – France, Finland, Denmark, Belgium, Portugal, Vietnam, to offer some examples – do so not on grounds of embryo rights but, nevertheless, according to the *perspective* of the growing embryo/foetus. This perspective becomes acutely important in the stages when the foetus is suspected to *feel* things, such as pleasure or pain, or if it could possibly *survive* in an incubator. The question of when the foetus is equipped to feel pain is disputed and infused by the political debates surrounding abortion. As a consequence there is no scientific consensus on the issue, but week 22 appears to be a good estimation (Bellieni 2012). Babies born as early as week 22, or even late in week 21, have been saved in neonatal care units (Edemariam 2007). It should be stressed, though, that babies born earlier than week 23 rarely survive, and that premature babies born very early – as a rule – suffer from a variety of severe health problems.

The scientific and technological means to map the life of the foetus and make it possible for prematurely born babies to survive outside the womb affect our views on the acceptable upper time limit of abortion. If the right to abortion is defended on the grounds that the foetus is a part of a pregnant woman's body, and *nothing else*, the possibility that the foetus might feel pain and might survive even if the pregnancy were to be terminated appears to undermine this view in such cases. However, should abortion be performed to save the life of the pregnant woman, or because the chances of the baby's survival without severe defects are slim, the right (or even obligation) to perform abortion in week 22 or beyond could be defended on these grounds instead of the 'my-body right' view.

What other developmental milestones in the life of an embryo/foetus should be taken into account in determining the limits of legal abortion? From a phenomenological perspective, the most obvious one is the pregnant woman's experiences of 'quickening' (Bornemark 2015; Young 2005). The first sensations the pregnant woman has of the foetus moving and kicking in her belly are, as a rule, felt in gestational weeks 18–20 (Sinha et al. 2012: 4). In the literature and on various webpages one finds reports of even earlier occurrences of quickening, so let us add two extra weeks (week 16) to be on the safe side. (In gestational weeks, before week 16 it is probably very hard, if not impossible, to distinguish foetal movements from bowel movements/gas.) This is a very significant occurrence because the woman can actually feel the presence of *another* human being inside her. This occurrence is very different from the experience of bodily alienation in illness that we have analysed in previous chapters.

Iris Marion Young, who published her classic piece on the phenomenology of pregnancy in 1983, argues that the experiences of pregnancy, including quickening, are not alienating in themselves (Young 2005). What alienates the life of pregnant and birthing women, according to Young, is the medical-technological gaze associated with the equipment of maternal care. Young's perspective is typical of early studies in phenomenology of medicine, assuming the medical perspective to be *inevitably* alienating and oppressive in nature, in contrast to a personally experienced, bodily transformation that would preserve the dignity and autonomy of the patient (Svenaeus 2009a). In contrast to this view, I would argue that medical science and the attention of doctors and nurses are not necessarily alienating or oppressive for the patient. It is certainly neither of these when medical technologies provide means to limit severe suffering and save lives, as is regularly the case in maternal care and birthing care. This critique notwithstanding, I think Young and other feminist scholars are right in pointing towards the risks of unnecessarily medicalizing pregnancy, and also in claiming that pregnancy, despite involving the experience of 'an alien', is not necessarily an *alienating experience* in this regard.

There is a clear difference between, for instance, the typical occurrence of morning sickness in early pregnancy and the events of quickening. The difference is between the experiences of the lived body as alien – in this case, in nausea – and the experiences of another living being in my body (compare the discussions in chapter three). The foetus may to some extent be perceived as an unwelcome stranger – particularly if the pregnancy is unwanted – but in most cases, quickening is referred to as the first *contact* with the baby to come. To feel the foetus is to feel the *togetherness* of mother and child, and this feeling is generally referred to by the pregnant woman not as alienating but as the feeling of a different, and in some ways, *fuller* state of being (Bornemark 2015). Many feminists developing arguments about the right to legal abortion appear to miss, or even gravely misconstrue, the experiences of the pregnant woman by portraying them in terms of being chained to an alien when it is rather a matter of perceiving the gradual arrival of a child. This is the case not only in Judith Jarvis Thomson's famous thought experiment of waking up in the hospital back to back with an unconscious violinist who has been plugged into your circulatory system (Thomson 2006), but also in instances comparing the foetus to, for instance, a fish that has taken up residence in the pregnant woman's body (see the criticisms found in Mackenzie (1992) and Mumford (2013)).

Admittedly, this way of attempting to specify the phenomenological conditions of normal pregnancy runs the risk of underestimating the individual differences between pregnancies. If pregnancy is unwanted for the woman, and, especially, if it has been brought about by rape, the pregnant woman may feel the presence of the foetus to be exactly alien in nature. This may also be the case if the woman is afraid of how the new state of being will change her life, even if she does not wish to have an abortion, say if she is afraid of the pains of giving birth or of becoming a mother. Even so, quickening may in such cases also serve as a 'counter alienating' experience in which the woman feels the foetus and exactly through this contact with a child to be accepts her pregnancy as a not entirely bad thing.

The experience of quickening appears to be a strong candidate for setting an upper limit for legal abortion from the phenomenological point of view. This idea is not new; it appears to have proliferated in many pre-modern societies and cultural contexts that did not explicitly forbid early abortions (Dworkin 1994: 35 ff.). However, contemporary medical technologies have affected not only our views on the life of the early embryo *in vitro*; they have also affected the way we establish the first contact with the child to come. As a routine part of obstetric care, ultrasound pictures of the foetus are currently made for reasons of determining a more exact date of gestation and looking for early signs of foetal abnormalities, such as Down's syndrome. Obstetric ultrasounds are routinely performed in most developed countries in the gestational interval of weeks 16–20 (and often earlier, see below). This time interval squares well with the first perceived movements of the foetus by the pregnant woman (quickening).

The differences between visual and physically felt proof of foetal life are significant, and it could be claimed that the pictures provided in the clinic are more to do with scientific documentation than with contact with the baby to come. However, the routine of listening to the heartbeats of the foetus while viewing it on the screen, and the provision of detailed, realistic pictures and videos by specialized commercial medical services, complicate the view that the ultrasound is only a medical-diagnostic tool (Mills 2011: 101–121). As a matter of fact, it could be argued that the pictures and videos of the foetus to be shared with others and put in the family album are perceived as *more* real than the sensations of foetal life felt in quickening, even from the perspective of the pregnant woman. Vision, in comparison to the other senses (hearing, touch, taste, and smell), has always been privileged as the ultimate access to things in the world, and this appears to apply even in pregnancy. Ultrasound 'opens up' the body of the pregnant woman, providing a new way of experiencing the presence of the foetus.

As mentioned above, diagnostic ultrasound is done in weeks 16–20 in most developed countries as part of standard maternal care. This time interval squares well with the events of quickening; and the technologically mediated contact with the foetus provided by the pictures, though it changes the experience of the pregnancy, does not change the view on the upper time limit of legal abortion. What complicates the matter of providing an upper time limit from the phenomenological point of view is the recent introduction in many countries of more or less routine ultrasound scans in a much earlier stage of pregnancy, roughly weeks 10–12. These earlier scans have been introduced because ultrasound is less invasive than tests of foetal DNA that involve the extraction of amniotic fluid. For a long time, such tests have been recommended in high-risk pregnancies (e.g. high age of the mother-to-be or other risk factors). Because the sampling of amniotic fluid requires inserting a needle into the uterus, it carries some risk of miscarriage. Early ultrasounds were introduced to scan for defects that could then be confirmed or denied by amniocentesis (and/or maternal blood serum tests). Early ultrasounds, however, are presently offered not only in cases of high-risk pregnancies but often as a standard part of maternal care. In the countries where early ultrasound has been introduced in combination with blood tests from the pregnant woman, the practice has led to the performance of a large number of abortions when tests indicate a high risk of Down's syndrome, which has subsequently radically reduced the number of babies born with this defect (Gordon 2015).

That a large number of babies with chromosomal or other congenital defects are never born because a life with such a defect is considered not to be worthwhile, and that the disabilities in question subsequently become rare or non-existent, might be problematic in itself. I will return to this ethical issue in the section below on choosing children. Our concern here, however, is how the early ultrasound affects our views and the arguments on legal abortion, from the phenomenological point of view. If early ultrasound is not employed as a routine test in maternal care, but only as a way of scanning high-risk pregnancies, it does not significantly change the analysis I have developed above. However, if early ultrasound is becoming part of standard maternal care, and is also being presented by the medical staff as a first opportunity to get to know the baby-to-come (which has already happened in some countries, such as Denmark), the phenomenology of a pregnancy's early weeks will radically change. That the same pictures made in weeks 10–12 to scan for medical defects also find their ways into the wallets and family albums of the prospective parents is deeply problematic, if we want to defend a right for women to legal abortion with an upper time limit of week 16 (the first possible experiences of quickening).

The child-to-come *appears* for the parents by way of the early ultrasound at a stage in pregnancy at which it was previously not identifiable as something distinct from the woman's body. From the perspective of the doctors, nurses, and midwives, this is considered a good thing, since they think it makes it easier for the woman to embrace the pregnancy and take good care of the foetus. The problem from the vantage point of legal abortion, however, is that some foetuses in an early stage of development take on the ethical standing of children-to-be, whereas others (that have not been scanned, or are aborted as a consequence of the scan) are not considered to have any significant ethical standing. This is clearly ambivalent, and the only way to remedy this inconsistency is either to adapt the upper time limit for legal abortion to the routine of the early ultrasound, or to apply early ultrasound only to high-risk pregnancies rather than use it as a standard way of establishing contact with the child-to-be. If we aim for the first, we should set the time limit for legal abortion at the same week such a test is scheduled in maternity care. If we aim for the second, the last week for legal abortion should be the earliest week of quickening. The law would obviously have to state a specific week rather than refer to events in individual pregnancies. That some (though not many) women would not have the option to choose abortion because they would find themselves beyond the time limit before they realized they were pregnant would be the price that would have to be paid for a phenomenological approach to legal abortion.

So far I have discussed how a phenomenological perspective on pregnancy will affect our views on legal abortion. Cases of pregnancies involving health risks for the pregnant woman open the way for a permissive (or even injunctive) view on abortion in stages later than the week spans of 10–12 or 16–20 that we have discussed so far. The reason for this is exactly the point of view of the pregnant woman and her state of bodily being, which we have considered as the primary focus for the phenomenological analysis. The remaining central reasons for abortion on grounds other than the woman's wish not to have a child (at the present time) are of embryonic/foetal defects identified through medical examinations and tests (and, possibly also, pregnancy as the result of rape). Since it appears not only cruel, but also pointless, to offer diagnostic tests without the option of abortion should the tests turn out positive, the challenging ethical question thus becomes what tests should be made available or be made mandatory in maternal care. This brings us to the issue of whether, and how, to choose the characteristics of children to be.

Choosing children

In his book *The Imperative of Responsibility: In Search of an Ethics for the Technological Age,* Hans Jonas offers the example of the newborn, 'whose mere breathing uncontradictably addresses an ought to the world around, namely, to take care of him' (Jonas 1984: 131). According to Jonas, the newborn child, by way of its sheer appearance, demands our attention and assistance in preserving his life and allowing him to prosper. The newborn ushers in an ethical appeal to shoulder responsibility for his vulnerable and dependent being that is similar to the claim that originates from the face of the other in Levinasian ethics (Levinas 1991). This claim targets a temporal dimension by addressing the need to resume responsibility for the future and the generations to come (Jonas 1984: 136). Jonas's main message in the book is the need to gain control of technologies that threaten the future of human life with their potential to destroy the ecological niches necessary for life on the planet (e.g. weapons of mass destruction, the plundering of natural resources, and industrial pollution). However, his example of the newborn child, who presents a 'you ought to take responsibility for me', is also interesting in the pre-birth context, even though Jonas himself never presented any consistent view on the rights or wrongs of abortion in the way he took a stand against cloning and genetic enhancement (Jonas 1987: 162–218).

It could be argued that the foetus presents a similar, although perhaps weaker, claim of a need to be taken care of by presenting itself to the pregnant woman *via* quickening, or to her and other close assumers of responsibility in the ultrasound image. Such a claim would challenge the woman's right to abortion, as well as other behaviours that would pose a risk to the health and life of the foetus. But what if the claim to be taken care of collides with knowledge about the future situation of the mother-to-be, or child-to-be, which makes the continuation of pregnancy to full term appear *irresponsible*? The responsibility to secure a future for the child when the pregnant woman judges her chances of taking good care of the newborn to be slim or non-existent, for financial or other reasons, could possibly be handled by way of adoption, which means that the challenge against the right to abortion in such cases still holds from the phenomenological angle. But what if the prediction of the future has to do with the baby's health and possibility for flourishing rather than with the mother? To knowingly give birth to a child with bodily defects that will lead to severe suffering and/or a radically shortened life, as is the case in disorders such as anencephaly, Edwards syndrome (Trisomy 18), muscular dystrophy, cystic fibrosis, or Tay-Sachs disease, appears irresponsible and immoral, at least if the pregnancy could have been terminated when the foetus was still in a non-viable or, better, pre-quickening stage. The diagnostic tests for such genetic diseases are available precisely to spare future human beings unnecessary suffering (Milunsky and Milunsky 2016).

This does not mean that such a human life would not be worth living in every case – this depends on the severity of the disorder and the circumstances of the individual case – but it could be predicted to be *considerably* more painful and alienated on the three related levels of suffering–flourishing that we identified in chapter two: embodiment, everyday actions, and core life-narrative values. An argument in favour of abortion in this context would include medical defects that tend to make a human life considerably worse when compared with normal circumstances, even if there will be fairly many healthy years before the onset of a painful and deadly illness suffering (Huntington's disease, for instance). In such cases, the suffering will be considerable as soon as the person comes to *know* about her inevitably falling ill in the future, and this suffering, on the level of life-narrative and core values, will also include knowledge about the risks of passing the disease on to children. The use of 'considerable' in the argument above is admittedly vague, but it should at least lead us to assume grounds in support of abortion also in cases when the pregnancy has developed beyond the week limits we have considered for abortion on non-medical grounds. When the defect can be predicted to lead to severe suffering and a radically shortened life for the child, the responsibility claim transforms into an obligation to abort on the part of the woman for the reason of avoiding undue suffering for the child to come.

The diagnostic tests on offer in maternal care scrutinize embryonic/foetal DNA or other biomarkers found in the amniotic fluid (or in the blood) of the pregnant woman, as well as bodily defects visible through the foetus's outer appearance in forms of imaging such as ultrasound (Milunsky and Milunsky 2016). The currently most debated test in prenatal diagnostics is the ultrasound scan to detect Down's syndrome (DS) by means of the NT procedure (nuchal translucency ultrasound scan), followed up by a blood serum test and/or amniocentesis, also called the combined ultrasound and blood (CUB) test. The questioning of ultrasound scanning for DS from an ethical point of view has been directed particularly towards early routine scanning beyond the boundaries of risk groups. Such testing inevitably leads to a rather high number of false positives, which lead to (unnecessary) invasive confirmative tests, and it also means that most of the foetuses correctly diagnosed with DS will be aborted. Recently, the possibilities of detecting genetic disorders through an analysis of the very small amounts of foetal DNA that can be found in the blood of the woman from very early on in pregnancy (NIPT) have been brought to the centre of attention (Dondorp et al. 2016; Morain et al. 2013). Such tests can be made to scan for genetic defects – or for genes associated with characteristics other than diseases – very early in pregnancy with very high accuracy. However, if the genetic disorders scanned for are rare, NIPT could nevertheless lead to a considerable number of false positives if the test is used to scan the whole population of pregnant women as opposed to only risk groups. (NIPT is short for 'non-invasive prenatal testing', which is potentially confusing, since a needle is injected to obtain the blood sample from the pregnant woman, but the use of 'non-invasive' is clearly meant with respect to the uterus in this case.)

The argument from critics against a recommended, more or less obligatory, early diagnostic test for DS in maternal care is that the tests lead to unnecessary abortions of foetuses at risk of carrying DS (especially when performed in an early stage of pregnancy) and that this is unfortunate because, first, these children may be unaffected (false positives); second, even if children have the syndrome, they may lead a good life; and third, the tests and the ensuing abortions (carried out in about 90 per cent of the positive cases) send the message to persons with DS and their families that these children are an unnecessary burden to society (Gordon 2015). In addition to these three concerns, one should mention that standard prenatal scanning for DS and other genetic disorders or diseases could lead to a less tolerant view in general of persons who are different from the healthy norm in our society in the future. (Why should we spend a lot of resources on alleviating sufferings that could have been prevented from the start?) While acknowledging these points of criticism, one should nonetheless take into consideration that even though a life with DS is not, as a rule, a life filled with suffering, it is without doubt a life that is more afflicted by medical problems than normal – a considerably higher risk of developing heart failure, neurological spasms, sleep apnoea, problems with speech, endocrine disturbances, gastrointestinal diseases, and mental disorders, to name the most prevalent (Hickey et al. 2012). One should also remember that a life with DS, even if it does not involve major medical problems, is fraught with intellectual disabilities and that it is, in most cases, a life that is shorter than other human lives.

The main problem associated with judging whether a life with DS is considerably more prone to suffering and/or considerably less prone to flourishing than a 'standard' human life is that this varies considerably from case to case. Some persons with DS appear to live happy and successful lives, whereas others suffer or are robbed of most normal life opportunities as a consequence of the syndrome. The prenatal tests cannot determine whether the child will be severely disabled or a case of 'high-performing' DS. However, the tests are able to determine with high accuracy – especially if we are considering ultrasound in combination with amniocentesis or NIPT – that the child will suffer from DS with standard complications in some degree of severity from the first day of birth. This is a primary difference in comparison with other (prenatal) genetic tests that determine statistical *risks* for developing diseases at some point in life – tests that are already around and will likely become increasingly common in the future with NIPT.

Most diseases are not single-gene disorders but multifactorial, involving many genes that determine risks for developing a disease in combination with environmental factors. We do not currently apply such diagnostic tests to determine risks that a child will develop, for instance, heart disease, various forms of cancer, ADHD, or depression at some point in life, because the risks associated with single genes or even combinations of many genes are too low and too uncertain to motivate abortion, even if the tests were to turn out positive. Perhaps the ultrasonic scanning for DS should be considered a low-risk test of this kind on the grounds that what the test should really determine, if it is to be relevant, is the risk of developing DS with *major* medical problems and *severe* intellectual disabilities, not DS as such. Whether the current diagnostic test is to be considered relevant or not depends on the size of the group of severe-suffering DS persons in relation to the group of mild-suffering DS persons. If the ratio is something like 20:80 we should probably not use the NT test as a standard procedure in maternal care. If the ratio is more like 80:20, the risk for severe-suffering DS is probably too high to justify not offering the test as a part of routine maternal care. I am currently unable to make the estimation, but I think this way of approaching the ethics of prenatal diagnostics for DS would be the best way to proceed. In making such an estimation, it should be kept in mind that the contented moods or even happy moods which persons with DS commonly appear to enjoy clearly count against considering such a life to be fraught with suffering from the phenomenological perspective, despite the fact that important ways to flourish may be closed as a result of intellectual disabilities.

Would a 50:50 ratio be enough to motivate scanning for DS in early pregnancy? Perhaps, but much depends on how criteria are set for the two groups of mild and severe DS. We will likely see many more risk-ratio and severity-issue discussions for a variety of diseases in the future if NIPT in early pregnancy is implemented as a standard part of maternal care. Since such risks linked to certain genes may also, in some cases, be 'risks' of developing characteristics that we treasure – emotional sensitivity or intelligence in the case of depression and bipolar disorder, for instance – it is a development that should be closely monitored and ethically scrutinized. A broad implementation of NIPT would likely lead to a much larger number of abortions performed to avoid giving birth to babies with risks for developing diseases and/or carrying genetic defects of various kinds. Such a development is ethically problematic for the different reasons that I have touched upon above: false-positive cases of abortions, abortions of embryos/foetuses that would have given rise to persons with lives that were not considerably worse than normal, stigmatizing effects for the persons who live with the diseases and disorders, and a less tolerant view in general of abnormalities in our society. However, replacing early ultrasound scanning for DS with NIPT alone would have one significant advantage in light of the phenomenological argument about abortion developed above. The embryo/foetus tested by means of NIPT would not appear to the parents the way the moving image of the foetus on the screen does, and it would not result in any family album photographs.

Designing babies

An issue that has been much discussed in bioethics is the future possibilities of designing babies *in vitro*, not only by scanning for disease risks (PGD), but also by selecting for or manipulating genes coding for various *characteristics* to be enhanced (e.g. height, beauty, intelligence, emotional stability, a long life, etc.) (Agar 2013; Buchanan et al. 2000; DeGrazia 2012; Habermas 2003; Hauskeller 2013; Malmqvist 2007, 2014; Parens 2015). The two main arguments in favour of such procedures are that it is the quality of life of the child-to-be that matters, not whether he or she will become diseased or not (Harris 2007; Savulescu 2005); and that it is the right of the future parents to design their offspring *in vitro* as they find fit, in the same way that they improve their children's characteristics by rearing and schooling them after they have been born (Agar 2004; Robertson 2003).

The first of these arguments is interesting from the point of view of the phenomenology of suffering and flourishing I have introduced in this book. Disease, as such, does not appear to be the morally relevant issue in genetic diagnosis but, rather, the embodied, world-opening, life-shaping moods that the future children will end up living in. However, even if scanning for severe diseases *in vitro* or in early pregnancy is done in order to avoid future suffering rather than disease (defect, disorder) per se, the phenomenological argument does not open to enhancement on similar grounds (Malmqvist 2014). The responsibility to avoid having children that we know will have a considerably more painful and alienated life than normal is not a responsibility to have children with genes that we think will make them considerably happier, with greater flourishing, than normal. We are responsible for offering our children the possibility to develop and flourish that would be precluded by severe diseases and defects, but we are hardly responsible for making their genome ultimately fit to prosper and succeed in this world. And even if we had such a strange parental responsibility, somehow trumping all other responsibilities we have to other, future human beings of this world, the project as such is fraught with difficulties in determining which lives are 'better' than normal (Hauskeller 2013: 185–186). As I have continuously stressed above, to flourish, from the phenomenological point of view, does not mean merely to feel happy, but to realize one's life in a way that identifies and brings about one's core life values. And how could the parents know in advance what the future child will be like, what she will treasure and find meaningful in *her* particular life?

This issue brings us to the second main argument of the enhancement enthusiasts: namely, that since parents currently have the right – in liberal democratic societies – to influence or even shape the core life values of their children by way of upbringing, why should they not enjoy the right to do so by way of genetic enhancement? The phenomenologist, however, has access to a way of thinking about human being – as embodied, narratively extended being-in-the-world – that can explain why the two situations of determining in advance by way of genes and attempting to influence and shape by way of child-rearing are not analogous. Freedom to choose one's way in life – autonomy is the term most often used in bioethics – is crucial to human flourishing, but such a freedom is possible only from the position of already being *someone* who can choose. Unless there is first someone who has not been chosen to be such-and-such but merely accepted and taken responsibility for *as* such, there is no freedom to be enjoyed. To flourish means to be true to *oneself* by identifying and living according to one's self-determined core life values, and it is crucial for such an attempt that one's genetically influenced characteristics have not been predetermined by others, including parents (Habermas 2003: 44–53; Malmqvist 2007). We should fear the situation of parents genetically enhancing their children to maximize their success in a capitalist society for the same reason that we should fear a totalitarian society designing offspring to fulfil different forms of utility functions (Huxley 2006). Choosing a partner with attractive characteristics, or even buying high-quality germ cells from a company, are admittedly also ways of enhancing offspring, but the way oocyte and sperm fuse in fertilization is still highly unpredictable as concerns the genetic set-up of the embryo (Brevini and Pennarossa 2013).

Abstaining from choosing the characteristics of children-to-be beyond the measures taken to save them from considerable, unnecessary suffering is ultimately a matter of avoiding instrumentalizing the practice of procreation. The relationship between parents and their children should be thought of as an empathic and dialogic relation of the same type as the one we explored in chapter 'four, yet one that is deeper and more fundamental in character than the one at work in the clinical encounter. At stake in this relation is not only the understanding and avoidance of unnecessary suffering but also the possibilities of human flourishing. Child-rearing should respond to the personal characteristics that a child, from birth onwards, already embodies and expresses, and continually support and guide the child's possibilities to develop these characteristics in a successful way. Providing a set of core life values certainly belongs to this process, but not in a way that would make it impossible or even too hard for the child to make adjustments in the set and change to a different type of life than the parents had hoped for and tried to make available.

Core life values are admittedly a rather inclusive concept, all the more so with the provision of Charles Taylor's specification of the three zones, which include moral values, the good life, and self-respect in the eyes of others (1989: 14–15). To teach a child how to behave morally, in the sense of caring for others and being just, could hardly be looked upon as some form of parental indoctrination. The crucial life-value choices of the child that need to be *guided* rather than plainly taught are about the contents of the good life, while self-respect in the eyes of others is related both to moral values and to the characterization of the good life.

The worry about enhancement through genetic selection and manipulation of the embryo, in proceeding to the non-disease domain, is therefore a concern that has to do with the impossibility of objectively determining the shape and content of a good human life in any detail, but also with the potential *instrumentalization* of the most important type of human relationship that exists – that between parents and their children. If the situations in which we assume responsibility for children get transformed into situations in which we design our offspring to be the type of persons we want them to be, they are being considered as means to attain our goals rather than as future ends in themselves. The term for responsibility, *Verantwortung*, used by Jonas (1984) and Habermas (2003) in the German originals of the books I have referred to above, captures this dialogical, non-instrumental duty – in a much better way than 'responsibility' can – through its implication of 'responding to' the child. To assume responsibility for someone means 'to answer to' his or her needs and wishes, and to know *how* to do this, the parent must *get to know* the child. The embryo to be implanted is clearly not a person one can have a dialogue with, nor is the kicking foetus or the screaming newborn child, but they are nevertheless persons in potential being who appear to the parent(s) as a 'you should take care of me'. Parents and others (e.g. medical staff, proxy caretakers) responsible for caretaking answer to a demand to exist and flourish from a vulnerable child-to-be, whom they will be given the possibility to know and love in the process of so doing, if they fulfil this imperative of responsibility.

Summary

The phenomenological analysis in the field of the ethics of early human life proceeds from the embodied perspective of the pregnant woman and from the imagined perspective of the embryo–foetus–newborn–child, informed by medical science and technologies. In the phenomenological way of addressing embryo ethics, abortion ethics, and the issues concerning possibilities to choose what types of children should be born by using prenatal diagnostic methods and germ line interventions, key terms are instrumentalization and taking responsibility.

Already by bringing embryo production outside the woman's body, the practice of IVF changes the ethical status of the pre-implanted, non-gastrulated embryo.

The technologies used to facilitate fertilization and make embryos in new ways *in vitro* underline that we are dealing with a new type of objects: embryos brought out of the environment that previously determined their form of potential being in a one-way manner. That *in vitro* embryos are not merely or only potential persons means that they may in some cases be legitimate objects and sources of material for medical research and treatments, provided the risks of instrumentalization of human life as such can be kept in check. The ethical standing of the embryo becomes more powerful and demanding as it develops beyond the stage of implantation and gastrulation and is in place in the uterus of a woman. Abortion ethics, in addition to instrumentalization worries, includes the questions of under what circumstances and within what time limits it is acceptable to end the life of an embryo/foetus in the womb. The experience of quickening appears to be a strong candidate for setting an upper limit for legal abortion from the phenomenological point of view. In quickening, the pregnant woman feels the presence of another human being inside her, and this is not, as a rule, an alienating event but rather a part and process of a different form of embodied being, in contact with a child-to-be, who demands protection and support to develop and flourish. In cases of being able to avoid giving birth to children who will suffer considerably more painful and alienated lives than normal, this responsibility for taking care of the child-to-be will be transformed into a responsibility to consider and/or have an abortion, including cases of pregnancies continued beyond the weeks of quickening or even, in some cases, beyond the weeks of viability.

An issue that has been much discussed in bioethics is the future possibilities of designing babies *in vitro*, not only by scanning for disease risks but also by selecting for or manipulating genes coding for various characteristics to be enhanced (e.g. height, beauty, intelligence, emotional stability, a long life, etc.). Abstaining from choosing the characteristics of children-to-be beyond measures taken to spare them considerable, unnecessary, meaningless suffering is ultimately a matter of avoiding instrumentalizing the practice of procreation. The relationship between parents and their children should be thought of as an empathic and dialogic relation, not a strategic engagement. At stake in this relation is not only the understanding and avoidance of unnecessary suffering but also the possibilities of human flourishing. Child-rearing should respond to the personal characteristics that the child from birth onwards, to a certain extent, already embodies and expresses, and continually support and guide the child's possibilities to develop these characteristics in the world at hand.

7

SURVIVING DEATH

The concept of death

Is it possible for a person to be dead while still breathing? This question arose in the 1960s and 1970s when new medical technologies made it possible to keep the heartbeat and respiratory function of brain-damaged individuals intact by connecting them to ventilators when they could no longer breathe by themselves. The reasons for challenging the aliveness of these persons were the fact that they would never become conscious again and, especially, that parts of their bodies could be used to help others in need if they were declared dead while blood was still perfusing their organs. These concerns led to the implementation of a complementary way to make a medical judgement of death in most countries of the world during the 1970s, 1980s, and 1990s: brain death. Accordingly, in addition to the traditional criterion of loss of cardiopulmonary function, a person may also be defined as dead if she has irreversibly lost all functionality of the brain even if the circulatory system of the body is being maintained by machines (Younger 2007).

Brain death is not the same thing as coma. Persons who are permanently comatose may still have intact brain stem functionality necessary for cardiopulmonary and other vital bodily functions. And the cerebral functions necessary for consciousness, which are absent in coma, may be only temporarily gone, as it is when people are anaesthetized, for instance. Brain death is also different from what is called a persistent or permanent vegetative state (PVS), in which a person is awake (or asleep) but not aware of what is going on. People in a coma or a vegetative state have not lost all the functions of the brain, and even though the doctors, after studying the damage done to their brains and assessing their long-term condition, may establish with very high likelihood that they will not regain consciousness, it is impossible to establish this beyond *all* doubt. These patients are kept alive by feeding tubes and nursing care, and they can live for years or even decades if nutrition and care of the body is maintained. The wishes of and conflicts between relatives and medical personnel concerning whether or how to allow these patients to die are legendary in bioethics (McMahan 2009).

In addition to brain death, coma, and vegetative state, two related conditions should be mentioned in which consciousness is *not* totally lost: minimally conscious state and locked-in syndrome. A person in a minimally conscious state may look much like a patient in a vegetative state except that awareness can be proved beyond reflexes and automated behaviours like swallowing or blinking when she is exposed to external stimuli. A person in a minimally conscious state is able to understand and respond to simple questions, expressing feelings by means of body language or moving a limb when asked to do so, for instance. A person in a locked-in syndrome is fully aware and conscious despite suffering from total, or nearly total, bodily paralysis. Cognitive functions of the higher brain are intact, while damage to the lower parts of the brain prevents the person from voluntarily moving any part of her body with the exception, in most cases, of vertical movement of the eyes and blinking. A person in a minimally conscious state may easily be mistaken for a patient in a vegetative state, or vice versa, because of the difficulties in establishing whether bodily responses are conscious or automated. And locked-in conscious states may easily go undetected, especially if the paralysis also affects eye movements and blinking. Recalling our phenomenological analysis of what it means to suffer on the three levels of lived body, being-in-the-world, and life narrative, locked-in syndrome appears to be not only a truly nightmarish condition but also a case of at least minimal, if severely restricted, embodiment. A locked-in person is, indeed, never totally locked in because she is able to see and hear what is going on around her and is also able to express herself by way of her eyes. Proprioception and bodily perception are also often present to some degree despite the paralysis (Bauby 1998).

Brain death, defined as the irreversible loss of all functions of the brain, can be established beyond all reasonable doubt by examining the type of damage done to the brain and establishing the absence of all electrochemical activity. In cases of brain death, the present ethical dilemma is not about whether but *when* to turn off the life-sustaining technology. The ventilator is actually not a *life*-saving technology anymore if the patient is declared brain dead, since he is then *dead* according to the law in most countries of the world at the present time. The ethical conflicts are instead about whether such patients should be kept in a state in which their organs are perfused with oxygenated and nutritious blood for the sake of others. Should they be treated for somebody else's – the organ receiver's – sake for a while rather than for their own good? Or, as phenomenologist Hans Jonas argued in a paper published in 1968 and continued to stress in following the implementation of brain death in medical practice and laws of various states in the United States, is this procedure nothing but the instrumentalization of the body of a patient who is still alive (1987: chapter 10)?

It should be pointed out that Jonas's wish and ethical claim was not that permanently comatose or brain-dead patients should be kept alive when the chances of their regaining consciousness and a life worth living were (close to) zero. His claim was that we are not entitled to declare them dead – rather than letting them die – in order to be able to use their bodies as 'organ banks', as he puts it (Jonas 1987: 219). Jonas is not alone in criticizing the idea and definition of brain death for being incoherent and pragmatically rather than scientifically motivated (see DeGrazia 2005: chapter 4; Younger 2007). There is no doubt something strange about claiming that patients with non-functioning brains who are kept on life- (!) sustaining technology, and who in some cases have been witnessed to go through puberty, heal wounds, fight off diseases, and even gestate a baby, are dead. These bodies, indeed, appear to have survived the death of their brains.

The main problem if we want to be able to use organs from patients with non-functioning brains for transplants is that we would *kill* them by doing so if we have not first declared them dead (the dead donor rule). An interesting possibility, which Jonas raises in the last postscript to his 1968 paper, written in 1985 when the legislation on brain death had already been put in place, is at least to turn the ventilator off and wait until the heart has stopped beating *before* removing the organs (Jonas 1987: 239). This would not be totally ideal from the perspective of preserving the organs, but the advantage would be that the medical staff would allow the patient to die – according to the traditional definition of death – before opening his body.

Since the need for organs has steadily increased – more about this below – the question has inevitably arisen of whether patients who are not fully brain dead, but still beyond hope of recovering from coma, could be used as organ donors when the life-sustaining equipment has been turned off – so-called donation after circulatory death (DCD). Donation following circulatory death has been in use for a long time, but since the functionality of organs deteriorates rapidly in the absence of blood flow, the transplant possibility is lost in most cases when people die sudden and unexpected deaths. The situation is different when the comatose patient is already in the hospital and hooked up to life-sustaining technology. It is then possible to prepare his body and the recipient of the organs for the transplant before turning off the machines and waiting for brain death to occur (five to ten minutes), followed by the operations. The ethical argument for moving towards donation after circulatory death in this controlled manner is that it will greatly increase the number of organs available. The argument against is that the doctors are letting the patient die in order to procure his organs for transplantation. This sounds grave – not only keeping patients alive for others' sake but actually letting them die – but the proponents of the procedure will respond that these comatose patients would have had their life sustaining technology turned off anyway, because of the next-to-zero likelihood of ever regaining consciousness and a life worth living.

The pro and contra arguments about brain-dead donation and DCD are similar to the ethical conflicts explored in the preceding chapter about using spare embryos from IVF treatments for research. The embryos would be wasted anyway, the proponent will argue, while the sceptic will bring up the issue of whether the embryos were not in fact foreseeably produced for research from the start. Are human lives *instrumentalized* in the process of producing embryos *in vitro* and using them for various purposes? A similar concern about the bodies of brain-damaged patients could be voiced in the case of organ donation when brain-dead or comatose patients are harvested for their organs rather than treated for their own good. In the following I will explore the practice of organ transplantation from a phenomenological point of view: what is it like to receive a new kidney or heart – these will be my main examples – and what forms and regulations of donation are compatible with avoiding instrumentalization? These questions will bring us back to the issues of what constitutes human life and personhood from the phenomenological point of view that we began to investigate in the preceding chapter.

The body as gift, resource, or commodity

A phenomenological exploration of organ transplantation will be tied to fundamental questions about what type of relationship we have to our own bodies, as well as what kind of relationship we have to each other as human beings sharing the same being-in-the-world as embodied creatures. Such an analysis could serve as an antidote to and possibly a remedy for a contemporary bioethics stuck in what Drew Leder aptly and poignantly calls 'a paradigm of disconnection' (2016: chapter 8). Leder's point is that contemporary organ-transplantation ethics disconnects the person not only from her body but also from other persons sharing the same kind of embodiment (see also Campbell 2009).

Organ transplantation as a life-saving technique took its first tottering steps in the 1950s. Since then it has expanded exponentially, in terms both of survival rates and the number of people on the waiting lists. Advances in immunosuppression, prevention of infection, and other improvements in medical measures have led to success, but as the technology has improved there has also been an increase in the number of patients who are considered suitable and in need of a transplant. The range of conditions for which transplantation is offered has widened, and transplantable organs now include kidney, liver, heart, pancreas, lung, uterus, intestines, and thymus. Dead donors can provide all of these organs, while living donation is restricted to one of the kidneys (the vast majority of cases) or sections of liver, lung, pancreas, and bowel. A consequence of the dramatic expansion in life-saving potentiality has been a worldwide demand for organs far exceeding their current availability from either living or cadaveric sources.

In connection with the transplantation of organs we have also witnessed medical developments related to the transfer between bodies of cells and tissues (sometimes regenerative), such as skin tissue, cornea, nerves, veins, heart valves, bone, tendons, bone marrow, blood, and gametes. We are moving into an era of 'tissue economies' – the transfer and circulation of human tissue on a global scale (Liljefors et al. 2012; Waldby and Mitchell 2006). 'Tissue engineering' – growing (parts of) organs from cells cultivated in the laboratory – might very well turn out to be a technology that makes organ donation superfluous in the future. Xenotransplantation – transplanting organs from pigs or other animals to humans – is another path forward that initially looked very promising but has been halted because of health risks for receivers (e.g. viruses migrating between species and various compatibility problems) (Sharp 2007).

There are three metaphors that guide contemporary thinking about organ transplantation as it is increasingly focused on in bioethical debates. Although the *gift* is the sanctioned metaphor for *donating* organs, the underlying perspective on the part of state authorities and medical organizations seems rather to be that the human body and its parts are to be understood as a *resource*. The recent switch in the laws of many countries from informed to presumed consent regarding organ donation from brain-dead patients is a clear sign of this (Weimar et al. 2008). The gift of your organs when you do not need them any more (when you are dead) is increasingly framed by the state as a gift you cannot refuse to give once you have been properly informed about what it means to others (life) and to yourself (no harm, since you are dead). To refuse to donate is considered irrational, assuming that you have been properly informed about the value of the gift in question, and consequently, this is a gift we should *expect* (presume) everyone to agree to. Organs are too precious to be wasted because people do not want to think about their own death before they pass away, or because they are simply irrational or egoistic, so the argument goes. (For a critique of this way of stating the alternatives, exploring the rich phenomenology and cultural aspects of brain death and consent to donate, see the work by Margaret Lock: *Twice Dead: Organ Transplants and the Reinvention of Death* (2002).)

The acute scarcity of organs, which generates a desperate demand in relation to a group of potential suppliers who are equally desperate (desperately poor), leads easily to the gift's becoming, in reality, not only a resource, but also a *commodity*. This is the third metaphor used in contemporary discourse to frame the ontology of the body in the case of organ transplantation. The transfer of body parts is increasingly organized in the form of a global transplant trafficking scene, which is illegal, but still a reality and an option for the rich (the buyers in North America and Western Europe) as well as the poor (the sellers in Asia and Eastern Europe). Poor people, with no or little property, have been selling their labour to the wealthy for a very long time. Now they are also selling parts of their bodies (kidneys) in order to mitigate their misery. That the misery in question is often aggravated rather than mitigated by the transplantations – the medical condition of the sellers is worsened and most of the money ends up in the hands of organ brokers and medical clinics – is the sad, present reality of organ trafficking (Lundin 2015).

While the resourcification of human bodies that proceeds by way of redefining death and assuming everybody's consent harbours a clear risk of instrumentalization, the commodification achieved by putting parts of the human body on the market is not only a clear example of the instrumentalization of the body but also of the *exploitation* of their poor owners (Malmqvist and Zeiler 2016). To add the 'free choice' of selling one's kidney to the severely restricted number of opportunities available for desperately poor people, instead of helping them and their children to a better life with both kidneys still in place, is hardly a liberation project. It is a cruel form of coercing and taking advantage of poor people on top of resourcifying their bodies.

The paradox of organ-transplantation ethics

The ethics of organ transplantation is tied to the question of what kind of relationship we have to our own bodies. How can it be that a person who is allowed (and, indeed, encouraged) to give parts of her body away is not allowed to sell the same parts to a buyer who is prepared to pay the price? How can I be the owner of something (my body) that I am still not allowed to sell? This is the paradox that haunts contemporary bioethics on this topic. Since the donation of organs is taken to presuppose ownership, how can this ownership rightly be restricted by the liberal state, especially if the selling in question could be organized in a legal manner which would benefit not only the buyers but also the sellers in question (Erin and Harris 2003)?

There are a number of strategies that philosophers have tried to apply to solve this problem, ranging from comparisons with other accepted ownership–right restrictions regarding one's own-body and person (e.g. prohibitions against slavery, suicide, or prostitution) to arguments stressing the bad consequences of organ markets (e.g. risks of exploitation of sellers, decreasing numbers of donations, threats to the altruistic society as such) (Campbell 2009). However, all these strategies appear to share one premise: in order to defend the gift metaphor one needs to take it for granted that we own our bodies. This premise is deeply ingrained in bioethics as it is practised today, especially in the United States and Great Britain: the liberal heritage with its focus on personal autonomy is a property-based model, which ever since Locke has been founded in the person's ownership of her body (Locke 1980; Nozick 1974). This ethics could be rights based – a person has a fundamental right to decide over her own body, a right which nobody can take away from her – or it could focus rather on autonomy and personal freedom as the guiding principles of bioethics in general (Engelhardt 1996). Notice, however, that it is Locke's philosophy – and not Kant's – which is the source of autonomy-based bioethics. What matters is that the individual makes an autonomous choice in the sense of a choice which is well informed and free from coercion, not that the choice in question is also a morally righteous choice (in line with the laws of practical reason). What is ethically sound to do in a situation is basically up to the individual as long as she does not harm the freedom of others.

The main current of thought supplementing personal autonomy in contemporary bioethics is utilitarianism (e.g. Singer 2011). Utilitarianism can be framed as a major alternative to rights-based ethics – if others could benefit more from my belongings or, indeed, organs than I do, they should have them, since future utility (and suffering) for everybody involved is what matters, not what happens to belong to me presently (and this includes my body and life). If liberalism (libertarianism), with its focus on personal autonomy and freedom, is the main defender of the body-as-commodity metaphor, utilitarianism could be viewed as the main defender of the body-as-resource metaphor.

Autonomy and utility could be looked upon as alternatives in bioethics, but in the literature they most often supplement and reinforce each other rather than compete. The main reason for this is that most utilitarian bioethicists consider the negative consequences of a restrained personal freedom to be too severe to actually foster the general happiness they want to promote. If the individual knows that the state can take his organs away at any point when it finds that others would have better use for them (the infamous thought experiment of an individual's being picked by the drawing of lots to donate his organs to several people in need every time more lives could be saved by this strategy), he would probably live in constant fear (unhappiness) and would try in every way possible to avoid ending up as a donator (seeking health care), which, in turn, would create major hazards in the organizing of happiness. The state in which everybody has to give up ownership of the body will simply never be the happy state, even though it was supposed to be so on the strength of its clever, utilitarian design. Human psychology is actually a major obstacle to human happiness from the utilitarian point of view.

Autonomy and utility team up not only in different sorts of ways in the books and articles of contemporary bioethics, but also in relation to the *practice* of organ transplantation, as I touched upon above. If the body belongs to each individual, yet is a potential resource for the welfare of other individuals in need of healthy organs, commodification lurks around the corner for logical as well as practical reasons. If I own it, why should I not be allowed to sell it? And if it is valuable, why should it not be assigned a price along with other valuable things in the world that have entered the market? At this point I would like to propose that a successful explication of the gift metaphor in the case of organ transplantation and a complementary defence of the ethical primacy of the *sharing* of organs need to be grounded in a philosophical anthropology which considers the implications of embodiment in a different and more substantial way than is generally the case in contemporary bioethics. Otherwise, the two questions above about the right to sell and buy organs will continue to haunt bioethics, and there will be no good answers. Phenomenology, as I will attempt to show, offers such an alternative, with the help of which we can understand why body parts could and, indeed, under certain circumstances, should be shared with others, but are not resources or properties to be sold (Diprose 2002).

Persons and their organs

Philosophers working in the field of bioethics often share a rather reductive, implicit view of what it means to be a person (self): it means being a rational agent striving to realize one's preferences (one of these preferences could be the utilitarian maxim of striving to maximize everybody's happiness). The body, in this view, admittedly plays a basic role in the life of a person, but it does so in a rather supplementary way. In order to be able to realize my preferences and take possession of things in the world, I happen to need a body. The body is the most basic thing I need (and own), but it is not really *me* – I am my thoughts, feelings, wants, memories, and so on, not my material body. The body of an individual could even be replaced, as in the teletransportation thought experiments found in the work of Derek Parfit, often referred to by bioethicists (1984). Another way of putting this, if one is a reductive materialist, is that I am my brain (McMahan 2009). The brain is thus the only organ that cannot be donated; if you offer your brain to be transplanted into another body, you become a receiver, not a donor, of organs.

It is doubtful whether the brain transplanted into a new body would still be the same person as before the operation (DeGrazia 2005: chapter 2). As brain scientists have pointed out for quite some time now, what the brain feels and thinks is determined by the way it is *connected* to the rest of the body. This goes not only for feelings, but also for thoughts, since thoughts are indeed made meaningful by the feelings that precede and feed into them (Damasio 1999). The brain cannot think in the vat, only in the body. What actually *would* happen if we were able to transplant a brain into a new body we simply do not know at this point. The practical difficulties of such a brain transplant appear overwhelming at present, but partly successful experiments involving the swapping of monkeys' heads have been carried out, and some surgeons believe the first human head will be transplanted in the not-too-distant future (Canavero 2013). The heart transplant was certainly considered impossible one hundred years ago, but it was still carried out in the late 1960s. Maybe the first human brain (head) will be transplanted in 2050 or so.

A good guess is that the brain-transplanted person would feel to some extent like the same person he was before the operation, especially if he has memories of the time preceding the transplant (which, indeed, appears to be necessary if he is even to understand the question we are confronting him with). Maybe he would say that he is the same person as before the operation, but also different in many important ways (consider, e.g., the possibility that he was a she before her (now his?) brain was transplanted). He would also, I think, say that these ways of being the same but still different are new to him in an important way. To get one's brain transplanted into a new body will probably be a different kind of personality change than going through an existential crisis (minus a new body). Maybe puberty, pregnancy, and amputee experiences could be helpful when we consider what getting a brain transplant (getting one's brain a new body) would be like, but these real-life examples will not get us the whole way.

The brain-transplant case is admittedly different from the prospect of getting not a whole new body (except the brain), but mainly a new limb or organ (a hand, a kidney). Some body parts are not as essential as others to the make-up of a person. This is true not only concerning which organs one could dispense with and still go on living without, but also concerning the cultural, lived aspects of bodily identity. Face transplants, for instance, touch deeply upon matters of identity, although the matters involved are not primarily related to survival, as in the case of a lung or heart transplant (Perpich 2010; Svenaeus 2012). In considering what it means to be a person, embodiment is consequently not to be thought about as a brain (or soul) using different bodily tools to find and make its way around in the environment (though 'tool' is indeed the etymological root of the word 'organ'). The person (self) does not own his body; he *is* his body as the central vehicle of his being-in-the-world. This is a basic phenomenological premise, most famously explored by Maurice Merleau-Ponty, but actually found already in the middle period of Edmund Husserl's works, as well as in the early Martin Heidegger, when the philosophers consider the implications of our *Leiblichkeit*, which is the German keyword for the topic of the lived body (Welton 1999). These phenomenological contributions to the philosophy of the body, which we have surveyed in previous chapters of this book, were made back in the 1910s through the1940s, but they are still relevant, not least to psychological, experimental approaches that make use of recent findings about the functions of the brain (Gallagher 2005).

The experience of undergoing kidney transplantation

In *Holograms of Fear*, novelist Slavenka Drakulić tells the story of her first kidney transplant, which takes place in Boston in 1986 (1993). Drakulić has left her homeland of Yugoslavia, her family, friends, and even her young daughter, in order to live in New York as a journalist. This radical decision is forced upon her not by political oppression but by a kidney disease (PKD). The medical care she is getting in Yugoslavia is not sufficient (she watches her fellow patients in the dialysis ward deteriorate and die), and she has poor chances in Yugoslavia of getting the transplant she needs to survive. In the book she tells how the disease and her dysfunctional kidneys force her to undergo dialysis every second day in the hospital for several hours:

> I had no choice. Every other morning at five o'clock I went for my dialysis at the hospital on 72nd Street. I didn't consider the possibility of not going. The healthy can choose. Life is simple when you're sick, as it is for people in jail or in the army. There are rules that are more than rules because breaking them can only mean one thing. At first this is non-freedom but later, it is just certainty. … Here the blood flows in streams: in veins, capillaries, pumps, rubber hoses, in clear plastic tubes, in cylindrical dishes with filters. As if the white room was woven with a red web. Everyone is quiet, deathly tired. They communicate in code, in subdued tones.
>
> (Drakulić 1993: 3–4)

To have dialysis treatment means that your life becomes *regimented* (Gunnarson 2016). This concerns not only the hours you have to spend connected to the dialysis machine but also the way you have to watch and regulate your body, diet, how much to drink, sleep, exercise, and so forth to keep the disease under control. But the deepest effect of kidney disease is that the body shows up in new and disconcerting ways that become central to your everyday experience, self-reflection, and life story.

The body becomes an obstacle and a threat, instead of my home territory and founding ground, but in this (and most other severe) case(s) of illness it also changes the ways I address the meaning of my life and my relationship to others on a social and narrative level. It should be noted that the bodily experiences in this case do not specifically make the *kidneys* appear – the way, for example, my finger appears to me as painful and needing attention when I hit it by accident when hammering nails. Rather, in kidney disease, my whole embodiment becomes plagued and obtrusive through pain, nausea, and bodily decay.

Waiting for a transplant, knowing that you are on the waiting list but with no knowing when, if ever, a suitable kidney will be found for you, is a distressing experience in itself. So is the fear of pain or dying as a result of the operation. You long desperately for a life with more freedom and fewer symptoms, but at the same time, the regime of dialysis becomes a habit and a kind of security you are afraid of leaving for the uncertainty of the operation, which is, certainly, a very dramatic event:

> 'Breathe, breathe.' An English voice penetrates the darkness in which I'm floating. … Terrified I try to suck in air, catch it with my open mouth, but something is inside, something is inside. It is smothering me, I have to retch it out. They are pulling out a long tube with a sudden jerk from my throat, tearing the membranes. A deep sigh. Then a sharp pain under my stomach cuts me in half. 'Your kidney is functioning.'
>
> *(Drakulić 1993: 42)*

Only slowly does Drakulić recover after the operation; it takes exercise and a lot of time to be able to sit up, stand, walk, eat, and so forth. Even going to the toilet is an effort and, in the specific case of kidney transplants, also a new and remarkable experience for the patient, since the kidneys have not been producing any urine for a long time.

Even in successful cases, when the new kidney functions properly and is not rejected by the immune system, life after a transplant is not like life before the disease stepped on to centre stage. To suffer from a disease that destroys one's kidneys and to receive a new kidney means that life becomes prolonged and normalized, but it never means that life becomes *quite* normal (the way it was before the onset of the disease), since you are at constant risk of renewed kidney failure and other problems (Gunnarson 2016). This leads to a life that is very self-regulated as regards the relationship to one's own-body. It often means a more anxious life, in the sense that one's basic trust in the body is gone (Carel 2013). But it could also mean a more reflective life, in the sense that one's finitude and the question of what is of real importance in life have come to the surface (Frank 1995). Finally, it will lead to thoughts about the lives of others and how they are connected to me, especially the particular other whose death (in the case of cadaveric transplant) or (in the case of living transplant) generous gift means life for me:

A lot of time will pass, then in a subway somewhere, a tall man will stop me. … 'Excuse me, I couldn't help myself, but you look so much like my late wife.' I'll stare at him, indifferent at first. I'll pretend that I have no idea what he is talking about. Perhaps I'll say I don't know any English. But something will force me to change my mind and I'll say: 'Yes. Yes, I probably do look like her. We are sisters, almost twins — you didn't know that she had a sister? You see this thin scar? It has almost disappeared, but this is where she moved in. We live well together, the two of us. Sometimes she gets a little obstinate. I can't keep her from spreading. Sometimes she chooses a smile, other times a gesture, or a walk — to show that she is here, that I am in her power. I think perhaps she wants to make me feel grateful. It's not my fault that she was killed.'

(Drakulić 1993: 73–74)

Kidney disease and transplantation leads to changes in selfhood (personhood) on the attuned levels of embodiment and being-in-the-world and in the patterns of existential self-reflection of the afflicted person. These patterns include the social and narrative realms, since my life story, spun in the web of my relations to others, is the place and structure in and by which existential reflections about my identity are carried out (see chapters two and four). This reflection may lead to various feelings and thoughts considering the origin and impact of the foreign kidney I now bear in my body (Sharp 2006). The scientific attitude to my new organ, an attitude that will be encouraged by the doctors, can easily be conquered by an attitude in which the kidney of the other harbours her identity in some way that has now been transposed to me. It might also lead to a thankfulness that becomes transformed into guilt – how have I earned this life that was made possible by the other person's death? In the case of a kidney, however, this process is made weaker by the fact that I cannot *feel* the new organ in me. The kidney is buried in the depth of my body in a way that disappears. The existential self-reflection spurred by the operation is also likely to be different in cases of living donation from family members or friends, who are neither foreign nor gone in the way a dead donor is.

The heart transplant

In the case of a heart, things are slightly different, not only when it comes to its symbolic character (life, love, goodness) in comparison to the kidney (what, really, is a kidney symbolic of?), but also regarding the extent to which the heart *shows up* to me, in illness and also in health. It is possible to direct one's attention to the activity of one's heart at any time, and in situations that make us react strongly emotionally it is almost impossible *not* to notice one's heart pounding in association with other bodily processes, such as blushing or sweating. In exercise, the heart (together with the rest of the body, of course) sets the limit for what we are able to accomplish, and these limits are clearly *felt* on the embodied level as intense heart and lung activity or pain and weakness of muscles when, for example, I run fast for a long time.

It is true that heart disease, just like kidney disease, does not always make itself known through the experience of pain in the heart itself; a heart attack is experienced as a chest pain radiating out through chest and arms, for example. But the possible irregularity in the rhythm of the heart's beating, which can be a powerful and frightening experience, nevertheless marks out the heart as a phenomenon that appears in a more singular manner than the kidney does, in at least some cases of heart disease.

Hearts have been transplanted since the late 1960s (the history of kidney transplantation dates back to the 1950s) (Tilney 2003). A heart transplant is a more dramatic and difficult operation than a kidney transplant, and it was not until the 1980s that surgical techniques and new immunosuppressive medications made it likely to survive more than a few days or weeks after having a heart transplant. To find a new heart for a dying patient is harder than finding a new kidney, for two simple reasons. Each person only has one heart, which makes living donation impossible. And hearts deteriorate much faster than kidneys outside the body, which means that there is a very limited window of opportunity to perform the transplant (kidneys last much longer if they are kept the right way). Hearts for donation will most often come from patients who have been put on ventilators as the result of accidents or sudden disease (stroke) and have then been declared brain dead while they are still connected to the machine that assists breathing and the circulation of blood that keeps the organs fresh.

In the early 1990s, the phenomenologist Jean-Luc Nancy underwent a heart transplant after a period of severe illness. He wrote about this event and the cancer that he subsequently suffered – probably as a result of the heavy dose of immunosuppressive medicine that post-transplantation patients have to take to prevent rejection of their grafts – in an essay, 'L'intrus', which was published in 2000 (Nancy 2008). Nancy's main figure for understanding the process he is undergoing is found in the essay's title (in English, 'The Intruder'):

> The intruder introduces himself forcefully, by surprise or ruse, not, in any case, by right or by being admitted beforehand. Something of the stranger has to intrude, or else he loses his strangeness. If he already has the right to enter and stay, if he is awaited and received, no part of him being unexpected or unwelcome, then he is not an intruder any more, but neither is he any longer a stranger. ... To welcome a stranger, moreover, is necessarily to experience his intrusion.
>
> *(Nancy 2008: 161)*

This way of conceptualizing the *intruder* (as a person, but also, as we will see, as a thing that intrudes in me, such as an organ) is very similar in structure to the analysis of bodily *alienation* in kidney disease and transplantation that we developed above and have generally found to be present in various cases of illness suffering throughout this book (not least the case of anorexia nervosa analysed in chapter three). When Nancy's analysis is coupled with the experience of illness and transplantation of the heart, the overlap becomes almost total:

> If my own heart was failing me, to what degree was it 'mine', my 'own' organ? Was it even an organ? For some years I had already felt a fluttering, some breaks in the rhythm, really not much of anything: not an organ, not the dark red muscular mass loaded with tubes that I now had to suddenly imagine. Not 'my heart' beating endlessly, hitherto as absent as the soles of my feet while walking. It became strange to me, intruding by defection: almost by rejection, if not by dejection. I had this heart at the tip of my tongue, like improper food. Rather like heartburn, but gently. A gentle sliding separated me from myself.
>
> *(Nancy 2008: 162–163)*

In comparison with the kidney failure experienced by Drakulić, we can see that the failing heart penetrates the experiences of Nancy to a far greater extent as regards the perception of the organ itself compared with the rest of his embodiment. But the alienation is also driven by the unique symbolic quality of the heart as the essence of life, goodness, and personal identity. Despite living in a scientific age, it is almost impossible to view the heart as a pure biological entity among others, as a 'pump' rather than the centre of our emotional life. The heart is loaded with meaning and identity; therefore the intruding heart (still his old one) separates him from himself.

A new heart (the transplanted heart) is certainly also an intruder, but it is an intruder that we would like to welcome. This is possible, however, only by 'experiencing his intrusion', as Nancy writes (2008: 161). This means the pains and plagues following the procedure of having the sternum cracked and the chest cut wide open in an operation that lasts several hours and during which the blood is circulated and oxygenated by a heart–lung machine. It also means suppressing the body's immune system to prevent it from attacking and rejecting the graft, something that will otherwise happen immediately after the operation or in due course. The graft is foreign, an 'intruder' in the body, which we have difficulties welcoming. But the immunosuppressive actions taken mean that other intruders (bacteria, viruses), lying dormant in the body or entering from outside, become a major threat. It also means that the regular outbreaks of uncontrolled cell division in the body, which are otherwise dealt with by the immune system, can now lead to cancer.

Nancy describes this multiple intrusion by organs, viruses, and cancerous cells, but also by medical technology and therapies. The latter make him *objectify* his own body – compare my analyses in chapters three and five – and in this way he becomes alienated from it in a way that aggravates the physical suffering:

> I end up being nothing more than a fine wire stretched from pain to pain and strangeness to strangeness. One attains a certain continuity through the

intrusions, a permanent regime of intrusion … This has always more or less been the life of the ill and the elderly: but that's just it, I am precisely not the one or the other. What cures me is what affects or infects me; what keeps me alive is what makes me age prematurely. My heart is twenty years younger than I, and the rest of my body is (at least) twelve years older than I.

(Nancy 2008: 169)

We all know what a heart or a kidney looks like; but it is still hard to imagine that *my* heart (or kidney) looks exactly like that right now when it is functioning within my body (Svenaeus 2010). The inner realm of the body is a messy, foreign zone with which we are rarely acquainted directly. It is foreign, despite being closest, because we have only a lived, subject-like experience of it and not, in addition to this, an object-like acquaintance, as in the case of my hand, which I can watch and touch from outside, or my face, which not only can be touched and watched in the mirror, but is also central for my subject-like appearance to others (Merleau-Ponty 2012).

Though both heart and kidney are hidden under the skin (visible only in the extreme situations of accidents, operations, and autopsies), the heart is 'mine' in a way that the kidney is not. This is probably due to the heart's being an organ that can be *felt* in its beating. Because of this, we consider the heart to be the *locus* of our feelings, a view that is upheld through a whole system of different bodily metaphors feeding our language with meaning (Lakoff and Johnson 2003). The heart is considered the heart (!) of selfhood and personality in many emotionally and culturally inter-nested ways, and therefore a heart transplant evokes questions of identity to a greater extent than a kidney transplant does.

Sharing organs in an embodied community

The donation of organs – living as well as dead donation – creates bonds between giver and receiver to a larger degree than we (the medical establishment) are currently ready to admit (Campbell 2009; Leder 2016; Sharp 2006). To acknowledge these more or less strong bonds in the bioethical analysis and debate, I think we would do better to describe and name the situations of organ donation as a form of *sharing* than as giving (or, indeed, selling) (Zeiler 2014). A person is sharing parts of himself rather than giving away his belongings in organ donation, because the parts that are transferred from one body to another are tied to the *existence* of the donor in one way or another. The organs are not belongings but parts of a person's embodiment, a lived bodily manner of existing in the world (Svenaeus 2016b). This does not mean that the receiver of a transplant, in standard cases such as living or dead kidney donation or in deceased donation of organs such as the heart, inherits parts of the donor's personality.

The identity issues involved in transplanting inner organs are better understood as giving rise to, or strengthening, bonds *between* persons than as transferring personality traits. When we share ourselves with others in donating organs we become connected in a way that resembles the way families are formed by way of procreation (Sharp 2006). The bonds in question are not entirely of the same type, certainly, but they represent forms of bodily *sharing* that tie people together in altruistic and *caring* ways. It is possible, certainly, to have children only in the interest of strengthening and widening one's own influence in the world, just as it is possible to 'donate' organs in exchange for money (the organ- and tissue-trade business), but in most (and laudable) cases the care felt and shown for the child or patient in need will contribute to non-selfish bonds being formed when body parts are shared.

The idea that we share organs in this way appears to be a promising alternative to the standard metaphors of gift, resource, or commodity in medical ethics (Zeiler 2014). Such an idea would be compatible with a *mandatory* consent (having to say yes or no) for all citizens of a society when they come of age, rather than having a voluntary consent – the body-as-gift metaphor – or a presumed consent – the body-as-resource metaphor – in place. It would be possible to opt out – to refuse to share one's organs when one is no longer in need of them – but not by way of neglecting to declare one's wishes. It is hardly reasonable or fair that persons who refuse to share just because they cannot be bothered to think about their own death should take advantage of other persons' organs when the supply is so limited. How to organize the mandatory consent procedure in practice and detail is a complicated issue, and the philosophical argument given above will not take us the whole way. Much depends on how health care in the society of mandatory consent is to be organized in terms of insurance and how to deal with cases of persons who refuse to state their views or want to change their minds for egoistic reasons. Nevertheless, the advantage of having a mandatory consent procedure, instead of the increasingly common assumed consent, in the case of dead organ donation is that this would force each and every person in a society to reflect upon and take a position on the relationship they have to their own-body and the bodies of others. Such an obligatory reflection procedure could also have positive effects in raising the numbers of living donations.

The idea of sharing our bodies though organ donation represents a view of justice that is founded on the empathy felt for suffering persons *in general*. Diseases fall upon us regardless of what we deserve, and the moral imperative must be to remedy this misfortune when we face suffering persons. The human embodied-vulnerable condition is the basic reason and responsibility for helping others in need, as we touched upon in the first two chapters of this book (MacIntyre 2001). In chapter four we explored the role of empathy in the clinical encounter and the way this feeling is embedded in a moral context guiding the actions of health-care professionals in attempting to help patients. Empathy, however, is not felt only *for* patients but also *by* patients in encountering the suffering of other persons. And everybody is, indeed, a potential patient in the sense of being a candidate for illness suffering in the near or distant future. Experiencing empathy for suffering persons in general, rather than for concrete others, is a kind of phenomenological border case, since it proceeds from an imaginative feeling about an unknown other supplied and informed by one's previous empathic encounters (Svenaeus 2015b). The sympathy and altruistic actions that could be the result of such empathy for mankind (and possibly for other suffering creatures as well) would at least incline the empathizer to solidarily share his organs, once he no longer needs them, with other persons.

The phenomenological view that we belong to our own bodies in a fundamental way, rather than the other way around, can work as an antidote to the influential organ–resource–commodity paradigm in contemporary bioethics (Leder 2016: chapter 8). The phenomenological account can deliver an argument explaining why body parts are not just another type of things to be traded but, rather, are fundamental parts of our self-being. We are born *as* a body coming from *another* body. The body makes our existence and appearance as persons possible, and it does so in a way that is related to how we depend on each other as finite human beings living in the world together. Rather than fearing that seeing parts of the human body as something more than useful biological material will create confusion and feelings of guilt in patients who receive new organs, health-care professionals would do better to acknowledge the bonds that are being created between people through organ transplantation, including cases of posthumous transplantation. To survive one's own death in the sense of having one's organs still functioning in other persons is a powerful image of what solidary sharing can accomplish.

Very early, early, and narrative persons

What about the risks of instrumentalization and exploitation associated with an ideal and policy of sharing one's organs? Could it become mere rhetoric and a cover-up for taking advantage of vulnerable people in resourcifying or even commodifying (parts of) their bodies? Would some people – the poor and powerless – be supposed to share their organs even before they are dead because other, rich and powerful people are said to have better use of them? In the novel by Kazuo Ishiguro, *Never Let Me Go*, we witness a science fiction scenario of a society in which every member has a clone made in middle age to serve as an organ donor (2005). The clones are certainly killed during the procedure of procuring their organs – usually at the age of thirty or so – but this is called 'to complete', and the clones are raised in communal estates by guardians who indoctrinate them into the view that their noble purpose is to serve their originals by donating when the time comes. The novel is centred on the abuse of the gift metaphor in this context, but could it not just as well have been modelled on the idea that some should *share* because this is the meaning and purpose in (of) their lives?

The ideal of sharing organs could certainly be abused, but the idea that *everybody* should *share* seems less likely to support the view that *some* should *give* because it is their role and purpose as arguably inferior beings (the clones in Ishiguro's novel are no different from other human persons in their abilities to suffer or flourish). Sharing sits well with the idea that every human being is equal. Or, rather, it fits with the idea that every *person* is equal on the strength of having self-consciousness, language, memory, and an ability to plan her actions, as we defined this concept in chapter six (DeGrazia 2005: 3–7). Sharing could serve as an ideal for living donation when the operation is not dangerous or harmful for the donor (kidney donation), but it would certainly prove to be counterproductive in this context if we introduced something like a compulsory kidney lottery, similar to the one discussed above in the context of dead donation (Harris 2006). Sharing, as I imagine the metaphor and ethical command in the context of organ transplantation, would primarily be something that everybody in a society is expected to do *when they are no longer a person*, because all essential capacities necessary for personhood and *the experience of being alive* will be inevitably and permanently gone.

In the previous chapter we began the exploration of what moral status and protection-worthiness should be assigned to creatures of *Homo sapiens* (or other species) in their successive stages of development. The *in vitro* embryo was found to have a significantly weaker status than the implanted and/or gastrulated embryo, a judgement that allowed its use in certain types of medical activities that destroy it in the process – research activities that seek cures for severe human diseases. The implanted and gastrulated embryo is certainly not a person either, but it is a human creature (animal) that will standardly develop into an organism that offers the possibility for all characteristics of personhood to appear, if its life does not end before this happens (miscarriage or abortion). With the term 'standardly' I intend the exceptions of severe defects, injuries, or diseases, or severe deficiency in parental care. Anencephalic foetuses never become persons and neither did Kaspar Hauser (at least not in the full narrative sense; see below).

Let us call the implanted and gastrulated embryo a *pre-person*. It lacks the ability to feel, and it can only make its presence announced by way of medical technologies (early ultrasound scan was the example analysed in chapter six). The phenomenological perspective, giving priority to the experience of pregnancy, led to the view that a significant change in moral status appears around the standard weeks of quickening when the pregnant woman can first feel the presence of the foetus inside her (weeks 16–20). However, at this point in gestational time, the foetus is neither viable outside the womb nor sentient, capacities that evolve in weeks 22–24 and are highly significant from the point of view of moral status. Let us call the *experiencing* foetus a *very early person*. It has embodied experiences of being alive and feeling its various states to be pleasurable or painful (Bellieni 2012; Zahavi 2005: chapter 5). As surveyed in chapter six, this calls for a responsibility to protect the foetus from this stage onwards, provided it is not suffering from a defect, injury, or disease that will make its future life as a person *considerably* more painful and alienated than normal on the three related levels of suffering and flourishing that we identified in chapter two: embodiment, everyday actions, and core life-narrative values.

The next significant stage in the life of a foetus is the birth that makes it into a *baby*. As we have seen, this is the event that Jonas associates with the ethical appeal to shoulder responsibility for the child's vulnerable and dependent being

(1984: 131). To kill a baby with the kind of severe defects we went through in the previous chapter – Edwards syndrome, muscular dystrophy, cystic fibrosis, or Tay-Sachs disease – is clearly a different thing than performing a late abortion of a foetus suffering from such disorders. The first act is rarely, if ever, permissible (we are discussing mercy *killing* here, not the withholding of life support); the second is sometimes even advisable. Birth is significant from an ethical point of view because the baby *presents* itself to the world – that is, to the persons who are there to take care of it – and this ushers in a different kind of responsibility than the foetus in the womb is capable of appealing for. Through birth the baby becomes, to use a metaphor found in the work of Emmanuel Levinas, a very early person with a *face* (Levinas 1991). To have a face in this context does not only mean to have the physical characteristics of eyes, nose, and mouth in place, it means that the child expresses a vulnerable, personal being by way of how it looks, sounds, feels, smells, and so on.

However, from the point of view of development of personhood, physical birth is not the next decisive event in the life of the foetus/baby after becoming sentient. This is, rather, the event that is sometimes called 'psychological birth': the child's opening to the world around it, and, most significantly, the communicative expressions and responses offered in face-to-face interaction with the parents (or other care persons) (Rochat 2009: 69). This is called the 'two-month revolution' in the development of the baby, and it shows that around this age the baby is not only experiencing basic feelings but is also entering the shared, intersubjective realm of a being-in-the-world (Rochat 2009: 67–78). Let us call the six-week-old baby an *early person*, who is now sharing the world with others and through successive developmental stages will become aware of things and persons in the world around him, and also of himself as an embodied creature capable of acting and expressing his wishes.

The next decisive step – I am certainly skipping most of the details in this sketchy overview – from the perspective of personhood is the one associated with passing what is known as the 'mirror test' (Zahavi 2005: chapter 7). This usually commences around eighteen months of age and is supposed to prove that the child – or animal other than *Homo sapiens* – is aware of himself in a *reflective* way (Rochat 2009: chapter 5). The test consists in putting the child in front of a mirror, but first, without the child's awareness, marking its forehead with a clearly visible dot or sticker. Before the age of eighteen months (roughly) the child will point towards the dot or sticker seen in the mirror; after eighteen months it will put its hand on its own forehead, realizing that the child in the mirror reflection is identical with itself.

Philippe Rochat, the well-known child developmental psychologist to whose path-breaking work, *Others in Mind: Social Origins of Self-Consciousness*, I have already referred above, convincingly argues that the birth of self-consciousness in a child is not only a cognitive move but also, and more importantly, an emotional recognition of oneself as somebody being seen and evaluated *by others* (Rochat 2009). Reflective self-consciousness means that the child becomes aware of itself as a 'me' in the eyes of others in addition to a pre-reflectively experiencing 'I', and this first feeling of me-ness is most often a feeling of embarrassment or shame (Rochat 2009: chapter 6). Interestingly, animals other than humans that have been reported to pass the mirror test (e.g. primates, corvids, dolphins, elephants) do not as a rule express such social feelings (at least not in a way that we humans fully understand). Complex social emotions appear to be unique to humans (and possibly some other species of the great apes), and they show the extent to which we as persons are dependent upon a network of social relations that demand a moral sensitivity nurtured by these very feelings (de Waal 2006; Steinbock 2014).

From the age of one and a half years the child is thus a *person* (having passed the very early and early stages) being aware of itself in a world shared with others. This standardly includes some use of language and a rudimentary memory as well as the capacity to plan actions ahead, so we have all the characteristics usually associated with personhood in place (DeGrazia 2005: 3–7). However, the command of language and the understanding of social roles and moral obligations are still very primitive and limited in the second year of child's life. Over the next three years the language abilities and temporal understanding of the child will develop in substantial ways. This allows for the emergence at around four and a half of what we could call a *narrative person*, with a picture and story of herself in which judgements concerning matters in the three strong evaluative fields of moral rights and obligations, the contents of the good life, and self-respect in the eyes of others have begun to be formed (Rochat 2009: chapter 9; Taylor 1989: 4 ff.).

Only *Homo sapiens* has so far been seen to develop into a creature that becomes a narrative person, and this is certainly significant in taking a position on the moral obligations we have towards other animals (or other creatures). Many animals are clearly sentient, and many are also communicative and capable of intentional actions in the same way human babies are from the age of roughly six weeks. However, this hardly means that these animals have the same moral status as very early or early human persons, respectively, since they will never *become* persons by the definition provided above. Some animals do become persons – if they are capable of self-recognition and social emotions – but they still do not have the same moral status as human persons, since they will never develop into *narrative* persons.

Do human persons who will never become narrative persons, for the reason of defects, diseases, or injuries, have the same moral entitlements as other human persons, who either already are or will normally become narrative persons? Why do the respect we show such human beings and the rights we bestow on them differ from the moral respect we show other animals with similar person-capacities? What about early human persons who will not even become persons by the definition above? Why should their moral status be more demanding than the moral status of other animals? To offer an example: some dogs certainly display more characteristics of the early person, and possibly also person, than some severely mentally disabled children do. Yet the respect we show such children and the resources we invest to give them a decent life are very different from what we do in the case of dogs. Or, at least, this should be the case in what most of us take to be a morally decent society. Lest we give in to some form of crude utilitarianism, assessing a life worth living only from the perspective of pleasurable or painful experiences, or a fascist division of people into groups of individuals who are either worthy of living or not worthy of living, we should find some way to philosophically *justify* the different moral status we bestow on such dogs and children.

I do not want to pretend that the phenomenological approach would enable us to find a brand-new argument solving this bioethical dilemma, which has been on the agenda for a very long time and discussed in many different contexts (e.g. ethics of infanticide, animal ethics, and disability rights studies). Yet I think the best arguments found in these debates converge in acknowledging the scope of the shared meaningful human *world* that the infant is entering at around the age of six weeks and becoming a self-conscious member of at the age of eighteen months. We do not welcome other animals to this life world of social and narrative meaning patterns in the same way we do with babies, at least not standardly. And other animals that become capable of reflective self-understanding do not do so in the *human way*, but according to meaning patterns that are peculiar to their species – to the ways they become 'enworlded' together as a group. The respect we show and the moral status we ascribe to humans who are very early persons, early persons, and persons, respectively, in comparison with other animals that enter these categories, is ultimately a respect for the complexity of the human life world as such in comparison with the situation of other animals. As touched upon in chapter two, some animals undoubtedly have a life world in the phenomenological sense, or even a primitive form of culture, as in the case of chimpanzees (de Waal 2006). But no animals other than humans come close to the complexity and sophistication displayed by the meaning patterns found in the world of narrative persons (Arendt 1998). If this way of ethically distinguishing between human and non-human animals is a case of 'speciesism', at least it is speciesism by way of culture and not by way of nature (DNA).

Late, very late, and post-persons

Having considered early person matters let us return to the main topic of this chapter: matters surrounding the death of human beings. Analogously to the way persons come into being they can also, in some cases, gradually disappear. Alzheimer's is a chronic neurodegenerative disease that usually starts slowly and gets worse over time. It is the major cause of dementia, which may also be caused by other diseases and injuries that affect the brain, such as stroke (WHO 2016a). At least 47.5 million people suffer from dementia, and there are 7.7 million new cases in the world each year. Dementia is a syndrome – most often of a chronic and progressive nature – in which there is deterioration in cognitive function beyond what might be expected from normal ageing. It affects memory, thinking, orientation, comprehension, calculation, learning capacity, language, and judgement. Consciousness is not affected. The impairment in cognitive function is commonly accompanied, and occasionally preceded, by deterioration in emotional control, social behaviour, or motivation.

In the early stage of dementia, the person suffers from symptoms such as forgetfulness, losing track of time, and getting lost in familiar places (symptoms that in milder forms are certainly part of normal ageing and might therefore go undetected or, alternatively, lead to false positives). In the middle stage, the person may become forgetful of recent events and people's names, get lost in her home environment, have difficulties finding the right words, need help with personal care, and go through behavioural changes. In the late stage, the person becomes unaware of time and place, has difficulties recognizing family members and close friends, becomes unable to take care of basic needs such as eating, dressing, and going to the toilet, loses the ability to walk, and may suffer personality change (WHO 2016a). Alzheimer's disease and most other forms of dementia lead to death. In the last stage, the patients are most often bedridden, conscious, and able to respond to verbal or non-verbal address, but are totally bereft of cognitive understanding of who they are and what is going on around them.

Dying from Alzheimer's, or dementia by another cause, is a cruel death, not least for relatives and close friends of the patient, but it is also an interesting process for phenomenological studies of personhood. It appears that in the case of going through the different stages of gradually progressing dementia we have a kind of mirror image of the gradual appearance of an early person, person, and narrative person in infancy and childhood. The early and middle stages of dementia correspond to the gradual appearance of (in the case of dementia, the gradual disappearance of) the narrative person. In the late and last stages we witness the person deteriorating gradually towards the form of early personhood that comes into being about six weeks after birth (the psychological birth of the baby) or even the very early forms preceding this event in which the baby or foetus is conscious and able to feel good or bad but nothing much beyond this. The stages that the Alzheimer's patient goes through in suffering and dying from this terrible disease we could call the stages of a *person* with a gradually deteriorating narrative, a *late person*, and, in some cases, a *very late person*, corresponding to person (eighteen months after birth), early person (six weeks after birth), and very early person (weeks 22–24 gestational time). Beyond this we have the stages of permanent coma and brain death discussed above that would be the equivalent to what we named the life of a pre-person in the womb. Let us call such permanently comatose and brain-dead patients *post-persons*.

Do late persons have the same moral status as early persons, very late persons the same moral status as very early persons, and post-persons the same moral status as pre-persons? Should we, in each case, treat them in the same way with regard to dignity, protection-worthiness, human rights, and the like? No, this does not follow, since we are, in the cases of persons affected by dementia in gradually progressing stages and post-persons, dealing with beings who are completing, rather than beginning, their life narratives. The manner in which we relate to these human beings and treat them must reflect this temporal and narrative structure that is characteristic of a human life when thought about and reflected upon (Ricoeur 1992: chapter 6). We treasure a two-month-old baby, not only for who she already is, but also for who she will *become* together with us. We love and respect a severely demented person, not only for who he is, but also for who he has *been*. Yet there are some lessons to be learned from the comparisons. Post-persons are no longer persons, but they are still *living human beings*, just as the implanted-gastrulated embryo and the early foetus are. The legal implementation of the concept of brain death reflects the practical concern that the post-person is, indeed, no longer a person. Permanently comatose patients are also post-persons, the main differences distinguishing these patients from the brain dead being the continuation of brain stem functionality for breathing and the difficulties of establishing beyond all doubt that they will never regain consciousness again.

What relationship holds between the living body of a human animal and the person that she will become, is, or was? The biological functions of the living body – significantly, the activities going on in the brain – constitute the possibility for personhood to appear. However, as I have argued throughout this book, the person is not a brain, but an embodied way of being-in-the-world together with others, staging self-understanding in the manner of a life narrative. David DeGrazia, in his impressive study *Human Identity and Bioethics*, to which I have referred many times above, argues that we must *either* be human animals *or* persons (DeGrazia 2005: chapter 2). We cannot essentially be both, since some human animals are clearly not persons (embryos and permanently comatose patients), and some persons are not human (other animals, possibly even artificially intelligent computers). I think this is a too-hastily drawn conclusion which fails to take into account the significance of the two different perspectives I have continually stressed and used throughout this book: the first-person perspective (including the second-person perspective) and the third- (or rather non-) person perspective. From the third-person perspective of science all living human beings are biological organisms (animals). Some such organisms reach a stage of complexity and sophistication that allows for the first-person, experiential perspective to occur. The person that develops from the very early and early stages of personhood towards the stage of having a full narrative does so by way of being introduced to a shared world in which the second-person perspective is primary and in which the third-person perspective has historically arisen as a way of scientifically engaging in explanations of why things in the world work as they do (including the human organism) (Svenaeus 2013b).

I thus propose a view that is similar to the one put forward by Lynne Rudder Baker in her study *Persons and Bodies: A Constitution View*: persons are constituted (meaning 'made possible') by their biological organisms (Baker 2000: chapter 8). This means that persons neither die nor are born in the physical sense; instead, they come to and go out of existence more or less gradually depending on the states of the biological organisms that constitute their beings. Biological organisms are internally organized things that resist entropy and reproduce using energy from their environment (Jonas 1966; Silver 1997). This means that individual human animals – which are one species of such creatures – come to life when the embryo is created (minus a couple of weeks to make sure that no split or fusion into or with other embryos occur; see chapter six) and die when the organism has broken down (i.e. is no longer internally organized and resisting entropy). Baker holds that only creatures that have achieved the level of what I have called narrative persons are persons, whereas I have given priority to an experiential first-person perspective without denying the significant steps taken when very early persons turn into early persons, persons, and narrative persons, respectively (or when narrative persons turn into persons, late persons, and very late persons, respectively) (Baker 2000: chapter 4).

The consequence of such a phenomenological view is that neither the brain-dead nor the permanently comatose patient is dead. But they are not persons, not even late or very late persons, anymore, since they are permanently non-conscious, lacking the *experiences* that are necessary for the first-person perspective to exist. What the philosophers, doctors, and politicians implementing the concept of brain death are trying to say is that the *person* is gone if the biological organism has reached a stage in which the brain has ceased to function entirely. This is right, but from the third-person, scientific perspective in which questions about *death* ought to be settled they are all wrong: the living body that once constituted the persistence of a person is not dead; it is, rather, fatally damaged and being kept *alive* with the help of medical technology (DeGrazia 2005: chapter 4; Younger 2007).

The relationship between a human living body and the person that, under certain circumstances, it makes possible is similar to the one that holds between disease and illness (see chapter three). Biological organisms become diseased, but only persons are ill and suffering – that is, experiencing their way of existing in an alienating mood (see chapter two). When we say that a biological organism – say, a worm or a brain-dead human being – *suffers* from a disease, we are using this word in a metaphorical sense. And when we say that a person has *died*, what we really mean is that the biological organism that once constituted his existence is no longer capable of doing so.

As we explored in chapter four, terminally ill persons do not die only in the sense of their bodies gradually ceasing to function; they are also experiencing a *being-towards-death* that is intensified and made acute by the ways they suffer (Aho 2016; Heidegger 1996: 235 ff.). This being-towards-death is enacted on the levels of lived embodiment, being-in-the-world with others, and identification of core life-narrative values. When a person has died and left behind a corpse she is no longer there. Yet the persons who are left behind are still *with* her, and they treat the dead body as something which is connected to the person it once constituted: they grieve over it, bury it (in some way), and erect a stone (or something similar) to keep the person in their memories (and in the memories of other people still to come) (Heidegger 1996: 238; Sartre 1992: 456–458).

What about post-persons in this regard? Are we with the permanently comatose (including the brain dead) in a more substantial, different sense than is the case with corpses? In many cases we feel that we are, because their still-living bodies appear to *express* the presence of a person in a way a corpse does not usually do. The presence of the permanently comatose (and possibly of some corpses, too) is *uncanny* to us in this regard, as their living bodies appear to be *lived* by a person who is gone (Freud 1959). But they are not, really, having experiences in such a way, and to the extent that doctors are able to judge with absolute confidence that these living bodies will never regain consciousness again, we do best in viewing the post-person as an anticipatory corpse.

Could we be *with* such bodies in a way that allows us to treat them with dignity: honour them, grieve for them, and still transplant their organs once we have turned off the ventilator and other medical equipment that keeps them alive? I believe this is possible, but to avoid instrumentalization, the treatment of such bodies must be governed by a respect for the persons and life narratives that they previously made possible. If we insist on giving priority to a medical-scientific or liberal-economic perspective on them and neglect to honour the shared being-in-the-world that they are still related to, resourcification and/or commodification lurk around the corner.

Summary

Persons may apparently survive their own death in two related manners: their bodies can be still alive although they are no longer embodying them (brain death and permanent coma) and the organs of their bodies can continue to function in the bodies of others, if transplanted, although their own bodies have ceased to function. We must distinguish between the biological organism (human animal) and the person that, at a certain stage of developmental complexity, it makes possible. Biological organisms are created and die, whereas persons come into existence as very early persons (sentience and viability at weeks 22–24 gestational time), early persons (psychological birth at about six weeks), persons (self-understanding at about eighteen months), and full narrative persons (around four and half years of age), and go out of existence suddenly (if the biological organism suddenly dies) or gradually (if the biological organism is breaking down due to diseases or injuries in a more gradual manner), passing through the possible stages of late, very late, and post-personhood.

The phenomenological analysis of personhood as embodied being-in-the-world staged in the form of a narrative together with other persons, heeding certain core life values, leads to an emphasis on the human body not as a property but as a thing constitutive of our very being. We belong to our bodies rather than the other way around, and the lived body is our fundamental way of feeling alive, expressing ourselves, responding to the expressions of others, and sharing a world with them through action and communication. We suffer due to our vulnerable bodies and the vulnerable relations we form with other vulnerable persons through our being-in-the-world. The suffering of other persons (including early and late persons) ushers in a responsibility to take care of them when they present themselves to us in vulnerable conditions. Empathy with particular other persons transforms into a general empathy for unknown others with regard to the possibilities of solidary sharing not only our worldly belongings but also parts of our bodies, if we are no longer in need of them and this can be done without violating the dignity of the person whose body it once was.

Coming to be in need of an organ transplant means going through a suffering process of alienation that concerns the person's embodiment, being-in-the-world, and core life-narrative values. Such a feeling of otherness in relation to the own-body can be healed by receiving a foreign organ that may become homelike due to the shared bodily nature of human beings. The dangers of instrumentalization in cases of retrieving organs and cells of the human body to help persons in need may be kept in check by making sure that parts of (pre- or post-) persons' bodies do not become resources or commodities but stay life-giving, person-constituting parts shared between persons.

REFERENCES

Agamben, G. 1998. *Homo Sacer: Sovereign Power and Bare Life*. Trans. D. Heller-Roazen. Stanford: Stanford University Press.

Agar, N. 2004. *Liberal Eugenics: In Defence of Human Enhancement*. Oxford: Blackwell.

———— 2013. *Truly Human Enhancement: A Philosophical Defense of Limits*. Cambridge, MA: MIT Press.

Ahlzén, R. 2002. The Doctor and the Literary Text – Potentials and Pitfalls. *Medicine, Health Care and Philosophy* 5(2): 147–155.

Ahmed, S. 2006. *Queer Phenomenology: Orientations, Objects, Others*. Durham, NC: Duke University Press.

Aho, J., and K. Aho. 2008. *Body Matters: A Phenomenology of Sickness, Disease, and Illness*. Lanham, MD: Lexington Books.

Aho, K. 2016. Heidegger, Ontological Death, and the Healing Professions. *Medicine, Health Care and Philosophy* 19(1): 55–63.

Arendt, H. 1998. *The Human Condition*. Chicago: Chicago University Press.

———— 2006. *Eichmann in Jerusalem: A Report on the Banality of Evil*. London: Penguin Classics.

Aristotle 2002. *Nicomachean Ethics*. Trans. C. Rowe. Oxford: Oxford University Press.

Arras, J. 2007. The Way We Reason Now: Reflective Equilibrium in Bioethics. In B. Steinbock, ed., *The Oxford Handbook of Bioethics*, 46–71. Oxford: Oxford University Press.

Baker, L. R. 2000. *Persons and Bodies: A Constitution View*. Cambridge: Cambridge University Press.

Battaly, H. D. 2011. Is Empathy a Virtue? In A. Coplan and P. Goldie, eds., *Empathy: Philosophical and Psychological Perspectives*, 277–301. Oxford: Oxford University Press.

Bauby, J.-D. 1998. *The Diving Bell and the Butterfly: A Memoir of Life in Death*. Trans. J. Leggatt. New York: Vintage Books.

Beauchamp, T. L., and J. F. Childress. 2013. *Principles of Biomedical Ethics*, 7th ed. Oxford: Oxford University Press.

Bellieni, C. V. 2012. Pain Assessment in Human Fetus and Infants. *The AAPS Journal* 14(3): 456–461.

Berti, E. 2003. The Reception of Aristotle's Intellectual Virtues in Gadamer and the Hermeneutic Philosophy. In R. Pozzo, ed., *The Impact of Aristotelianism on Modern Philosophy*, 285–300. Washington, DC: Catholic University of America Press.

Birnbacher, D., and E. Dahl, eds. 2008. *Giving Death a Helping Hand: Physician-Assisted Suicide and Public Policy. An International Perspective*. Dordrecht: Springer.

Bishop, J. 2011. *The Anticipatory Corpse: Medicine, Power, and the Care of the Dying*. Notre Dame, IN: University of Notre Dame Press.

Boorse, C. 1997. A Rebuttal on Health. In J. Humber and R. Almeder, eds., *What is Disease?*, 1–134. Totowa, NJ: Humana Press.

Bordo, S. 2003. *Unbearable Weight: Feminism, Western Culture, and the Body*. Berkeley: University of California Press.

Borgmann, A. 2005. Technology. In H. Dreyfus and M. Wrathall, eds., *A Companion to Heidegger*, 420–432. Oxford: Blackwell.

Bornemark, J. 2015. Life Beyond Individuality: A-subjective Experience in Pregnancy. In J. Bornemark and N. Smith, eds., *Phenomenology of Pregnancy*, 251–278. Huddinge: Södertörn Philosophical Studies.

Bowden, H. 2012. A Phenomenological Study of Anorexia Nervosa. *Philosophy, Psychiatry, & Psychology* 19(3): 227–241.

Brassington, I. 2007. On Heidegger, Medicine, and the Modernity of Modern Medical Technology. *Medicine, Health Care and Philosophy* 10(2): 185–195.

Braude, H. D. 2012. Affecting the Body and Transforming Desire: The Treatment of Suffering as the End of Medicine. *Philosophy, Psychiatry, & Psychology* 19(4): 265–278.

Brevini, T. A. L., and G. Pennarossa. 2013. *Gametogenesis, Early Embryo Development and Stem Cell Derivation*. Dordrecht: Springer.

Brown, M. T. 2007. The Potential of the Human Embryo. *Journal of Medicine and Philosophy* 32(6): 585–618.

Buchanan, A., D. W. Brock, N. Daniels, and D. Wikler. 2000. *From Chance to Choice: Genetics and Justice*. Cambridge: Cambridge University Press.

Bulik, C. M. 2005. Exploring the Gene–Environment Nexus in Eating Disorders. *Journal of Psychiatry & Neuroscience* 30(5): 335–339.

Campbell, A. V. 2009. *The Body in Bioethics*. London: Routledge.

Camus, A. 1960. *The Plague*. Trans. R. Buss. London: Penguin.

Canavero, S. 2013. HEAVEN: The Head Anastomosis Venture Project Outline for the First Human Head Transplantation with Spinal Linkage (GEMINI). *Surgical Neurology International* 4 (Suppl.): S335–S342.

Canguilhem, G. 1991. *The Normal and the Pathological*. Trans. C. R. Fawcett and R. S. Cohen. New York: Zone Books.

Carel H. 2008. *Illness: The Cry of the Flesh*. Stocksfield, UK: Acumen.

———2013. Bodily Doubt. *Journal of Consciousness Studies* 20(7–8): 178–197.

——— and I. J. Kidd. 2014. Epistemic Injustice in Healthcare: A Philosophical Analysis. *Medicine, Health Care and Philosophy* 17(4): 529–540.

Carrithers, M., S. Collins, and S. Lukes, eds. 1985. *The Category of the Person: Anthropology, Philosophy, History*. Cambridge: Cambridge University Press.

Cassell, E. J. 2004. *The Nature of Suffering and the Goals of Medicine*, 2nd ed. Oxford: Oxford University Press.

Charon, R. 2006. *Narrative Medicine: Honoring the Stories of Illness*. Oxford: Oxford University Press.

Chiurazzi, G. 2012. *Pathei Mathos:* The Political-Cognitive Value of Suffering. In J. Malpas and N. Lickiss, eds., *Perspectives on Human Suffering*, 23–32. Dordrecht: Springer.

Cholbi, M., and J. Varelius, eds. 2015. *New Directions in the Ethics of Assisted Suicide and Euthanasia*. Dordrecht: Springer.

Colombetti, G. 2014. *The Feeling Body: Affective Science Meets the Enactive Mind*. Cambridge, MA: MIT Press.

Conrad, P. 2007. *The Medicalization of Society: On the Transformation of Human Conditions into Treatable Disorders*. Baltimore, MD: Johns Hopkins University Press.

Cooper, M., and C. Waldby. 2014. *Clinical Labor: Tissue Donors and Research Subjects in the Global Bioeconomy*. Durham, NC: Duke University Press.

Coplan, A., and P. Goldie, eds. 2011. *Empathy: Philosophical and Psychological Perspectives*. Oxford: Oxford University Press.

Damasio, A. R. 1999. *The Feeling of What Happens: Body and Emotion in the Making of Consciousness*. New York: Harcourt Brace.

Decety, J., ed. 2012. *Empathy: From Bench to Bedside*. Cambridge, MA: MIT Press.

DeGrazia, D. 2005. *Human Identity and Bioethics*. Cambridge: Cambridge University Press.

———— 2012. *Creation Ethics: Reproduction, Genetics, and Quality of Life*. Oxford: Oxford University Press.

Derrida, J. 1978. *Writing and Difference*. Trans. A. Bass. Chicago: University of Chicago Press.

Devisch, I. 2013. *Jean-Luc Nancy and the Question of Community*. London: Bloomsbury.

Devolder, K. 2015. *The Ethics of Embryonic Stem Cell Research*. Oxford: Oxford University Press.

de Waal, F. B. M. 2006. *Primates and Philosophers: How Morality Evolved*. Princeton, NJ: Princeton University Press.

Diprose, R. 2002. *Corporeal Generosity: On Giving with Nietzsche, Merleau-Ponty, and Levinas*. Albany: State University of New York Press.

Dondorp, W. J., G. C. Page-Christiaens, and G. M. de Wert. 2016. Genomic Futures of Prenatal Screening: Ethical Reflection. *Clinical Genetics* 89(5): 531–538.

Downie, R. S., and J. Macnaughton. 2007. *Bioethics and the Humanities: Attitudes and Perceptions*. London: Routledge.

Drakulić, S. 1993. *Holograms of Fear*. Trans. E. Elias-Barsaic and S. Drakulić. London: Women's Press.

Drummond, J. J., and L. Embree, eds. 2002. *Phenomenological Approaches to Moral Philosophy: A Handbook*. Dordrecht: Kluwer.

DSM-5. 2013. *Diagnostic and Statistical Manual of Mental Disorders*. Washington, DC: American Psychiatric Association.

Dunne, J. 1997. *Back to the Rough Ground: Practical Judgment and the Lure of Technique*. Notre Dame, IN: University of Notre Dame Press.

Dworkin, R. 1994. *Life's Dominion: An Argument About Abortion, Euthanasia, and Individual Freedom*. New York: Vintage Books.

Edemariam, A. 2007. Against All Odds, *The Guardian*, 21 February, www.theguardian.com/society/2007/feb/21/health.lifeandhealth.

Elliott, C. 1999. *Bioethics, Culture and Identity: A Philosophical Disease*. London: Routledge.

———— 2003. *Better than Well: American Medicine Meets the American Dream*. New York: Norton & Company.

———— 2010. *White Coat, Black Hat: Adventures on the Dark Side of Medicine*. New York: Beacon Press.

———— and T. Chambers, eds. 2004. *Prozac as a Way of Life*. Chapel Hill, NC: University of North Carolina Press.

Engelhardt, H. T. 1996. *The Foundations of Bioethics*. New York: Oxford University Press.

Erin, C. A., and J. Harris. 2003. An Ethical Market in Human Organs. *Journal of Medical Ethics* 29(3): 137–138.

Fallon, P., M. A. Katzman, and S. C. Wooley, eds. 1994. *Feminist Perspectives on Eating Disorders*. New York: Guilford Press.

Fielding, H. A. 2001. The Finitude of Nature: Rethinking the Ethics of Biotechnology. *Medicine, Health Care and Philosophy* 4(3): 327–334.

Figal, G. 1995. *Phronesis* as Understanding: Situating Philosophical Hermeneutics. In L. K. Schmidt, ed., *The Specter of Relativism: Truth, Dialogue, and Phronesis in Philosophical Hermeneutics*. Evanston, IL: Northwestern University Press.

Foltz, B. V. 1995. *Inhabiting the Earth: Heidegger, Environmental Ethics, and the Metaphysics of Nature*. New York: Humanity Books.

Foucault, M. 1990. *A History of Sexuality, Vol. 1: An Introduction*. Trans. R. Hurley. New York: Random House.

Frank, A. W. 1995. *The Wounded Storyteller: Body, Illness, and Ethics*. Chicago: Chicago University Press.

——— 2002. *At the Will of the Body: Reflections on Illness*. Boston: Houghton Mifflin.

Frankl, V. E. 1986. *The Doctor and the Soul: From Psychotherapy to Logotherapy*. New York: Vintage Books.

Freeman, L. 2014. Toward a Phenomenology of Mood. *The Southern Journal of Philosophy* 52(4): 445–476.

Freud, S. 1959. The Uncanny. In *Collected Papers*, vol. 4, 368–407. Trans. Joan Riviere. New York: Basic Books.

Fuchs, T. 2000. *Psychopathologie von Leib und Raum: Phänomenologisch-empirische Untersuchungen zu depressiven und paranoiden Erkrankungen*. Darmstadt: Steinkopff Verlag.

——— 2003. The Phenomenology of Shame, Guilt and the Body in Body Dysmorphic Disorder and Depression. *Journal of Phenomenological Psychology* 33(2): 223–243.

Fulford, K. W. M. 1989. *Moral Theory and Medical Practice*. Cambridge: Cambridge University Press.

Gadamer, H.-G. 1977. *Philosophische Lehrjahre: Eine Rückschau*. Frankfurt am Main: Suhrkamp Verlag.

——— 1994. *Truth and Method*. Trans. J. Weinsheimer and D. G. Marshall. New York: Continuum.

——— 1996. *The Enigma of Health: The Art of Healing in a Scientific Age*. Trans. J. Gaiger and N. Walker. Stanford, CA: Stanford University Press.

——— 1998. *Aristoteles, Nikomachische Ethik VI: Herausgegeben und übersetzt von Hans-Georg Gadamer*. Frankfurt am Main: V. Klostermann.

Gallagher, J. 2014. First Womb-Transplant Baby Born, *BBC News*, 4 October, www.bbc.com/news/health-29485996.

Gallagher, S. 2005. *How the Body Shapes the Mind*. Oxford: Oxford University Press.

———, ed. 2011. *The Oxford Handbook of the Self*. Oxford: Oxford University Press.

Gawande, A. 2014. *Being Mortal: Illness, Medicine and What Matters in the End*. London: Profile Books.

Goldie, P. 2000. *The Emotions: A Philosophical Exploration*. Oxford: Oxford University Press.

——— 2012. *The Mess Inside: Narrative, Emotion, and the Mind*. Oxford: Oxford University Press.

Gómez-Lobo, A. 2004. Does Respect for Embryos Entail Respect for Gametes? *Theoretical Medicine and Bioethics* 25(3): 199–208.

Gordijn, B., and R. Chadwick, eds. 2008. *Medical Enhancement and Posthumanity*. Dordrecht: Springer.

Gordon, O. 2015. Living with Down's Syndrome: 'He's not a list of characteristics. He's my son', *The Guardian*, 17 October, www.theguardian.com/society/2015/oct/17/living-with-downs-syndrome-hes-not-list-characteristics.

Green, R. M., and N. J. Palpant, eds. 2014. *Suffering and Bioethics*. Oxford: Oxford University Press.

Guignon, C. 2004. *On Being Authentic*. London: Routledge.

Gunnarson, M. 2016. *Please be Patient: A Cultural Phenomenological Study of Haemodialysis and Kidney Transplantation Care*. Lund: Lund Studies in Arts and Cultural Sciences.

Gustafsson, L. 1990. *The Death of a Beekeeper*. Trans. J. K. Swaffar and G. H. Weber. London: Collins Harvill.

Habermas, J. 1971. *Hermeneutik und Ideologiekritik*. Frankfurt am Main: Suhrkamp Verlag.

———— 2003. *The Future of Human Nature*. Trans. W. Rehg, M. Pensky, and H. Beister. Cambridge: Polity.

Halpern, J. 2001. *From Detached Concern to Empathy: Humanizing Medical Practice*. New York: Oxford University Press.

Halse, C., A. Honey, and D. Boughtwood. 2008. *Inside Anorexia: The Experiences of Girls and their Families*. London: Jessica Kingsley.

Harris, J. 2006. The Survival Lottery. In H. Kushe and P. Singer, eds., *Bioethics: An Anthology*, 2nd ed., 491–496. Oxford: Blackwell.

———— 2007. *Enhancing Evolution: The Ethical Case of Making Better People*. Princeton, NJ: Princeton University Press.

Hatab, L. J. 2000. *Ethics and Finitude: Heideggerian Contributions to Moral Philosophy*. Oxford: Rowman & Littlefield.

Hauskeller, M. 2013. *Better Humans? Understanding the Enhancement Project*. Durham, NC: Acumen Publishing.

Healy, D. 1999. *The Antidepressant Era*. Cambridge, MA: Harvard University Press.

Heidegger, M. 1977. *The Question Concerning Technology and Other Essays*. Trans. W. Lovitt. New York: Harper & Row.

———— 1978. Das Ding. In *Vorträge und Aufsätze*. Pfullingen: Neske.

———— 1996. *Being and Time*. Trans. J. Stambaugh. Albany: State University of New York Press (page references are to the German original found in the margins of the English translation).

———— 2001. *Zollikon Seminars: Protocols—Conversations—Letters*. Trans. F. Mayr and R. Askazy. Evanston, IL: Northwestern University Press (page references are to the German original found in the margins of the English translation).

Hickey, F., E. Hickey, and K. L. Summar. 2012. Medical Update for Children with Down Syndrome for the Pediatrician and Family Practitioner. *Advances in Pediatrics* 59(1): 137–157.

Hodge, J. 1995. *Heidegger and Ethics*. London: Routledge.

Horwitz, A. V., and J. C. Wakefield. 2007. *The Loss of Sadness: How Psychiatry Transformed Normal Sorrow into Depressive Disorder*. New York: Oxford University Press.

Hursthouse, R. 1999. *On Virtue Ethics*. Oxford: Oxford University Press.

Huxley, A. 2006. *Brave New World*. New York: HarperCollins.

Hyun, I., A. Wilkerson, and J. Johnston. 2016. Revisit the 14-Day Rule. *Nature* 533: 169–171.

Ihde, D. 2010. *Heidegger's Technologies: Postphenomenological Perspectives*. New York: Fordham University Press.

Ishiguro, K. 2005. *Never Let Me Go*. New York: Random House.

Jaspers, K. 1997. *General Psychopathology*, 2 vols. Trans. J. Hoenig and M. W. Hamilton. Baltimore, MD: Johns Hopkins University Press.

Jonas, H. 1966. *The Phenomenon of Life*. New York: Harper & Row.

———— 1984. *The Imperative of Responsibility: In Search for an Ethics for the Technological Age*. Chicago: Chicago University Press.

———— 1987. *Technik, Medizin und Ethik*. Frankfurt am Main: Suhrkamp Verlag.

Jones Pellach, P. 2012. The Suffering of Job: He is Every Person and No-One. In J. Malpas and N. Lickiss, eds., *Perspectives on Human Suffering*, 99–112. Dordrecht: Springer.

Jonsen, A. R. 1998. *The Birth of Bioethics*. Oxford: Oxford University Press.

Kaufman, S. R. 2006. *…And a Time to Die: How American Hospitals Shape the End of Life*. Chicago: University of Chicago Press.

Kierkegaard, S. 1997. The Joy of It: That One Suffers Only Once but Is Victorious Eternally. In *Christian Discourses: The Crisis and a Crisis in the Life of an Actress*, 95–105. Trans. H. Hong and E. Hong. Princeton, NJ: Princeton University Press.

Krakauer, E. L. 1998. Prescriptions: Autonomy, Humanism and the Purpose of Health Technology. *Theoretical Medicine and Bioethics* 19(6): 525–545.

Kramer, P. 1994. *Listening to Prozac*. London: Fourth Estate.

Lakoff, G., and M. Johnson. 2003. *Metaphors We Live By*, 2nd ed. Chicago: University of Chicago Press.

Leder, D. 1990. *The Absent Body*. Chicago: University of Chicago Press.

———— 2016. *The Distressed Body: Rethinking Illness, Imprisonment, and Healing*. Chicago: University of Chicago Press.

Levinas, E. 1991. *Totality and Infinity*. Trans. A. Lingis. Dordrecht: Kluwer.

———— 1998. Useless Suffering. In *Entre nous: On Thinking-of-the-Other*, 91–101. Trans. M. B. Smith and B. Harshav. New York: Columbia University Press.

Liang, P., Y. Xu, X. Zhang, C. Ding, et al. 2015. CRISPR/Cas9-mediated Gene Editing in Human Tripronuclear Zygotes. *Protein and Cell* 6(5): 363–372.

Liljefors, M., S. Lundin, and A. Wiszmeg, eds. 2012. *The Atomized Body: The Cultural Life of Stem Cells, Genes and Neurons*. Lund: Nordic Academic Press.

Lindemann, N. H., ed. 1997. *Stories and Their Limits: Narrative Approaches to Bioethics*. London: Routledge.

Lock, M. 2002. *Twice Dead: Organ Transplants and the Reinvention of Death*. Berkeley: University of California Press.

Locke, J. 1980. *Second Treatise of Government*. Indianapolis, IN: Hackett Publishing.

Lundin, S. 2015. *Organs for Sale: An Ethnographic Examination of the International Organ Trade*. Trans. A. Cleaves. New York: Palgrave Macmillan.

MacIntyre, A. 1985. *After Virtue: A Study in Moral Theory*. London: Duckworth.

———— 2001. *Dependent Rational Animals: Why Human Beings Need the Virtues*. Chicago: Open Court.

Mackenzie, C. 1992. Abortion and Embodiment. *Australian Journal of Philosophy* 70(2): 136–155.

———— and N. Stoljar, eds. 2000. *Relational Autonomy: Feminist Perspectives on Autonomy, Agency, and the Social Self*. Oxford: Oxford University Press.

————, W. Rogers, and S. Dodd, eds. 2014. *Vulnerability: New Essays in Ethics and Feminist Philosophy*. Oxford: Oxford University Press.

Madison, G. B. 2013. *On Suffering: Philosophical Reflections on What It Means to Be Human*. Hamilton, Ontario: McMaster Innovation.

Mahowald, M. B. 2004. Respect for Embryos and the Potentiality Argument. *Theoretical Medicine and Bioethics* 25(3): 209–214.

Malmqvist, E. 2007. Analysing Our Qualms about 'Designing' Future Persons: Autonomy, Freedom of Choice, and Interfering with Nature. *Medicine, Health Care and Philosophy* 10(4): 407–416.

———— 2014. Reproductive Choice, Enhancement, and the Moral Continuum Argument. *Journal of Medicine and Philosophy* 39(1): 41–54.

———— and K. Zeiler, eds. 2016. *Bodily Exchanges, Bioethics and Border Crossing: Perspectives on Giving, Selling and Sharing Bodies.* Abingdon, Oxon: Routledge.

Malson, H. 1998. *The Thin Woman: Feminism, Post-Structuralism and the Social Psychology of Anorexia Nervosa.* London: Routledge.

Mauron, A., and B. Baertschi. 2004. The European Embryonic Stem-Cell Debate and the Difficulties of Embryological Kantianism. *Journal of Medicine and Philosophy* 29(5): 563–581.

McMahan, J. 2009. Death, Brain Death, and Persistent Vegetative State. In H. Kushe and P. Singer, eds., *A Companion to Bioethics*, 2nd ed., 286–298. London: Wiley-Blackwell.

Meacham, D., ed. 2015. *Medicine and Society, New Perspectives in Continental Philosophy.* Dordrecht: Springer.

Melzack, R., and P. D. Wall. 1996. *The Challenge of Pain.* London: Penguin Books.

Merleau-Ponty, M. 2012. *Phenomenology of Perception.* Trans. D. A. Landes. London: Routledge.

Mills, C. 2011. *Futures of Reproduction: Bioethics and Biopolitics.* Dordrecht: Springer.

Milunsky, A., and J. Milunsky, eds. 2016. *Genetic Disorders and the Fetus: Diagnosis, Prevention, and Treatment.* Hoboken, NJ: John Wiley.

Morain, S., N. F. Greene, and M. M. Mello. 2013. A New Era in Noninvasive Prenatal Testing. *The New England Journal of Medicine* 369(6): 499–501.

Moran, D. 2000. *Introduction to Phenomenology.* London: Routledge.

More, M., and N. Vitra-More, eds. 2013. *The Transhumanist Reader.* Malden, MA: Wiley-Blackwell.

Mumford, J. 2013. *Ethics at the Beginning of Life: A Phenomenological Critique.* Oxford: Oxford University Press.

Nancy, J.-L. 2008. *Corpus.* Trans. R. A. Rand. New York: Fordham University Press.

Nordenfelt, L. 1995. *On the Nature of Health: An Action-Theoretic Approach*, 2nd ed. Dordrecht: Reidel.

Nozick, R. 1974. *Anarchy, State, and Utopia.* New York: Basic Books.

Nussbaum, M. 1990a. The Discernment of Perception: An Aristotelian Conception of Private and Public Rationality. In *Love's Knowledge: Essays on Philosophy and Literature*, 54–105. Oxford: Oxford University Press.

———— 1990b. Reading for Life. In *Love's Knowledge: Essays on Philosophy and Literature*, 230–244. Oxford: Oxford University Press.

———— and C. R. Sunstein, eds. 1999. *Clones and Clones: Facts and Fantasies about Human Cloning.* New York: Norton & Company.

Oregon Health and Science University (OHSU). 2013. Human Skin Cells Converted into Embryonic Stem Cells: First Time Human Stem Cells Have Been Produced via Nuclear Transfer. *Science Daily*, May 15, www.sciencedaily.com/releases/2013/05/130515125030.htm.

Palacios-Gonzalez, C., J. Harris, and G. Testa. 2014. Multiplex Parenting: IVG and the Generations to Come. *Journal of Medical Ethics* 40(11): 752–758.

Palmer, R. E. 1969. *Hermeneutics: Interpretation Theory in Schleiermacher, Dilthey, Heidegger, and Gadamer.* Evanston, IL: Northwestern University Press.

Parens, E. 2015. *Shaping Our Selves: On Technology, Flourishing, and a Habit of Thinking.* Oxford: Oxford University Press.

Parfit, D. 1984. *Reasons and Persons.* Oxford: Oxford University Press.

Pedersen, R. 2010. *Empathy in Medicine: A Philosophical Hermeneutic Reflection.* Oslo: University of Oslo, Faculty of Medicine.

Pellegrino, E. D., and D. C. Thomasma. 1993. *The Virtues in Medical Practice.* Oxford: Oxford University Press.

Perpich, D. 2010. Vulnerability and the Ethics of Facial Tissue Transplantation. *Journal of Bioethical Inquiry* 7(2): 173–185.

Polivy, J., and C. P. Herman. 2002. Causes of Eating Disorders. *Annual Review of Psychology* 53(1): 187–213.

Prinz, J. J. 2011. Is Empathy Necessary for Morality? In A. Coplan and P. Goldie, eds., *Empathy: Philosophical and Psychological Perspectives*, 211–229. Oxford: Oxford University Press.

Ratcliffe, M. 2008. *Feelings of Being: Phenomenology, Psychiatry and the Sense of Reality.* Oxford: Oxford University Press.

——— 2015. *Experiences of Depression: A Study in Phenomenology.* Oxford: Oxford University Press.

Rehmann-Sutter, C., M. Düwell, and D. Mieth, eds. 2008. *Bioethics in Cultural Contexts: Reflections on Methods and Finitudes.* Dordrecht: Springer.

Reiser, S. J. 2009. *Technological Medicine: The Changing World of Doctors and Patients.* Cambridge: Cambridge University Press.

Ricoeur, P. 1992. *Oneself as Another.* Trans. K. Blamey. Chicago: University of Chicago Press.

Riis, S. 2011. Towards the Origin of Modern Technology: Reconfiguring Martin Heidegger's Thinking. *Continental Philosophy Review* 44(1): 103–117.

Rizzolatti, G., L. Fadiga, V. Gallesa, and L. Fogassi. 1996. Premotor Cortex and the Recognition of Motor Action. *Cognitive Brain Research* 3(2): 131–141.

Robertson, J. A. 2003. Extending Preimplantation Genetic Diagnosis: The Ethical Debate. Ethical Issues in New Uses of Preimplantation Genetic Diagnosis. *Human Reproduction* 18(3): 465–471.

Rochat, P. 2009. *Others in Mind: Social Origins of Self-Consciousness.* Cambridge: Cambridge University Press.

Rodin, S., L. Antonsson, C. Niaudet, and K. Tryggvason. 2014. Clonal Culturing of Human Embryonic Stem Cells on Laminin-521/E-cadherin Matrix in Defined and Xeno-Free Environment. *Nature Communications* 5: article no. 3195.

Rose, N. 2007. *The Politics of Life Itself: Biomedicine, Power, and Subjectivity in the Twenty-First Century.* Princeton, NJ: Princeton University Press.

——— and J. M. Abi-Rached. 2013. *Neuro: The New Brain Sciences and the Management of the Mind.* Princeton, NJ: Princeton University Press.

Ruin, H. 2010. *Ge-stell*: Enframing as the Essence of Technology. In B. W. Davis, ed., *Martin Heidegger: Key Concepts*, 183–194. Durham, NC: Acumen Publishing.

Russon, J. 2003. *Human Experience: Philosophy, Neurosis, and the Elements of Everyday Life.* Albany: State University of New York Press.

Sanders, M., and J. Wisnewski. 2012. *Ethics and Phenomenology.* Lanham, MD: Lexington Books.

Sartre, J.-P. 1973. *Existentialism and Humanism.* Trans. P. Mairet. London: Methuen Publishing.

————— 1992. *Being and Nothingness: A Phenomenological Essay on Ontology*. Trans. H. Barnes. New York: Washington Square Press.

Saul, R. 2014. *ADHD Does Not Exist: The Truth About Attention Deficit and Hyperactivity Disorder*. New York: HarperCollins.

Savulescu, J. 2005. New Breeds of Human: The Moral Obligation to Enhance. *Reproductive Biomedicine Online* 10 (Suppl.): S36–S39.

—————, R. ter Meulen, and G. Kahane, eds. 2011. *Enhancing Human Capacities*. Malden, MA: Wiley-Blackwell.

Scarry, E. 1985. *The Body in Pain: The Making and Unmaking of the World*. New York: Oxford University Press.

Schechtman, M. 1996. *The Constitution of Selves*. Ithaca, NY: Cornell University Press.

Scheler, M. 2009. *The Nature of Sympathy*. Trans. P. Heath. London: Routledge.

Sharp, L. A. 2006. *Strange Harvest: Organ Transplants, Denatured Bodies, and the Transformed Self*. Berkeley: University of California Press.

————— 2007. *Bodies, Commodities, and Biotechnologies: Death, Mourning, and Scientific Desire in the Realm of Human Organ Transfer*. New York: Columbia University Press.

Silver, L. 1997. *Remaking Eden*. New York: Avon Books.

Singer, P. 2011. *Practical Ethics*, 3rd ed. Cambridge: Cambridge University Press.

Sinha, S., L. Miall, and L. Jardine. 2012. *Essential Neonatal Medicine*, 5th ed. Chichester, West Sussex: Wiley-Blackwell.

Slatman, J. 2014. *Our Strange Body: Philosophical Reflections on Identity and Medical Interventions*. Amsterdam: Amsterdam University Press.

Slote, M. 2007. *The Ethics of Care and Empathy*. London: Routledge.

Solomon, A. 2006. Emotions in Phenomenology and Existentialism. In H. Dreyfus and M. Wrathall, eds., *A Companion to Phenomenology and Existentialism*, 291–309. London: Blackwell.

Spiegelberg, H. 1972. *Phenomenology in Psychology and Psychiatry: A Historical Introduction*. Evanston, IL: Northwestern University Press.

Stanghellini, G., and T. Fuchs, eds. 2013. *One Century of Karl Jaspers' General Psychopathology*. Oxford: Oxford University Press.

Stein, E. 1989. *On the Problem of Empathy*. Trans. W. Stein. Washington, DC: ICS Publications.

Steinbock, A. J. 2014. *Moral Emotions: Reclaiming the Evidence of the Heart*. Evanston, IL: Northwestern University Press.

Stempsey, W. E. 2006. Emerging Medical Technologies and Emerging Conceptions of Health. *Theoretical Medicine and Bioethics* 27(3): 227–243.

Stueber, K. R. 2006. *Rediscovering Empathy: Agency, Folk Psychology, and the Human Sciences*. Cambridge, MA: MIT Press.

Sullivan, D. 2001. *Cosmetic Surgery: The Cutting Edge of Medicine in America*. New York: Rutgers University Press.

Svenaeus, F. 2000. *The Hermeneutics of Medicine and the Phenomenology of Health: Steps towards a Philosophy of Medical Practice*. Dordrecht: Kluwer.

————— 2003. Hermeneutics of Medicine in the Wake of Gadamer: The Issue of *Phronesis*. *Theoretical Medicine and Bioethics* 24(5): 407–431.

————— 2007a. Do Antidepressants Affect the Self? A Phenomenological Approach. *Medicine, Health Care and Philosophy* 10(2): 153–166.

————— 2007b. A Heideggerian Defense of Therapeutic Cloning. *Theoretical Medicine and Bioethics* 28(1): 31–62.

———— 2009a. The Phenomenology of Falling Ill: An Explication, Critique and Improvement of Sartre's Theory of Embodiment and Alienation. *Human Studies* 32(1): 53–66.

———— 2009b. The Ethics of Self-Change: Becoming Oneself by Way of Antidepressants or Psychotherapy? *Medicine, Health Care and Philosophy* 12(2): 169–178.

———— 2010. What is an Organ? Heidegger and the Phenomenology of Organ Transplantation. *Theoretical Medicine and Bioethics* 31(3): 179–196.

———— 2011. Illness as Unhomelike Being-in-the-World: Heidegger and the Phenomenology of Medicine. *Medicine, Health Care and Philosophy* 14(3): 333–343.

———— 2012. Organ Transplantation and Personal Identity: How Does Loss and Change of Organs Affect the Self? *Journal of Medicine and Philosophy* 37(2): 139–158.

———— 2013a. Depression and the Self: Bodily Resonance and Attuned Being-in-the-World. *Journal of Consciousness Studies* 20(7–8): 15–32.

———— 2013b. Naturalistic and Phenomenological Theories of Health: Distinctions and Connections. In H. Carel and D. Meacham, eds., *Human Experience and Nature: Examining the Relationship between Phenomenology and Naturalism*, 221–238. Cambridge: Cambridge University Press.

———— 2015a. The Phenomenology of Chronic Pain: Embodiment and Alienation. *Continental Philosophy Review* 48(2): 107–122.

———— 2015b. The Relationship Between Empathy and Sympathy in Good Health Care. *Medicine, Health Care and Philosophy* 18(2): 267–277.

———— 2016a. The Phenomenology of Empathy: A Steinian Emotional Account. *Phenomenology and the Cognitive Sciences* 15(2): 227–245.

———— 2016b. The Lived Body and Personal Identity: The Ontology of Exiled Body Parts. In E. Malmqvist and K. Zeiler, eds., *Bodily Exchanges, Bioethics and Border Crossing: Perspectives on Giving, Selling and Sharing Bodies*, 19–34. London: Routledge.

Taylor, C. 1989. *The Sources of the Self: The Making of Modern Identity*. Cambridge, MA: Harvard University Press.

———— 1991. *The Ethics of Authenticity*. Cambridge, MA: Harvard University Press.

Thomson, J. J. 2006. A Defence of Abortion. In H. Kushe and P. Singer, eds., *Bioethics: An Anthology*, 2nd ed., 25–41. Oxford: Blackwell.

Tilney, N. L. 2003. *Transplant: From Myth to Reality*. New Haven: Yale University Press.

Tolstoy, L. 2015. *The Death of Ivan Ilyich and Other Stories*. Trans. N. Pasternak Slater. Oxford: Oxford University Press.

Toombs, S. K., ed. 2001. *Handbook of Phenomenology and Medicine*. Dordrecht: Kluwer.

van der Burg, W. 2009. Law and Bioethics. In H. Kushe and P. Singer, eds., *A Companion to Bioethics*, 2nd ed., 56–64. Oxford: Blackwell.

Vanheule, S., and I. Devisch. 2014. Mental Suffering and the DSM-5: A Critical Review. *Journal of Evaluation in Clinical Practice* 20(6): 975–980.

Waldby, C., and R. Mitchell. 2006. *Tissue Economics: Blood, Organs, and Cell Lines in Late Capitalism*. Durham, NC: Duke University Press.

Weimar, W., M. A. Bos, and J. J. Busschbach, eds. 2008. *Organ Transplantation: Ethical, Legal and Psychosocial Aspects: Towards a Common European Policy*. Lengerich: Pabst.

Welie, J. V. M. 1999. *In the Face of Suffering: The Philosophical-Anthropological Foundations of Clinical Ethics*. Omaha, NE: Creighton University Press.

Welton, D., ed. 1999. *The Body: Classic and Contemporary Readings*. Oxford: Blackwell.

Wierciński, A., ed. 2005. *Between Description and Interpretation: The Hermeneutic Turn in Phenomenology*. Toronto: The Hermeneutic Press.

Wiggins, O. P., and A. C. Allen, eds. 2011. *Clinical Ethics and the Necessity of Stories: Essays in Honor of Richard M. Zaner*. Dordrecht: Springer.

Wilkins, S. M. 2016. Strange Bedfellows? Common Ground on the Moral Status Question. *Journal of Medicine and Philosophy* 41(2): 130–147.

World Health Organization (WHO). 2016a. *Dementia: Fact Sheet*, www.who.int/mediacentre/factsheets/fs362/en/.

——— 2016b. *Obesity and Overweight: Fact Sheet*, www.who.int/mediacentre/factsheets/fs311/en/.

Young, I. M. 2005. Pregnant Embodiment: Subjectivity and Alienation. In *On Female Body Experience: 'Throwing Like a Girl' and Other Essays*, 46–61. Oxford: Oxford University Press.

Younger, S. J. 2007. The Definition of Death. In B. Steinbock, ed., *The Oxford Handbook of Bioethics*, 285–303. Oxford: Oxford University Press.

Zahavi, D. 2005. *Subjectivity and Selfhood: Investigating the First-Person Perspective*. Cambridge, MA: MIT Press.

——— and Overgaard, S. 2012. Empathy without Isomorphism: A Phenomenological Account. In J. Decety, ed., *Empathy: From Bench to Bedside*, 3–20. Cambridge, MA: MIT Press.

Zaner, R. M. 1981. *The Context of Self: A Phenomenological Inquiry Using Medicine as a Clue*. Athens, OH: Ohio University Press.

——— 2004. *Conversations on the Edge: Narratives of Ethics and Illness*. Washington, DC: Georgetown University Press.

Zeiler, K. 2010. A Phenomenological Analysis of Bodily Self-Awareness in Pain and Pleasure: On Bodily Dys-appearance and Eu-appearance. *Medicine, Health Care and Philosophy* 13(4): 333–342.

——— 2014. Neither Property Right Nor Heroic Gift, Neither Sacrifice Nor Aporia: The Benefit of the Theoretical Lens of Sharing in Donation Ethics. *Medicine, Health Care and Philosophy* 17(2): 171–181.

——— and L. Folkmarson Käll, eds. 2014. *Feminist Phenomenology and Medicine*. Albany: State University of New York Press.

INDEX